AQUAMAN AND THE
WAR AGAINST OCEANS

Encapsulations: Critical Comics Studies

Aquaman and the War against Oceans

Comics Activism and Allegory
in the Anthropocene

RYAN POLL

UNIVERSITY OF NEBRASKA PRESS   LINCOLN

The University of Nebraska Press is part of a land-grant institution with campuses and programs on the past, present, and future homelands of the Pawnee, Ponca, Otoe-Missouria, Omaha, Dakota, Lakota, Kaw, Cheyenne, and Arapaho Peoples, as well as those of the relocated Ho-Chunk, Sac and Fox, and Iowa Peoples.

Library of Congress Cataloging-in-Publication Data
Names: Poll, Ryan, 1975– author.
Title: Aquaman and the war against oceans: comics activism and allegory in the Anthropocene / Ryan Poll.
Description: Lincoln: University of Nebraska Press, [2022] | Series: Encapsulations: critical comics studies | Includes bibliographical references and index.
Identifiers: LCCN 2022002703
    ISBN 9781496225856 (paperback)
    ISBN 9781496233691 (epub)
    ISBN 9781496233707 (pdf)
Subjects: LCSH: Aquaman (Fictitious character) | Environmentalism in literature. | Sea in literature. | Human ecology in literature. | Allegory. | Comic books, strips, etc.—History and criticism. | Johns, Geoff, 1973– —Criticism and interpretation. | BISAC: LITERARY CRITICISM / Comics & Graphic Novels | NATURE / Ecosystems & Habitats / Oceans & Seas | LCGFT: Literary criticism.
Classification: LCC PN6728.A68 P65 2022 | DDC 741.5/973—dc23/eng/20220208
LC record available at https://lccn.loc.gov/2022002703

Set and designed in Minion by N. Putens.

CONTENTS

ILLUSTRATIONS

SERIES EDITORS' INTRODUCTION

Martin Lund and Julia Round

Aquaman and the War against Oceans takes a deep dive into the murky depths of the titular, understudied superhero. Ryan Poll's in-depth analysis of The New 52 *Aquaman* explores the ways in which this comic dismantles the human-versus-nature binary that has been used to marginalize the Global Ocean and its vital role in our lives. The resulting book explores how and why Aquaman—and the Ocean—matters, as both disrupt and challenge assumptions around what we consider to be human and problematize the associated ideologies of humanism, racism, genderism, ableism, and capitalism. Poll shows how Aquaman is an effective figure to depict and explore the environmental violences that take place all around us, while probing the character's potential as a tool to develop progressive ecological thought.

This approach has much to teach us about the world around us and the possibilities for reading comics—and other stories—allegorically, as sustained and developed metaphors that can reconfigure reality. It engages with questions of representation and representability that are key to comics studies and that this series seeks to explore. In the creation of comics or graphic novels, "encapsulation" refers to the artistic and cognitive process whereby panels, images, words, and page layout create meaning and engage the reader. These connotations of selection and design underpin the aims of the Encapsulations series. This series of short monographs offers close readings of carefully delineated bodies of comics work with an emphasis on expanding the critical range and depth of comics studies.

By looking at understudied and overlooked texts, artists, and publishers, Encapsulations facilitates a move away from the same canonized texts. Instead, the series uses more diverse case studies to explore new and existing critical theories in tune with an interdisciplinary, intersectional, and global approach to comics scholarship. With an eye to breaking established patterns and forging new opportunities for scholarship, books in the series advance the theoretical grounding of comics scholarship and broaden critical knowledge of global comics. By showcasing new interdisciplinary perspectives and addressing emerging conceptual, formal, and methodological problems, Encapsulations promotes new approaches, contributes to the diversity of comics scholarship, and delves into uncharted sections of the comics archive.

Compact, affordable, and accessibly written, books in the Encapsulations series are addressed to the interested general reader as well as scholars and students. These volumes provide teachable, critical texts that foster a deeper general understanding of comics' cultural and historical impact, promote critical public literacy, and expand notions of what's worthy of academic study. We are proud to launch this endeavor with *Aquaman and the War against Oceans*.

ACKNOWLEDGMENTS

I am deeply grateful to so many people who made this book possible. First and foremost, I want to thank my home institution, Northeastern Illinois University, a public university whose diversity creates the most enriching, rewarding, and generative environment. I am so blessed to enter classes where I consistently become a pupil. Our students sacrifice so much to be in college, to attend classes, and to become coproducers of new knowledges, new narratives, and new ways to organize a more socially responsible and responsive world. Thank you to all students, past, current, and future. I am thankful to so many, but to single out a few who have helped clarify my thinking, broaden my aesthetic understanding, and sharpen my politics, I thank Jon Antol, Nadia Askar, Lauren Barry, Ulisa Blakely, Elias Cepeda, Jo Ann Colagiacomi, Sebastian Contreras, Heidi Curran Bojorges, Brendan Dabkowski, Martin Davis, Emily DeLeon, Zach Franks, Clif Frei, Joshua Friedberg, Dr. Kristina Garcia, Marlene Garcia, Scott Glass, Megan Guerin, Mark Gunter, Carlos Gutierrez, Carl Hauck, Samantha Hernández, Kathryn Hudson, Neil Huff, Shamsa Islam, Hussain Khemani, Hans Kim, David Knudson, Vanessa Macias, Sherilyn Maddex, Jasmine Rodriguez, Rebeca Ruiz, Katie Sall, Angelica Sanchez, Karina Sanchez, Raquel Gomez Savoy, Gus Segovia, Josh Smith, Kimara Smith, Daniela Tapia, Jennifer Velazquez, Kathryn Velez, and so many more. I am grateful to be part of a public university.

This project began with a conference talk I gave at the Midwest Popular Culture Association / American Culture Association in 2016 on Aquaman and Ocean pollution. I thought it was a one-off talk, on the margins of my scholarly work. But I am blessed that, by chance, Sean Guynes, an incredible editor and visionary scholar, was in the audience that day and encouraged me—for years—to follow through on this project. I was hesitant for myriad reasons, but Sean helped me see the potential and importance of a longer Aquaman project. And finally, I acquiesced. Sean's vision, faith, and energy were the initial tides that pulled me forward.

Everyone at the University of Nebraska Press has been incredible in guiding me through the publishing process with patience, understanding, insight, and encouragement. I am grateful to the entire team for everything, but I want to express my deep gratitude to my acquiring editors, Bridget Barry and Heather Stauffer, and to my project editor, Sara Springsteen. Thank you all for humanizing the process, making me feel like part of an institutional family, and for helping in every way.

I am so fortunate to work with an incredible copy editor, Jeremy Hall. Jeremy is a writer's dream. He saved me from numerous embarrassing errors and became my teacher in the process. Thank you, Jeremy, for reading my manuscript with care, patience, and dedication. Of course, all errors are mine. I am also deeply grateful for my indexer, Amron Gravett, who was wonderful in understanding this project on all levels. Amron, thank you for your critical artistry.

I am deeply indebted to the series editors, Martin Lund and Julia Round. Both were tremendous in their guidance and their invaluable criticism throughout the entire process, from the initial proposal to the final revisions. This project is richer because of their commitment. Both Martin and Julia became more than editors—they became friends. To me, this is the highest compliment imaginable.

I was a neophyte in superhero studies when I began this

project, and I discovered the most welcoming, generous, big-hearted community of scholars, including Eric L. Berlatsky, Carolyn Cocca, and Sika A. Dagbovie-Mullins. I am at a loss of words for the unbelievable support from Frederick Luis Aldama and Marc DiPaolo. Both were beyond generous with their time, feedback, and care.

I need to loop back to my home institution, Northeastern Illinois University. I am constantly in an environment with students whose intelligences far exceed my own. Two in particular were invaluable to this project: Katelyn Juerjens and Jenn Lee. Katelyn helped me at every stage of this book's development, from being a critical interlocutor to being one of the best critical readers of my work. Katelyn read numerous drafts of each chapter with a critical eye and offered invaluable criticism. And Jenn Lee was gracious to read and edit this book in its entirety, offering salient corrections and suggestions. I am so grateful to you both, and I can't wait to call you Professor Juerjens and Professor Lee in the near future!

I love my job, and I love academia. But the world that loves me back, the world that is my foundation, is my family. Thank you to all the Polls, Rushes, Kesselmans, Martons, Wassermans, Slutzkys, Karters, Teplitskys, and Beens. While this book was being finished, I gained a new brother and two amazing nephews—Paul, Ryan, Izaak, love you guys!! Mom, Dad, Reid, Marissa, Bubbie, Zadie, Grandpa, and Grandma, you have all nourished and believed in my dreams from the beginning. No matter where I go in life, no matter what I do, you all will always be there.

When my first book was published, I had one son. Now, I am blessed to have three children. Dylan, Noah, Emmy, you three are everything. Even though it may seem that my superhero name is No Fun Dad, I hope you know—and more importantly feel—how much I love each of you. Of all the titles I've earned in my life, the most important is "dad." I love watching all three of you grow and experiment with ways to be in the world and, equally important, to build a better world. You each fill my life with meaning, laughter, play, imagination, and insights that daily turn me into a student. I hope you each always remain my teacher.

Ally, in a watery world that often feels as if I am drowning, you're always my life jacket and my lighthouse. I love you to the bottom of the Ocean, across the Ocean floor, and throughout this world that is more magical and wondrous than our concepts can hold. Thank you for being my swimming partner through life (and a much better swimmer), no matter what the conditions, no matter how strong the swells, no matter what tempests threaten. It's easy to swim through pacific waters. True love is someone who helps you through the rough patches. Nothing would be possible without you and your love.

Finally, this book is dedicated to my best friend and chosen brother: Jordan Feldman. Life isn't the same without you. You filled every space with love and laughter, and you made this world richer, more beautiful, and more meaningful in every way possible. You are loved, and you are missed. But as the Ocean teaches, nothing is truly lost; everything just assumes a different form. You live on in so many ways, in so many forms, including in so many hearts, especially mine.

AQUAMAN AND THE
WAR AGAINST OCEANS

Introduction

In the final decades of the twentieth century and into the twenty-first, Aquaman had become a perennial punchline in popular culture. This trope is exemplified in myriad cultural texts, including *Entourage, Family Guy, Robot Chicken, South Park*, and *SpongeBob SquarePants*. On *The Big Bang Theory* (2007–19), a television show about a group of self-identified nerds, when one of the show's central characters must dress as Aquaman for a superhero costume party, he protests, "Aquaman sucks!"[1] His Aquaman costume tellingly resembles the iteration from the 1967–68 cartoon *The Superman/Aquaman Hour of Adventure*. In this version, Aquaman began to resemble Fred Jones from *Scooby-Doo*, a campy representation repeated in the long-running animated show *Super Friends* (1973–86), which replayed in syndication for decades.[2] (The resemblance between Aquaman and Fred Jones is no coincidence; both cartoons were produced by Hanna-Barbera.) In the early twenty-first century, Aquaman had been figured as a worthless superhero because his superpowers were contained to the ocean, a geography implicitly posited as outside of and beyond Human concerns and affairs. As exemplified by *The Big Bang Theory*, even self-identified nerds, those typically outside and critical of dominant narratives of power, agreed that Aquaman "sucks."

1

When writer Geoff Johns began his multiyear reimagining of Aquaman (2011–14) for The New 52—a massive overhaul and rebranding of all DC superheroes to make them more modern and accessible to more diverse audiences—he began his transformation by acknowledging the pervasive discourse that posited Aquaman as an object of ridicule. In issue 1 of The New 52 *Aquaman* (September/November 2011), a blogger approaches the superhero and asks, "So how's it feel to be a punchline? How's it feel to be a laughingstock?"[3] As the blogger makes explicit, this trope circulates widely in various forms and networks: "I'm sure you've heard all the jokes and seen all the skits from *Saturday Night Live* on YouTube."[4] Johns begins his modern Aquaman iteration by addressing a popular discourse that had previously existed primarily outside DC's curated history and, hence, beyond Aquaman's sanctioned story world. Put differently, this once outside discourse had become so mainstream and normative that it needed to be addressed explicitly from the outset and made internal, and even central, to the superhero's narrative. In this sense, we can say that one of the narrative engines of The New 52 *Aquaman* is an ideological battle for respect and dignity—both for Aquaman and, by symbolic extension, the ocean.

Johns's complex and layered multiyear run as the sole writer of The New 52 *Aquaman* from 2011 to 2014 can be understood as a concerted effort to counter this dismissive discourse by narrating how and why Aquaman matters. He matters because the oceans matter. The discourse that makes Aquaman the object of ridicule is a judgment not just on Aquaman's value but, symbolically, of the ocean's value as well. The blogger who confronts Aquaman with a barrage of hostile questions concludes with a rhetorical challenge: "How's it feel to be nobody's favorite super-hero?"[5] This rhetorical question is animated by a hierarchical value system in which Aquaman—a conspicuous symbol of the ocean—is at the bottom. And to be at the bottom of this hierarchical structure is to be beyond Human concern, care, and even visibility.

This book argues that, far from being a joke, Aquaman—under the direction of Geoff Johns (writer), Ivan Reis (penciller), Joe Prado (inker), and Rod Reis (colorist)—becomes a salient figure for mapping the environmental violences that constitute the Anthropocene, as well as a popular icon for developing a progressive ecological imagination.[6] As the comics series foregrounds, the global ocean is a salient geography in understanding and narrating the entangled violences that constitute the Anthropocene. Although the ocean is largely unseen and illegible in the dominant knowledge regimes of modernity, The New 52 *Aquaman* challenges this normative paradigm by visualizing and narrating how the Anthropocene is transforming the ocean into a vast and deep graveyard.

Aquaman is a symbol of the Ocean, a geography that covers more than 70 percent of Earth's surface and a geography that is central to a healthy and sustainable planet.[7] (From this point forward, I will capitalize the word *Ocean*, which I will use interchangeably with *Oceans*, because as maritime historian Eric Paul Roorda, the editor of *The Ocean Reader: History, Culture, Politics*, argues, the "stylebook spelling of 'ocean' diminishes it as a geographic reference. To capitalize Ocean is to challenge the conventional wisdom that the seas can be taken for granted. They cannot.")[8] Earth is a water planet, yet paradoxically, in dominant discourses, the Ocean is frequently positioned as peripheral to Human affairs. The New 52 *Aquaman* seeks to challenge and change this conception.

The Global Ocean, as political geographer Philip E. Steinberg argues, is a "social construction."[9] Every culture redefines the Ocean in relation to their histories and worldviews. How we socially construct and engage with the Ocean changes how we perceive and conceive it. That is, the Ocean's metaphoricity and materiality are inextricable.[10]

The New 52 *Aquaman*'s centering on the Ocean challenges the Anthropocene's narratives and epistemologies. Maritime historian Helen M. Rozwadowski writes, "The vast expanse of the world ocean, the dominant feature of planet Earth, has remained at the edges of our histories. . . . Writers have embedded a terrestrial bias in virtually all stories about the past." Rozwadowski continues, "Dry land is the presumed norm."[11] The normative Humanities and the normative Human—ideological constructs that I am capitalizing throughout to highlight their artificiality—have a "terrestrial bias," and The New 52 *Aquaman*, I argue, is an attempt to break this pervasive bias. The comics intervention in this bias becomes all the more urgent because in the twentieth century, as literary and environmental scholar Steve Mentz argues, the Ocean became "displaced . . . from the center of" the dominant "cultural imagination."[12] The marginalization of the Ocean coincides with the rise of "terracentrism," a concept that "refers to people's tendency to consider the world and human activity mainly in the context of the land and events that take place on land."[13] Tellingly, the marginalization of the Global Ocean and the subsequent rise in terracentrism overlaps with the history of Aquaman, whose debut was in *More Fun Comics* 73 in 1941.

Aquaman, this project contends, is a progressive, popular figure for narrating the Ocean's central role in imagining politics beyond the myopic, violent paradigm of the surface world, beyond the prism of the Anthropocene. The Anthropocene names and recognizes a new geological age defined by unprecedented "human-driven chemical, physical, and biological changes to the Earth's atmosphere, land surface, and oceans."[14] In this new geological age, Humans have become "geological agents," affecting species and geographies everywhere.[15] As Jan

Zalasiewicz, Mark Williams, and Colin N. Waters write, the term *Anthropocene* signifies how the contemporary world is "undergoing rapid environmental change" as evident by "the clearing of rainforests for agriculture, the eutrophication of lakes and shallow seas by fertilizer run-off, depletion of fish stocks, acid rain, and global warming"[16] As these examples suggest, one of the primary geographies in which the Anthropocene's devastation is most evident is the Ocean.

However, despite being a central geography in which to see and understand the violences of the Anthropocene's unfolding, the Oceans are frequently projected, in Humanistic theories, as an externality, an unthought of and uncared for geography beyond the Human. As The New 52 *Aquaman* highlights, the Anthropocene develops and expands by refusing to recognize the Ocean as a complex geography worthy of study, respect, and dignity. The dominant world order is enabled, in large part, by not seeing the Global Ocean, by practicing and perpetuating an aggressive form of ecological ignorance. By turning toward the Global Ocean, the horrors of the Anthropocene become visible—horrors that are typically kept hidden, buried, and external to dominant discourses and epistemologies.

Central to The New 52 *Aquaman*, both the comic and hero, is to dismantle a central ideology of the Anthropocene, one that positions the Human as beyond nature. This conceptual work is allegorized by Aquaman. Aquaman, whose birth name is Arthur Curry, is a superhero who lives between two worlds: the surface and the Ocean world. His father is Human and worked as a lightkeeper, and his mother is from the Ocean and was once Queen of Atlantis, an underwater kingdom. The intimacy and coupling of Arthur's parents—one Human and the other from the Ocean—was forbidden by both the surface and the Ocean world. Yet their intimacy, their willingness to defy the dominant social order of their respective worlds, is a form of utopian world making that leads to their mixed-race son, Arthur Curry, the future Aquaman.[17] In The New 52 *Aquaman,* Arthur negotiates both sides of his hyphenated identity, between land and sea. Initially, Arthur is "lost" (the name of an early comic issue in the series) and hapless, not at home in either the Human or Ocean world. However, by the end of Johns's narrative run, Arthur learns to see that his hyphenated identity is not a marker of shame but a source of epistemic strength. As stated late in The New 52 *Aquaman,* Arthur's mission is "to unite land and sea."[18] To see the Oceans and land as one—to decenter the terrestrial bias that structures normative epistemologies and narratives—is a radical ecological and activist project and one, I will argue, that critiques all forms of hierarchical thinking that reign on the surface world, from capitalism to racism.

The ideological divide between the surface and the Ocean is a foundational feature of the Anthropocene. In the Anthropocene, the surface world is the world of Humanism—an ideological category, as I will later elaborate, that excludes most biological humans—and global capitalism. From the perspective of the surface world, the Ocean is figured as a form of nature, a social construct that is projected as mere background and external to Human affairs. The New 52 *Aquaman* critiques this ideological divide at the heart of the Anthropocene by making visible how the two worlds are interrelated and internal to each other.

Arthur's efforts to show that the surface and Ocean worlds are dialectically conjoined can be understood as allegorizing the critical project of the "blue humanities." The blue humanities critique hegemonic forms of Humanism that posit and reify Humans as divorced from other species and ecologies, including, most prominently, the Ocean. In contrast to the Humanities' myopic frame, the blue humanities encourage innovative and creative thinking to help forge new paradigms and philosophies to think about how human and marine life are interconnected and how the Ocean, like its surface counterpart, must be historicized.[19] Aquaman, this project contends, is an accessible figure for thinking through the blue humanities and for teaching Ocean literacy more generally. Aquaman, like nearly all superheroes, is a figure of hope who refuses to capitulate to cynicism and who embodies the utopian principle that another political order is both possible and winnable.

Aquaman is one of the most conspicuous political figures in mainstream U.S. superhero comics. Although the aquatic hero has many iterations since his debut in 1941, central to Aquaman's identity is his birthright. Aquaman comes from a royal family, and his destiny is to be king of the underwater Kingdom of Atlantis. Myriad story lines have centered on Aquaman wrestling with his role and responsibility as king and what it means to rule and care not just for a particular underwater kingdom but for all the Ocean. As a comic and figure, Aquaman is an allegory about politics beyond the myopic paradigm of Humanism—the belief that Humans are at the center and measure of all social relations, a hubristic paradigm exemplified in the name *Anthropocene* ("Anthro-" has its roots in the Greek word for "human," *anthrōpos*).[20] As King of Atlantis, Aquaman moves beyond the narrow Humanist definition of politics that concerns itself only with Human citizens, and instead he wrestles with what it means to rule, lead, protect, and be responsible for multiple species. This is a radical conception of citizenship that includes all marine species and a radical conception of politics that recognizes all geographies as political geographies. Aquaman, in short, helps bring politics into the twenty-first century by making the concept of ecology central to the concept of the political.

How, this project queries, do we read *Aquaman* comics differently by reading the underwater protector through and against the prism of the Anthropocene? The New 52 version of *Aquaman*, and subsequent iterations, actively works to realize a new world order, one beyond the Anthropocene. Aquaman works to bridge the ideological and material divides between the surface and the Ocean world, working to show how the two worlds profoundly influence one another and how the two are intertwined. In contrast to the logic of the Anthropocene, the Human and Ocean worlds are not two competing worlds, but rather, they are mutually constitutive. In a 2018 interview, Ivan Reis, the primary penciller working with Johns on The New 52 *Aquaman*, explains that *Aquaman* stories matter because of the story world's primary geography: "The ocean serves a few different purposes in that it's able to host different stories and bring up different questions about the problems of the planet, including environmental issues."[21] Reis foregrounds that in The New 52 iteration, Aquaman is an environmental hero.

Moreover, Reis stresses Aquaman's hyphenated identity. Reis emphasizes that "Aquaman lives in two worlds," the surface and the Ocean, that are ideologically viewed as separate, distinct, and noncompatible.[22] Aquaman's mixed heritage has conspicuous racial resonances. Reading allegorically—a method I practice throughout this project—Aquaman can be read as a mixed-race superhero.[23] This allegorical reading became literalized with the casting of Joseph Jason Namakaeha Momoa, better known as Jason Momoa, to play Aquaman in the 2018 movie that is largely based on Johns, Reis, Prado, and Reis's narrative run.[24] Momoa is Hapa, a Hawaiian word used to describe someone of mixed heritage.[25] (*Hapa* was originally a derogatory term used to describe "mixed-race children of plantation guest workers from the Philippines, Korea, China and Japan, and the women they married in Hawaii in the early part of the 20th century."[26] Today, though, *Hapa* is a term widely embraced by mixed-race Hawaiians.)[27] In the following pages, I chart the transformation of Aquaman from a blue-eyed, blond-hair white superhero into a Hapa superhero and the wider implications of this sea change in representation and politics.

The New 52 *Aquaman*, I argue, imagines the Ocean as a geography that disrupts and challenges what Sylvia Wynter critically calls "the regime of the Human" and the intertwining ideologies that constitute this regime, which includes Humanism, racism, genderism, ableism, and capitalism.[28] In conjunction with this critique, The New 52 *Aquaman*, I contend, begins a process in DC comics, movies, and television in which the Ocean transforms from a white imaginary into one that is explicitly Black, brown, feminist, queer, and Indigenous.

Visualizing a New Oceanic Imaginary

While The New 52 iteration of Aquaman can be read allegorically as a mixed-race superhero who champions a more diverse, complex, multispecies worldview, phenotypically, he could not be any whiter. While the series becomes a trenchant critique of white supremacy (see chapter 4), its visual iconography initially seems to perpetuate the troubling racist imaginary prevalent in mainstream U.S. superhero comics, an imaginary that aligns "heroism" with "white privilege," "white supremacy," and masculinity.[29] In The New 52 rebranding, Aquaman is initially identified by his physicality and prowess (and his white appearance). In the opening issue, Aquaman is presented as a hypermasculine badass, an identity that echoes Peter David's extensive run two decades prior. Beginning in 1994, David, collaborating with artists Martin Egeland, Brad Vancata, and Tom McCraw, worked to negate the iconicity popularized by *Super Friends*. In contrast to the clean-cut, cheerful, Boy Scout aesthetic, David's Aquaman wears a perpetual scowl; his hair is long and unruly; he sports a full, ungroomed beard and mustache; and in the second issue of David's run, *Aquaman* 2

(August/September 1994), his left hand is gruesomely severed.[30] Eventually, Aquaman chooses a harpoon as a prosthetic, becoming harpoon-handed.[31]

The New 52 *Aquaman* seems to reproduce and even enhance David's aesthetic. The collective team of Johns, Reis, Prado, and Reis foreground that Aquaman is a superhero whose spectacular powers extend to all geographies, including the surface world. In the opening pages of issue 1, Aquaman performs superhuman feats that have never been seen in previous iterations. Three masked and armed bank robbers speed through the crowded streets of Boston in an armored truck. The truck outpaces the pursuing police cars, threating to escape, when suddenly, in the middle of the street, Aquaman appears. Upon seeing Aquaman, one of the robbers fires a machine gun. The bullets, though, ricochet off Aquaman's armored body. The truck speeds toward Aquaman, still anticipating an easy kill. However, Aquaman unexpectedly smashes his fist into the speeding car's hood, causing the vehicle to flip into the air. Immediately thereafter, Aquaman leaps over multistory buildings.[32] In the series' inaugural issue, Aquaman resembles less a watery superhero and more DC's most iconic superhero, Superman.

Yet despite these awesome, superhuman powers on full display, the surface world still sees Aquaman as a joke. In this opening sequence, the three bank robbers and the trailing police officers are shown in panels that are visually parallel and vertically connected, one on top of the other. Both robbers and police are positioned in vehicles, both groups face the same direction (right), and both groups ridicule Aquaman (fig. 1).[33] Although they occupy opposite sides of the law, both robbers and police have a shared sensibility in their attitude toward

1. Criminals and cops visually analogous. "The Trench, Part 1," Geoff Johns (writer), Ivan Reis (penciller), Joe Prado (inker), and Rod Reis (colorist), *Aquaman 7*, no. 1, The New 52 (New York: DC Comics, September/November 2011).

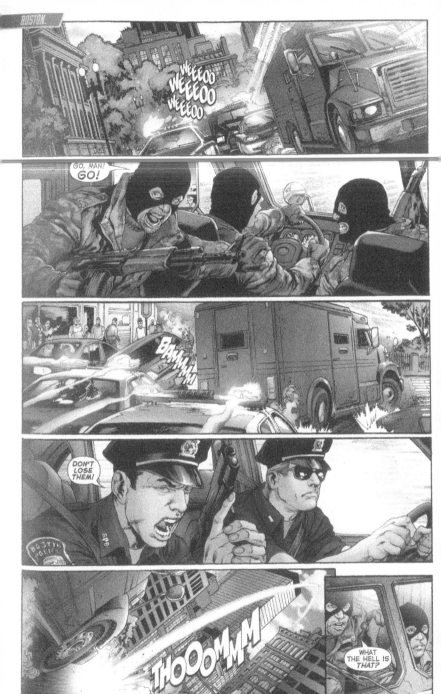

the marine superhero. When the robbers see Aquaman in the middle of the road, one bursts out into laughter, and another derisively states, "Bye-bye, tuna man."[34] Analogously, after Aquaman thwarts the robbers' escape plan, one police officer says, "I can't believe we just got upstaged by Aquaman." And another officer replies, "The boys at the station are never gonna let us hear the end of this."[35] No matter what Aquaman does, he can't escape the pervasive discourse that he is a laughingstock.

Ultimately, The New 52's objective to remake Aquaman into a respected and celebrated superhero succeeded. To the surprise of many, Aquaman transformed from a marginal superhero with flagging sales to one of DC's best-selling comics. Moreover, The New 52 series became a primary source for the big-budget 2018 DC movie Aquaman, for which Johns received story credit and for which he was a cowriter; the movie also borrowed heavily from the visuals of Ivan Reis. Defying expectations, Aquaman became the highest-grossing film in the DC Extended Universe (DCEU) to that point and the highest-grossing film based on any DC superhero, surpassing every Batman movie, including The Dark Knight Rises.[36] In the span of one decade, Aquaman became a globally recognized (and profitable) icon of the Global Ocean.[37]

In contrast to dominant surface narratives that posit the Ocean as marginal to modernity, The New 52 Aquaman visualizes how the Ocean is central to the flourishing of all species and geographies. The series achieves this task through a perhaps unexpected literary device: allegory.[38] The word allegory literally means "other speaking."[39] It is a literary device committed to hearing and making legible voices made other by reigning ideologies. The New 52 Aquaman makes visible the Ocean's myriad voices, a geography rendered invisible and inaudible by the dominant culture of globalization. By allegorically giving voice to the Ocean, The New 52 Aquaman narrates how

Oceanic life is under assault by the everyday practices and institutions of the Anthropocene, including most prominently by global capitalism.

While The New 52 *Aquaman* is primarily an ecological narrative, multiple, interlocking allegories develop within the comics' pages. As the series suggests, the Ocean is a space beyond Humanity—a space inhospitable and resistant to Human projects and ideologies—and paradoxically, an all-too-Human space, a geography inextricable from the histories and structures of capitalism, genderism, and racism. In conjunction with following the allegorical narratives of Aquaman, this project also follows Mera, Aquaman's romantic partner and fellow aquatic superhero, whom I read as both a victim of systemic gender violence and as an allegory of ecofeminism; Orm, Aquaman's half brother, who becomes an allegory for an autonomous, agential Ocean that declares war on Humanity and capitalism; and Black Manta, one of the few African American supervillains in mainstream U.S. comics. As I argue, Black Manta allegorizes the progressive promise of the Ocean, and conversely, his narrative highlights how anti-Black racism structures all geographies, including the underwater Kingdom of Atlantis. As this book argues, by contextualizing and closely reading Johns, Reis, Prado, and Reis's narrative run, an ecological imagination is inextricable from formations of class, gender, and race. Although the Ocean is frequently projected as alien to Human society and culture, signs of "civilization" are everywhere in the Ocean, from racialized slavery to pervasive plastics. Therefore, I read The New 52 *Aquaman* within wider critical discourses, including ecological Marxism, ecofeminism, posthumanism, Black Atlantic studies, critical Black studies, queer theory, and Indigenous studies.

This book—the first academic study of Aquaman—analyzes the interconnected allegories that develop in The New 52 iteration. While there are myriad studies of allegory in fiction, what does comics allegory mean? More specifically, how does the collective of Johns, Reis, Prado, and Reis develop allegories both verbally and visually? The series develops progressive and regressive allegories that center on the Ocean, but such allegories do not remain confined there. Instead, the allegories multiply and branch out in perhaps unexpected directions. What starts as an allegory about the Ocean becomes intertwined with allegories of genderism, racism, nationalism, and fascism.

Aquaman and the War against Oceans makes several, intersecting arguments. First and foremost, the project contends that The New 52 *Aquaman* offers a complex, yet accessible, allegory of the Ocean's central position in the making of modernity. By centering on the Ocean, as The New 52 *Aquaman* does, many things become visible that are predominately disavowed in the dominant regimes of visibility and intelligibility. The New 52 *Aquaman* visualizes the Ocean as the victim of a centuries-long war waged by colonial capitalism. Understanding the Ocean as historically conditioned and shaped by Human economies and activities challenges how the Anthropocene views the Ocean. Roorda writes, "Because the Ocean can't be plowed, paved, or shaped in ways the eye is able to discern, it has seemed to be constant, while the land has changed drastically over the centuries."[40] This ideological projection of the Ocean as stable and fixed, as beyond history, blinds Humanity from seeing the horrors accumulating beneath the visible surface. The New 52 *Aquaman* visualizes, in a popular medium and genre, that the Global Ocean is a space of history and a space being drastically transformed by Human institutions and economies.

In many ways, the Ocean is a geography alien and inhospitable to Humans. However, the Ocean is central to the production and reproduction of the modern world. Modernity has been created and enabled by two types of ships: the slave ship and container ship. Maritime historian Marcus Rediker avers, the slave ship is "the vessel that made the world-transforming commerce possible, . . . the mechanism for history's greatest forced migration, . . . [and] the instrument that facilitated Europe's 'commercial revolution,' its building of plantations and global empires, its development of capitalism, and eventually its industrialization." As Rediker concludes, "In short, the slave ship and its social relationships have shaped the modern world."[41] In the twentieth century, when *Aquaman* was created and circulated, modernity became shaped by a different ship. Today, most of the world's cargo is transported on the Global Ocean, and at the center of this revolutionary expansion of global capitalism is the container ship. Since its invention in the 1950s, the container box "has become one of the most important mechanisms for the global spread of capitalism."[42] By the end of the twentieth century, "ninety-five percent of world trade by weight, and two-thirds by value, is carried by ship."[43] Paradoxically, though, despite being at the center of global trade, the Ocean remains largely invisible in the dominant social imagination. As Allan Sekula and Noël Burch argue in their 2010 documentary, despite being a geography in which 90 percent of the world's cargo travels, the Ocean remains a "forgotten space."[44] The Ocean is not simply a watery road to carry commodities around the globe; it's a living, complex geography that is being choked to death.

In the Anthropocene, the Ocean is central for studying how Humanity is transforming Earth. Postcolonial and environmental scholar Elizabeth M. DeLoughrey asserts, "The Anthropocene has catalyzed a new oceanic imaginary in which, due to the visibility of sea rise, the largest space on earth is suddenly not so external and alien to human experience."[45] This "new oceanic imaginary," DeLoughrey continues, "has inspired an increase in a body of literature, art, film, and scholarship concerned with our watery futures."[46] The New 52 *Aquaman*, I contend, is an important contribution to this emergent Oceanic imaginary.

The Global Ocean is a salient space for studying the devastating effects of the Anthropocene, and moreover, centering on the Global Ocean, as The New 52 *Aquaman* does, helps develop and expand social and ecological imaginations. Historian David Gange writes, "Many writers have recognised that tides, currents and waves link many parts of the world that have been artificially divided by national borders drawn on land."[47] In contrast to the dominant social imagination that has "been obsessed with land and territory," a range of postcolonial thinkers from Édouard Glissant to Edward Kamau Brathwaite argue that the Ocean, "with its depth and flux, with tidal time that moved backwards as well as forwards—could generate an entirely different worldview."[48] Reading allegorically, The New 52 *Aquaman* becomes a popular and accessible bridge to such radical thinkers.

Visualizing the Anthropocene

As The New 52 *Aquaman* narrates and visualizes, the Anthropocene is transforming the Ocean into a wasteland. The Anthropocene is a recent periodization that recognizes how Humans have become "geological agents," radically reshaping geographies everywhere and, hence, radically transforming life everywhere.[49] Postcolonial scholar Dipesh Chakrabarty writes, "To call ourselves geological agents is to attribute to us a force on the same scale as that released at other times when there has been a mass extinction of species."[50] And indeed, as scientists across the disciplines recognize, we are in the midst of the sixth great extinction.[51]

In 2007, four years prior to the publication of The New 52 *Aquaman*, scientists from all over the world convened at the UN Convention on Biological Diversity and shared sobering and alarming statistics. UN Secretary-General Ban Ki-moon summarized, "Biodiversity is being lost at an unprecedented rate. . . . Every hour, three species disappear. Every day, up to 150 species are lost. Every year, between 18,000 and 55,000 species become extinct."[52] On the conservative side, that's more than one thousand times the average extinction rate. Other scientists, though, argue that we're closer to ten thousand times more than the average extinction rate.[53] Regardless of the exact ratio, there is a broad scientific consensus that we are living in the "greatest wave of extinctions since the disappearance of the dinosaurs."[54] And the reason is because of Human activities and economies.[55] Paradoxically, this everyday mass extinction is unfolding beyond the "everyday" of global capitalism, ideologically outside the capitalist regime of visibility and legibility.

In an August 2011 article, published one month before The New 52 officially launched, zoologist Robert M. May wrote, "It is a remarkable testament to humanity's narcissism that we know the number of books in the U.S. Library of Congress on February 1, 2011, was 22,194,656, but cannot tell you—to within an order-of-magnitude—how many distinct species of plants and animals we share our world with."[56] This "narcissism" is one of the animating ideologies of the Human, an ideological category implicitly critiqued throughout The New 52 *Aquaman*. As May implies, Humans have created an artificial world that imagines itself as divorced from other species and from nature more generally. This ideological deracination encourages Humans to neither see nor care about the apocalypse that Humans are both causing and living through. As May writes, "We are astonishingly ignorant about how many species are alive on earth today, and even more ignorant about how many we can lose yet still maintain ecosystem services that humanity ultimately depends upon."[57] This is both narcissism and hubris. This structural ignorance and indifference is at the heart of the Anthropocene and fuels the acceleration of the sixth great extinction.

If we are "astonishingly ignorant" about the species on the surface world, this ignorance is redoubled when it comes to the Ocean.[58] In 2010, one year before the official launch of The New 52, the Census of Marine Life published the results of their ten-year project "that recorded the diversity, distribution, and abundance of life in the ocean."[59] This was a collective, international effort in which more than 2,700 scientists from eighty nations participated and contributed. Still, despite this international effort, 91 percent of all Oceanic species remain unknown.[60]

As The New 52 *Aquaman* allegorically narrates, the Global Ocean is one of the most important geographies to study in order to understand the entangled violences that constitute the Anthropocene. The comic's turn toward the Ocean is a turn away from normative ways of seeing and a turn away from the dominant grids of intelligibility. Turning toward the Ocean, in other words, is turning toward the alien. Today, Humans know more about outer space than about the Global Ocean, a fact articulated at the beginning of the 2018 blockbuster movie *Aquaman*.[61] The Ocean's alien status is what attracted Johns to Aquaman in the first place. As Johns explained in a 2011 interview, his transition from writing Green Lantern comics to Aquaman comics was not a complete departure; Johns was moving from one alien world to another alien world. Whereas Green Lantern narratives take place throughout the galaxy, Aquaman is an Earth-born and Earth-bound superhero. Paradoxically, though, from the perspective and regime of the Human, Aquaman is an alien. As Johns explains, Green Lantern and Aquaman are, in many ways, analogous figures: "I've been writing Green Lantern for a long time and one of the reasons I've enjoyed it is because the depth of stories you can tell is pretty endless with Space and everything." Johns continues, "With Aquaman there's actually the opposite of Green Lantern in that it's inward toward our world, the unknown in our oceans and the depths of the seas . . . fish that should be extinct, things that just baffle science."[62] As Johns recognizes, Green Lantern and Aquaman are analogous figures in that both live in worlds alien to Humanity. But there is a key difference. Green Lantern and Aquaman narratives move in opposite directions. Green Lantern's narratives frequently move away from Earth, farther into outer space, whereas Aquaman's narratives move "inward toward our world," toward inner space.

Although the dominant genre of the Human treats the Global Ocean as marginal to society, the Global Ocean is "the planet's largest and most important habitat," covering more than 70 percent of Earth's surface.[63] Moreover, the Global Ocean offers more than 99 percent of Earth's "habitable living space."[64] The turn to the Global Ocean is a turn to the heart of Earth's biodiversity and to the heart of the ecological crisis that is largely kept offshore from Humanity's consciousness and imagination. Far from a geography alien to the human species, the Ocean is essential to human survival, a primary source of fresh water, food, energy, climate regulation, and oxygen. In fact, scientists "estimate that 50–80% of the oxygen production on Earth comes from the Ocean."[65]

The New 52 *Aquaman*'s creative team—led by Johns, Reis, Prado, and Reis—exemplify how the medium of comics is well positioned to help visualize the Anthropocene as a continuous assault on the Global Ocean, an assault largely unseen in modernity's regime of visibility and legibility. Turning to the Global Ocean to understand, critique, and see beyond the Anthropocene places the creators of The New 52 *Aquaman* in good company. One of the scientists who coined and popularized the periodizing term *Anthropocene* is Eugene F. Stoermer, a marine biologist.[66]

In conjunction with highlighting how Humanity is conducting a full-frontal assault on the Ocean, one that has been unfolding for centuries, The New 52 *Aquaman* also highlights how the surface world is not unified or homogenous. Rather, as the series suggests, the dominant conception of the Human is what Sylvia Wynter identifies as a particular "genre of the human," one predicated on "slavery, conquest, and colonialism."[67] The idealized conception of the Human—posited as universal humanity—is a particular body that is raced as white, gendered as male, sexualized as heterosexual, and without legible disabilities or deficiencies.[68] As becomes evident when analyzing characters such as Mera and Black Manta, the surface world is primarily structured by hierarchies of gender and race. In this sense, the "Anthropocene" is perhaps a misleading periodization. As Joni Adamson and other scholars from feminist, Indigenous, critical race, and postcolonial perspectives insist, "We have never been Anthropos."[69]

Aquaman as Comics Activism?

Since his debut in 1941, Aquaman has been fighting for justice in a geography not always recognized as a battleground for such. Aquaman was not the first marine superhero in U.S. comics. In 1939 Namor, the Sub-Mariner, debuted; soon thereafter, writer-artist Bill Everett's creation was acquired by what would become Marvel Comics.[70] However, I think it's a mistake to read Aquaman as derivative of the Sub-Mariner. In his early years, the Sub-Mariner was marked by his hatred of Humanity, all of whom he tellingly calls "the Americans."[71] In his debut, the Sub-Mariner kills two deep-sea divers and brings their dead bodies to his aquatic home, where his mother congratulates him on the kill.[72] The Sub-Mariner is an ecological figure, and in his early iteration, he was an "anti-human figure" who waged war on Americans, consistently attacking all signs and symbols of civilization.[73] Comics historian Les Daniels writes, "Although the Sub-Mariner acted like a villain, his cause had some justice, and readers reveled in his assaults on civilization. His enthusiastic fans weren't offended by the carnage he created as he wrecked everything from ships to skyscrapers."[74] In a 1940 issue, for example, the Sub-Mariner threatened to flood and destroy Manhattan.[75] Charlie Boatner writes that in his early adventures, the Sub-Mariner resembles less a superhero and more a "cornered wild beast."[76] The Sub-Mariner has good reason to hate Humans, or Americans; as shown in his debut issue, Americans are destroying the Sub-Mariner's home and countless species due to their reckless drilling, polluting, and exploding.[77]

In contrast to the early iteration of Sub-Mariner, Aquaman, from the outset, cared about marine life and Human life equally. In fact, in Aquaman's debut, the marine superhero fights Nazis on the high seas.[78] Aquaman debuted in *More Fun Comics* 73, with a cover date of November 1941. However, the comic appeared on shelves on September 25, months before the United States officially entered World War II. (This dating practice became a signature feature of mainstream comic books to enhance their shelf life and forestall the ideology that a commodity is expired and anachronistic after its stamped cover date.) As fascist regimes spread throughout Europe, Aquaman—like so many comic heroes at the time—can be read as a form of progressive propaganda. While a reigning ideology of isolationism and "America First" became entrenched in the United States, Aquaman became a figure of social justice who saw beyond the myopic borders of the nation-state.

In the late 1930s and early 1940s, myriad comic book creators formed an early iteration of "comics activism" against fascism.[79] Many of the creators in this movement were authors and artists whom the Nazis classified as subhuman, including

Jerry Siegel and Joe Shuster, creators of Superman; Jack Kirby and Joe Simon, creators of Captain America; Will Eisner, creator of the Spirit; and Bob Kane and Bill Finger, creators of Batman.[80] All these writers and artists were Jewish, as was Mort Weisinger, the son of Jewish immigrants from Austria, who is the cocreator of Aquaman.[81] As scholars have argued, the superhero genre has "its roots in the Jewish experience."[82] Collectively these authors and artists used creative, symbolic, and accessible ways to make visible the horrors of the Nazi regime at a time when the United States' official position was one of neutrality, as fascism mushroomed across countries and continents. Early issues of *Superman, Captain America*, and even *Aquaman* were trying to change the political narrative through the increasingly popular medium of comic books.[83]

In Aquaman's debut, authored by Weisinger, the titular superhero rescues "refugees and hospital workers" from a Nazi U-boat attack.[84] In this opening narrative, the Ocean is recognized as a political space, an ideological battlefield, and a geography of justice and injustice. The debut opens with a Nazi U-boat firing a torpedo at "an unarmed ship" that "speeds over the high seas on an errand of mercy."[85] This ship is transporting people whom a fascist regime has deemed disposable and killable. The ideology of Nazism insists that only certain people matter and that everyone beyond this narrow circle of care is unworthy of life. The fascist project demarcates who shall be on the side of life and who shall be disposable, killable, and unmournable. Put differently, fascist ideology demarcates the Human—an ideological category—from the subhuman and animal. To be seen or posited as outside the kingdom of Humanity is to be marked for unimaginable forms of suffering and violence. In contrast, Aquaman becomes a figure of radical empathy, someone who recognizes the value of all life, both human and nonhuman.

When all seems lost for these political refugees and humanitarian workers—the latter risking their lives to do the work that the United States judged as beyond its responsibility—Aquaman saves the day. The image of a "defenseless ship carrying refugees" historically echoes the MS *St Louis*.[86] On May 13, 1939, two years prior to the debut of Aquaman, 937 Jews were allowed to leave Nazi Germany aboard the luxury liner MS *St. Louis*. This Nazi-sanctioned project was largely a publicity stunt to illustrate the point that no nation-state actually wanted Jews. And the Nazi gamble paid off. The MS *St. Louis* initially went to Cuba—and the Cuban government refused to allow any Jews to enter their country. The ship then went to the United States, a nation-state twice the size of all of Europe. Still, the isolationist nation-state refused to allow a single Jew to disembark. The same story played out in Canada. Eventually, the ship was forced to return to Europe, and many of the passengers ended up in concentration camps and killed.[87]

On the opening pages of his debut, Aquaman saves a cruise liner carrying refugees. Since his 1941 debut, Aquaman has been an icon of justice, an identity reinforced by Aquaman being a founding member of the Justice League, which debuted in March 1960, during one of the most important social justice movements in U.S. history: the civil rights movement. Justice, of course, is as much a social construct as the Ocean or nature. Justice has different valences to different people at different times. As I will demonstrate in the following pages, the concept of justice that circulates in The New 52 *Aquaman* is complex, contradictory, and historically conditioned.[88]

While Aquaman's activism during World War II was primarily directed against the growing threat of fascism, from the perspective of the Ocean, World War II was paradoxically a blessing. Paul Greenberg, author of *Four Fish: The Future of the Last Wild Food*, writes, "World War II, while one of the most devastating periods in history for humans, might be called 'The Great Reprieve' if history were written by fish." Greenberg continues, "With mines and submarines ready to blow up any unsuspecting fishing vessel, much of the North Atlantic's depleted fishing grounds were left fallow and fish increased their numbers significantly."[89]

In The New 52 *Aquaman*, published seventy years after the hero's debut, activism manifests in myriad forms. "Comics activism," as defined by Martin Lund, is a commitment and practice of comic book writers and artists to use the medium of comics to make visible violences that are illegible to the dominant culture. For Oceanic activism, this means exposing and moving beyond the dominant culture's terrestrial bias. This physical and conceptual journey offshore, one that The New 52 *Aquaman* explicitly undertakes, changes our vocabulary and our horizon of visibility.[90]

Perhaps the most conspicuous form of comics activism in The New 52 *Aquaman* occurs in issue 17 (February/April 2013) when a collective of ecoactivists called the Sea Devils attempt to halt two massive ships slaughtering a pod of whales. As the Sea Devils race in two red speedboats toward massive, industrial fishing ships, they are shocked by the extensive slaughter that has already taken place. The first three pages of the comic are saturated in blood. Hues of red soak everything, including the boats, clothing, and even speech bubbles.[91] The issue opens in a world of death. One of the activists shares that according to their intel, these hunting ships have "only been here for twenty minutes." In response, another exasperated activist asks, "Then how did they kill so many so fast?"[92] The industrial fishermen achieved this by using new technologies that make their labor more efficient and effective but that cause systemic, widespread, and unprecedented violence below the surface, outside the hegemonic vision of global capitalism (fig. 2).

The fishermen using more powerful weapons to extract a greater sea harvest discloses the violent logic of capitalism's war on nature. Capitalism, in its pursuit of ever-greater profits, seeks more advanced and effective technologies in order to turn everything, including the natural world, into a more controllable, predictable, and increasingly profitable industry. In the age of the Anthropocene, fishing has transformed into an industry. Industrial factory fishing has created a new ecology of destruction that marine life may never fully recover from.[93] The captain and crew are not one-dimensional villains. Rather, they are fishermen trying to survive in an increasingly competitive marketplace.

The whale slaughter is so extreme because the weapons being used originate from Atlantis, the underwater kingdom to which Aquaman is the rightful heir. These more lethal fishing weapons can and should be read not as a disruption of everyday practices but, rather, as an extension of the capitalist norm. These fishing vessels using Atlantean weapons for slaughter can be read as icons of "mammoth factory ships" that "heralded the era of industrial fishing," a devastating era in Oceanic history and a salient index of the Anthropocene.[94] The artwork in this issue visualizes these industrial fishing boats as hulking war machines, signifying how the surface world, the world of capitalism, is at war with the Ocean.

After halting the whale hunt, Aquaman approaches the Sea Devils and voices a hegemonic, surface-world perspective: "People call the Sea Devils eco-terrorists."[95] The Sea Devils are seen as terrorists because they threaten the logic of global capitalism. The hegemonic labeling of the Sea Devils highlights how justice is a complex, socially constructed concept. What the Sea Devils understand and practice as justice—working to stop the industrial fishing complex from slaughtering an endangered species—is, from the perspective of capitalism, a form of terrorism.

As visualized in The New 52 *Aquaman*, the Global Ocean has become a degraded, desecrated space from which capitalism extracts as many resources as it wants and into which capitalism dumps as much waste as it desires. There are several interconnected processes transforming the Global Ocean in unprecedented, destructive ways, many of which are visualized and allegorized in The New 52 *Aquaman*: overfishing, pollution, increased acidification (a result of climate change), and habitat destruction. Every year, billions of pounds of waste are dumped into the Global Ocean, including ten million tons of plastic each year.[96] This systemic dumping of garbage into the Oceans cannot be blamed on Humans—an abstract, ideological category that actively excludes people of color, women, disabled subjects, ethnic minorities, refugees, and all nonnormative populations and bodies that are cast outside of the Human. Rather than blaming Humans in general for the sixth great extinction and, therefore, distributing the blame equally to everyone, it is better and more effective to recognize the structure that enables these systemic and everyday violences: colonial capitalism. As Anna Tsing writes in *The Mushroom at the End of the World*, "The most convincing Anthropocene timeline begins not with our species but rather, with the advent of modern capitalism, which has directed long-distance destruction of landscapes and ecologies."[97]

Capitalism is creating a world of death, a concept aesthetically developed throughout The New 52 *Aquaman* through various means, including coloration. In depicting the scene of the whale slaughter, colorist Rod Reis saturates everything in red. When the leader of the Sea Devils barks into a megaphone, "Captain

2. Sea Devils attempt to halt a whale massacre. "Throne of Atlantis, Epilogue," Geoff Johns (writer), Paul Pelletier (penciller), Sean Parsons (inker), and Rod Reis (colorist), *Aquaman* 7, no. 17, The New 52 (New York: DC Comics, February/April 2013).

Moller! You are breaking the laws of the International Whaling Commission! You will cease your activities immediately!" the leader's speech balloon is outlined in thick layers of red, visually echoing the whales' blood pooling on the Ocean's surface on the top of the page.[98] In fact, the entire page bleeds red: the Sea Devils' speech balloons are outlined in red, their clothing is red, and even their small motorboats are red. This coloration presents a world drowning in blood (fig. 2).

Tellingly, this density of red is broken by Arthur's voice. In this sequence, when Arthur speaks, his language is framed by thick, green caption boxes. Within this green frame—the iconic color of the modern environmental movement—Arthur reflects, "For years, I've tried to fight my birthright."[99] In contrast to capitalism's world order that is soaked in blood, Arthur's emergent narrative, framed in green, calls for a new world order. When he states that he "tried to fight" his "birthright" to become ruler of Atlantis, the caption box appears at the bottom of the page, as if sunken. But when we turn the page, green caption boxes proliferate. This dominance of green corresponds with Arthur explicitly assuming the activist role as protector of the Oceans.

As I will explore in chapter 1, when The New 52 *Aquaman* opens, Arthur tries to disavow his relation to the Ocean in an attempt to pass as Human. Tellingly, it is when Arthur sees this scene of activism that he recognizes the folly of his ways. From this point forward, Arthur commits himself to the activist cause of Ocean protector. As the green caption boxes multiply, Arthur renounces his Humanity and, instead, claims a new identity. At the center of the page, Arthur arches his arms back and yells in fury, "I am the king of the seven seas. . . . I am Aquaman."[100] This declaration occurs on a two-page spread that represents a new social order. In previous pages, the industrial fishing complex was at the top of a Human-imposed hierarchy, killing anything and everything in its grasp. But in this two-page spread, Arthur and his fellow Atlanteans are at the top, riding the crest of a wave. They look down at the captain and crew of the industrial fishing ship, which is now smashed and destroyed, visually suggesting a new social order in which the kingdom of the Ocean supersedes the kingdom of the Human.[101]

When Arthur destroys the industrial fishing boat, he tells the captain, "You're done hunting for good." To which the captain replies, "I have a license."[102] At this juncture, there are two forms of justice being evoked: Human law, which in the dominant culture of global capitalism is synonymous with justice, and ecological justice, which always exceeds and frequently clashes with Human law. (This conflict between forms of justice will be further explored in chapter 3.) The fishing captain is licensed by the state to kill. Therefore, he is acting within the law. Several pages earlier, some members of the fishing crew become nervous by the fast-approaching Sea Devils, whose leader blares into the megaphone that international laws are being "broken" and that "the authorities are on their way." The captain, though, assures his crew that the appropriate authorities "were well paid."[103] From the captain's perspective, this is a sanctioned killing.

At this moment, Arthur is still willing to recognize Human institutions (the law, the state) in which all non-Human life is killable. But then something changes. After a brief negotiation, Arthur snaps. This breaking point occurs within a discourse of "rights." As Arthur approaches the captain with an angry yet still-controlled demeanor, the captain tells him, "You have no right!"[104] From the perspective of the law, the state, and capital—three inextricable and interdependent formations—Arthur and, by extension, all marine life have no rights. Arthur has no jurisdiction or authority to end this sanctioned hunt. And it is at this moment that Arthur loses his cool. With one hand, he yanks the captain into the air and declares, "I have every right. These are my Oceans." In the next panel, shown in close-up, Arthur hauls the captain inward, mere inches from his face, and spews, "And you're trespassing."[105] In this sequence, Arthur extends the discourse of rights to include the Global Ocean.[106] The discourse of rights, tellingly, is justified through the discourse of capitalism. Arthur figures the industrial fishing ship as "trespassing" on what is now metaphorically figured as private property. Moreover, Arthur uses the possessive voice when declaring, "I have every right. These are my Oceans."

It's important to recognize the fish that Johns chose as the symbol that galvanizes Arthur to renounce his Humanity and to claim his responsibility and stewardship of the Global Ocean. At the issue's onset, the industrial fishing ships were sanctioned to hunt humpback whales. In the late twentieth century, humpback whales had become icons of a new paradigm for thinking about and framing marine life. This paradigm shift occurred, in large part, because of popular culture. In 1958, while working for the U.S. government at SOFAR station off the coast of Bermuda, Frank Watlington was listening patiently for Russian submarines, using underwater hydrophones. Instead of finding traces of the "enemy," Watlington instead discovered and began recording humpback whale songs. Prior to this "discovery," the Human kingdom had been largely ignorant of these songs. The humpback song became a symbol for the complex languages that flourished in the Ocean's depths, beyond the sensory, everyday world of Humans. Marine biologist Philip Clapham describes whale song as "probably the most complex in the animal kingdom."[107]

A decade after his recordings, the U.S. Navy authorized Watlington to turn his recordings over to budding whale scientists Roger Payne and Scott McVay. The latter turned these songs into an album that could be packaged and released for mass consumption. This act of mass publicity was informed by an activist intention. Payne and McVay figured that if the masses could hear whale songs and, hence, hear and appreciate their language, they would change their minds about marine life and demand that whale killings cease immediately. Like Johns, Reis, Prado, and Reis three decades later, they used the genre of popular culture to engage in activist work. In 1970 the album *Songs of the Humpback Whale* was released. The album came with a forty-eight-page booklet in English and in Japanese, documenting the current crisis many whale species faced due to Human hunting. Surprisingly, *Songs of the Humpback Whale* became a best-selling album. (To date, it remains the best-selling nature-sound record of all time.) Moreover, these whale songs became incorporated into human songs, creating a new hybrid form of music.[108] The power of popular culture is exemplified by this album. It created a sea change in human perception and conception. David Rothenberg writes, "As whale song entered the realm of popular artistic inspiration, so it began to be taken more seriously by science."[109] Moreover, this popular-culture intervention was instrumental in creating "worldwide support for a global moratorium on whale hunting passed by the International Whaling Commission in 1986."[110] In the late twentieth century, humpback whales became an icon for marine intelligence, language, and aesthetics. Yet what was once an icon of perhaps a new respect for the Global Ocean becomes narrated in The New 52 *Aquaman* as a momentary ecological victory that is now drowned by capitalism's will to destroy.

In response to this whale slaughter, Arthur and several members of Atlantis's army rush to the crime scene. Murk, the leader of the "frontline army of the great nation of Atlantis," proclaims with a belligerent snarl, "Today, the sea is red with the blood of the sacred singers."[111] From the perspective of Atlantis, a kingdom part of the Ocean's ecology, this is a slaughter of "sacred" beings, an egregious, unspeakable crime. From the perspective of capitalism, though, this slaughter is a profane, everyday occurrence. Murk reminds his fellow Atlanteans that Humans consistently "return to kill again. They always do."[112] As Murk articulates, the only way for the Ocean's diversity to have a future is to recognize that the surface and marine world are at war—a war that has lasted for centuries. And the appropriate response, Murk argues, is to fight back.

Arthur, though, does not fight back. Instead, he works to realize a new world order: "to unite land and sea."[113] This should be construed as an activist project. To see the Ocean and land as one—to decenter the terrestrial bias that structures normative epistemologies—is a radical ecological project that critiques all forms of hierarchical organization that reign on the surface world, including capitalism, genderism, and racism. In The New 52 Aquaman, this activism assumes a form that may seem counterintuitive. In contrast to the direct activism represented by the Sea Devils, Johns, Reis, Prado, and Reis develop their activism primarily through the form of allegory.

Reading Allegorically

In an interview leading up to the launch of The New 52 Aquaman, IGN journalist Joey Esposito praised Johns for his previous representation of Aquaman in Brightest Day (2010–11). Esposito shares that one of his "favorite moments" is when Aquaman confronted an oil spill. He then asks Johns, "How big of a role will these sort of environmental issues play in the series?" Johns replies, "I think probably it'll be more metaphorical than literal with this book."[114] As Johns indicates in this interview, The New 52 Aquaman challenges readers to interpret metaphorically, a reading strategy, I argue, that must be applied both at the level of content and form.

While Johns makes explicit the privileging of metaphor, I want to suggest that The New 52 *Aquaman* is better understood as a specific form of metaphor—an allegory. When a metaphor is "sustained" and "developed," it becomes an allegory.[115] Allegories stretch and open narratives to diverse voices. As stated earlier, *allegory* literally means "other speaking." Allegory listens to the voice of the other, the voice made other by reigning ideological regimes. In contrast to the dominant culture that silences othered voices, allegory tries to listen and hear others speak. In this sense, allegory can be understood as a mode that refigures what ideologically passes as reality.

Following Walter Benjamin, scholars recognize that allegories flourish when reality is in crisis, when the dominant paradigms for understanding the world begin to crack and crumble.[116] As DeLoughrey summarizes, "After Benjamin, it is generally agreed that allegory signals an era of calamity and a way of responding, inadequately but necessarily, to crisis."[117] The New 52 *Aquaman*, I contend, can be read as an accessible allegory of the multiple, intersecting crises organized under the periodization the Anthropocene.[118] Most prominently, The New 52 *Aquaman* develops multiple, critical allegories that help make visible how, in the Anthropocene, the Global Ocean has become a site of an unceasing colonial-capitalist onslaught causing slow and systemic death in all Oceanic regions.

Allegory is not a unified, monolithic aesthetic concept. In *Allegory and Ideology*, for example, Fredric Jameson distinguishes between progressive and regressive allegories. Regressive allegories reduce the world's complexities and contradictions into simplified, easily digestible narratives. In such reductive allegories, allegorical figures have a "point-to-point" correlation.[119] In this regressive form, the voice of the other becomes perfectly translatable and easily incorporated into the dominant culture.[120] Such regressive allegories fail to recognize non-Human animals, for example, as complex, diverse, and dynamic beings that exceed Human paradigms and worldviews. Regressive allegories, Jameson argues, support hierarchical structures such as Humanism.[121] In the dangerous worldview textualized and reproduced by regressive allegories, only Humans are posited as complex and pluralistic; all non-Human animals are reduced to simplified and often singular meanings.

In contrast, progressive allegories have "multiple meanings."[122] Such allegories are polysemous, offering complex, layered meanings that challenge and transgress Human paradigms. Progressive allegories unsettle and upset the reigning social order's categories, classifications, and codifications. Therefore, progressive allegories can be an important form in developing an ecological imagination. Progressive allegories remove the Human from the center of meaning making and story worlds and, moreover, gesture toward the multiplicity of social relations and meanings that defy and exceed the myopic, hierarchical paradigms of the Anthropocene.

Allegories proliferate during times of crisis and convey a deep "dissatisfaction with what it terms the literal level, the surface."[123] In this sense, allegories are analogous to the Ocean. Like the Ocean, allegories invite us to dive beneath the surface and to see and study a world invisible from a surface perspective. Allegories flourish when subjects question what the dominant culture insists is a stable, secure reality. They thrive when the hegemonic conception of the world is seen as contingent and historical, rather than fixed and eternal. Progressive allegories don't offer solutions; rather, they ask questions and gesture toward the plurality of meanings and social relations beyond reigning paradigms such as Humanism, racism, genderism, and capitalism.

Allegory is a device, a genre, a theme, and an interpretive act.[124] In *The Political Unconscious*, Jameson provocatively argues that all interpretations can be described as allegorical acts.[125] Allegory, in other words, can be internal to a cultural text, and it can be external to the text. In other words, critics can read a text as allegorical even if the text itself is not intrinsically allegorical. This interpretative process is called *allegoresis*.[126] Allegoresis is an interpretive mode, or as Jameson writes, "the reading of a text as though it were an allegory."[127] In *The Political Unconscious*, Jameson argues that allegorical readings are processes that "open . . . the text to multiple meanings."[128] This reading practice, Jameson emphasizes, is deeply political. Throughout this study, I analyze the comic allegories internal to The New 52 *Aquaman* and practice allegoresis, illustrating the progressive energy of reading comics as allegory even when the text seems outside of or refuses such a paradigm. In this sense, I read with the text; at other times, adjacent to the text; and still at other times, against the text.

So let's allegorically dive in.

1

Deep in the Trenches

Monsters, Humanism, and Ecological Allegories

Ocean activism frequently foregrounds the profound spiritual bond between Humans and the Ocean. This spiritual bond was highlighted in 1998, the year that the United Nations declared the International Year of the Ocean.[1] To participate in this international appreciation and promise of global stewardship, the United States hosted its first and, thus far, only "National Ocean Conference" (July 11–12, 1998). The 244-page conference guide begins with a quote from then president Bill Clinton: "If we want our children to inherit the gift of living oceans, we must make the 21st century a great century of stewardship of our seas."[2] The "gift" of the Ocean was on full display during the conference, which was held in Monterey Bay, California, overlooking the United States' largest marine sanctuary. This setting symbolized the political success Ocean activism can achieve.

One of the conference's keynote speakers was marine biologist Sylvia Earle, who summarized some of the key points from her best-selling book, *Sea Change: A Message of the Oceans*. In the book, Earle writes, "The *living ocean* drives planetary chemistry, governs climate and weather, and otherwise provides the cornerstone of the life-support system for all creatures on our planet. . . . If the sea is sick, we'll feel it. If it dies, we die. Our future and the state of the ocean are one."[3] This discourse of

Human-Oceanic unity is animated by a strong sense of spirituality in which the Ocean becomes posited as an ecological symbol of harmonious interdependency and interconnectedness. This discourse of spiritual unity was reinforced by a widely distributed pamphlet at the conference in which then First Lady Hillary Clinton informed the audience that "seventy-one percent of our planet is ocean and seventy-one percent of our body is saltwater. . . . There is this extraordinary connection between who we are as human beings and what happens in this magnificent body of water."[4] This activist discourse works to make the Ocean legible not as an alien other but, rather, as our spiritual home that signifies balance, tranquility, and oneness. The Ocean produces a state of being that transcends the ontic world. Freud identifies this blissful state as an "oceanic feeling."[5]

This discourse that posits a deep connection between Humans and Oceans pervades prominent forms of U.S. Ocean activism. Rachel Carson, who is widely recognized as one of the founders of the modern U.S. environmental movement, uses spiritual language throughout her sea trilogy, which includes *Under the Sea-Wind* (1941), *The Sea around Us* (1951), and *The Edge of the Sea* (1955).[6] Such activists insist that by learning to see the Ocean beyond a utilitarian paradigm (for example, only seeing the Ocean as a geography from which fish can be extracted), we learn to see how deeply connected we are to the non-Human world, and hence, we can learn to break from the paradigm that posits Humans as divorced and deracinated from nature. In a U.S. context, seeing the Ocean through an aesthetics of awe, mystery, connectivity, and oneness is popularized through a variety of mass-media texts, including popular nature documentaries such as *The Blue Planet* (2001) and *Oceans* by Disneynature (2010).

If we understand The New 52 *Aquaman* as a form of comics activism, then it's telling that it disavows this spiritual discourse and, instead, represents the Ocean as threatening and monstrous. The New 52 *Aquaman*'s first narrative arc, "The Trench" (issues 1–4, September/November 2011–December 2011 / February 2012), seems to mediate the Ocean through the genre of horror. The trench—the name for this fictional species, in addition to the depression on the Ocean floor—initially seem to be nothing more than killing machines who breach the surface and attack random citizens along the Maine coastline and who threaten the entire East Coast of the United States. In this sense, "The Trench" narrative arc, and its artwork in particular, seems to perpetuate the popular and pervasive trope of the Ocean as a malignant and ever-present threat to Humans. This trope represents the Ocean as replete with unseen, unknown creatures from the deep sea that are a constant source of terror to Human communities. In a modern U.S. context, this trope is popularized by movies such as *Jaws* (1977), *Deep Blue Sea* (1999), *The Reef* (2010), *Piranha 3D* (2010), *The Meg* (2018), *47 Meters Down: Uncaged* (2019), *Underwater* (2020), and, turning to television, the institutionalized ritual of Shark Week, which began on the Discovery Channel in 1988 and has repeated every year since.

Initially, the trench appear as monsters that exceed and escape Human frameworks of understanding. As Aquaman descends to the deepest parts of the Ocean, beyond Human epistemology, he encounters an ecosystem beyond his ken. As the narrative unfolds, though, the trench prove to be not monsters but a species suffering greatly due to radical transformations to their home ecology. This chapter analyzes the trench as an allegory for how capitalist institutions are radically transforming all Earth's ecologies, including the so-called alien Ocean.[7] As "The Trench" narrative unfolds, we learn that the trench are coming ashore for food because their habitat is becoming a dead zone. This narrative arc, I argue, is an allegory for the proliferation of dead zones throughout the Global Ocean due to late capitalism. But as with all progressive allegories, there is no one-to-one correlation. The trench's meanings are multiple. The trench signify ecological forms of death and, I argue below, racialized forms of death.

"The Bottom of the Atlantic Ocean"

The first page of The New 52 *Aquaman* issue 1 minimizes and marginalizes Human language. At the top left of the page, a caption box reads, "The bottom of the Atlantic Ocean."[8] These are the only words on the page, tellingly located outside the panel that showcases the artwork of Ivan Reis (penciller), Joe Prado (inker), and Rod Reis (colorist) (fig. 3). From the outset, there is a disjunction between images and words. The artwork presents a space beyond Human language and comprehension, a space of various shades of gray and black that resist the Human eye, which has become the central apparatus for meaning making in modernity. The page layout visually challenges the romantic discourse of the Ocean's mystical unity and oneness. Rather than a cohesive, full-page panel, the Ocean is represented by three vertical panels, each stretching the length of the page. This divided sea foregrounds the gutters and, hence, the empty white space, highlighting the challenges and impossibility for Human artwork to represent the Ocean. In a very real way, as this opening image suggests, the Ocean is alien to Human paradigms and modes of meaning making, including aesthetics. The prominent gutters make readers aware of the failure to fully represent the Ocean's enormity, complexity, diversity, and dynamics. In this sense, the artwork of Reis, Prado, and Reis makes visible Steinberg's claim that cultural representations of

3. The trench ascend from their home ecology. "The Trench, Part 1," Geoff Johns (writer), Ivan Reis (penciller), Joe Prado (inker), and Rod Reis (colorist), *Aquaman* 7, no. 1, The New 52 (New York: DC Comics, September/November 2011).

the Ocean are always incomplete and always rife with "gaps."[9] Oceanic representations are persistent encounters with the "unrepresentable."[10]

While robotic technologies can now illuminate the Ocean floor with full-spectrum and incandescent lamps and, thereby, expand the reach of Human exploration and exploitation, Reis, Prado, and Reis represent the Ocean floor as beyond scientific probing and categorization.[11] From these alien depths, what appears to be a threatening monster emerges. This humanoid figure resembles monsters that circulate in popular culture. In conjunction with its blackness, its open mouth reveals elongated, sharp teeth, resembling a piranha's mouth. Moreover, its hollow, black eyes negate the Humanist cliché that positions the eyes—Human eyes with pupils—as a window to the soul. Without pupiled eyes, according to this logic, there is no soul and, hence, no interiority.

This humanoid figure's eyes and open mouth echo the blackness of its surroundings. Visually, this figure is inextricable from its environment, a conjoining reinforced by a shared coloration and shading. This conjoining, though, is challenged by the opening panel. When the comic begins, this figure emerges from a geographic trench, removing itself from what appears to be its native ecology, and swims toward the top of the page, toward the surface. On the next page, we see that there is not just one monster; rather, there are myriad monsters, hordes moving to the surface. From the outset, the collective team of Johns, Reis, Prado, and Reis place us in a genre of allegory. These monsters are called "the trench," sharing a name with their home environment. Put differently, these monsters are explicit allegories of their ecology, embodying their home ecology.

Before following the trench to the surface, I want to tarry at "the bottom of the Atlantic Ocean" to delineate a history and a theory that will become more prominent as this book progresses. Although geographically distant from the surface world, the trench is not a geography "alien" from the Human. Rather, this is a space that should be recognized as a Black graveyard.[12] During the Middle Passage, a journey in which the diversity of African peoples became "Black," the Atlantic Ocean became an archive of Humanity's racialized barbarity. In *Poetics of Relation*, Édouard Glissant writes that when a slave ship needed to lighten its load, "it was easiest just to . . . [toss] cargo overboard, weighing it down with balls and chains. These underwater signposts mark the course between the Gold Coast and the Leeward Islands."[13] In the capitalist, colonial discourse that anchors and steers the dominant narratives of modernity, "cargo" is code for Black lives. Rather than being lost to time, these bodies and histories become, in Glissant's materialist poetics, "underwater signposts" that cover the Atlantic Ocean floor.

Collectively, these "underwater signposts" form a different sign system than the one privileged on land. In contrast to the sign systems studied in the Humanities' "linguistic turn," indexed by thinkers such as Saussure, Lacan, and Derrida, the submarine signs at the center of Glissant's meditation are unseen and unknown in the dominant, landed institutions of modernity. And yet despite this ontological rift between landed and maritime sign systems, the significations and narratives buried in the Oceans are essential to understanding the bloody history of modernity.

Glissant's book opens with the voices of two Caribbean poets. The first is from Derek Walcott, "Sea is History," and the second is from Edward Kamau Brathwaite, "The unity is sub-marine."[14] Taken together, these two epigraphs open a paradigm that counters and critiques the dominant narrative of modernity. For the sake of time, I want to look briefly at Walcott's poem, which connects to Glissant's text to form a literary "archipelago . . . laden with palpable death."[15] The poem begins with a series of questions that intervene in the dominant logic of modernity that wishes to locate history away from the watery part of the world:

> Where are your monuments, your battles, martyrs?
> ~~Where is your tribal memory? Sirs,~~
> in that grey vault. The sea. The sea
> has locked them up. The sea is History.[16]

The poem begins by announcing modernity's epistemic limits. The sea's vast archive of African history—repressed in dominant European and American knowledge regimes—remains "locked . . . up" and imprisoned in the Atlantic's "grey vault." The fact that Walcott even needs to ask, "Where are your monuments, your battles, martyrs? / Where is your tribal memory?" signifies a dominant colonial culture in which subjects are taught *not* to understand the Ocean as a space of history. "The Sea Is History" challenges this logic and posits the Atlantic Ocean as a "submarine" archive of anti-Black violence, terrorism, and genocide.

Focusing on the Black Atlantic, Glissant develops an alternative paradigm for understanding history. Against the West's concept of history as "linear" and committed to "generalization," a singular story in which all particulars and specificities are either "assimilated" or "annihilated,"[17] Glissant develops a theory in which history becomes spatialized.[18] For Glissant, history "does not pass, it accumulates."[19] The history of modernity, birthed during the Middle Passage, accumulates at the bottom of the Atlantic Ocean and stretches toward the surface. In his important study *Specters of the Atlantic: Finance Capital, Slavery, and the Philosophy of History*, Ian Baucom writes, "If, for Glissant, modernity is the globalization of relation, then a relational modernity also has a ground, and that ground is alluvial, Atlantic, submarine. If time does not pass (or even recover itself in a lightning flash) but accumulates, then the segment of time we call modernity piles up from a starting point, and that starting point is the ramified system of transatlantic slavery."[20] The bodies and narratives accumulating in the Atlantic Ocean signify that racialized slavery is not located in the distant past but, rather, is a violence that continues to haunt and structure the present.

To understand the genocides, terrors, and horrors of history, we must turn to the Ocean. The Global Ocean is a geography and medium that is both radically alien to the Human and, at the same time, profoundly shaped by Human institutions. The Ocean as a site of violence and suffering is visualized throughout The New 52 *Aquaman*.

At the comics' onset, the Ocean is visually saturated in darkness and coded as a monstrous order. From the beginning, "the bottom of the Atlantic Ocean" seems to be a geography far removed from Human societies and institutions. However, as "The Trench" narrative arc makes clear, this ecology proves to be not an alien space but, rather, one structured by the everyday violences of colonial capitalism. In this narrative arc, such violences become manifest by the trench; and in rising to the surface, the trench allegorize the return of the repressed. This return, as I will argue in the next sections, has profound ecological and racialized significations.

Monsters of Late Capitalism

Reis, Prado, and Reis visually encode the trench as monsters, and Johns's narrative seems to reinforce this identity. In contrast to Humans, who are ideologically defined by their capacity for reason, self-discipline, and creative self-expression, the trench initially appear as simple-minded organisms without attributes that commonly elicit Human empathy and care. When we are first introduced to the trench in issue 1 (September/November

2011), they "speak" mostly in monosyllabic words. On the second page, when they first speak, there are twelve visible words, and only one word has more than one syllable: the disyllabic "above."[21] The word they become most associated with, the word they repeat again and again, is "food." In issue 2 (October/December 2011), the trench repeat the word "food" ten times. And the final issue of the narrative arc, issue 4 (December 2011 / February 2012), is titled "Food for the Trench." The trench rush toward the surface world in search of food, and once they breach the water's surface, they become killing machines. They kill indiscriminately and ferociously, first attacking fishermen (issue 1) and, later, attacking a coastal town in Maine, in which they randomly and insatiably kill men, women, and children (issues 2 and 3). In case the trench's identity as monsters wasn't explicit enough on a visual level, Humans throughout the narrative arc refer to them as "monsters."[22] The trench destroy and terrorize Human society. They are the monstrous other.

When Humans respond to the trench with an aggressive militarized show of force (issue 3, November 2011 / January 2012), Aquaman instead takes a contrasting approach and tries to understand why the trench are attacking the surface world. Our interpretation, our allegoresis, should follow Aquaman's empathetic approach. To see the trench as a complex species worthy of understanding is to challenge and critique the ideological category of "monsters." The monster, a pervasive trope that circulates everywhere in popular culture, in all media and all genres, is an ideological category with profound political and racial ramifications. To think more about the ideologies and politics of monsters mandates that we ask: To whom does the category of *monster* apply? The ideological labeling and projection of *monster* onto a body or bodies transforms a potential *who* (a pronoun that demarcates a subject with interiority) into a *what* (a pronoun that strips beings of any depths, rights, respect, and dignity). To be labeled a monster, in other words, is an ideological transformation from a potential subject into an object that is outside the discourse and community of Humanity and, therefore, beyond the epistemology of Humanism.[23]

Monsters are the projection and product of Humans and the ideology of Humanism. In 1966, two decades removed from European fascism sanctioning and implementing which ethnicities and groups should live and which can be tortured and killed with impunity and without mourning—that is, which humans are recognized as Humans and which are not—Foucault predicted the death of the Human. In the aftermath of the Holocaust and Gulags, Foucault foresaw a new epistemology emerging. In *The Order of Things* Foucault anticipates what would later be called "posthumanism." Foucault understood that the Human is not a biological category but an ideological one that is socially constructed. Foucault concludes *The Order of Things* by suggesting that the regime of the Human is coming to an end. The book concludes, "Man is an invention of recent date. And one perhaps nearing its end."[24] In its dominant form, Man is a gendered, racialized, classed, and able-bodied form. Despite Humanity's claim of universality, it is a myopic category that excludes most biological humans.[25]

The dominant form of Humanism is inextricable from the structures of whiteness, masculinity, able-bodiedness, heteronormativity, capitalism, Christianity, and anthropocentrism. Humanism's cloak of universality seeks to conceal that it is a philosophy built on exclusion, degradation, and devaluation. More specifically, it is a philosophy predicated on the continual construction of "others," a term closely aligned with "monsters." Philosopher Rosi Braidotti writes that the "Eurocentric paradigm" of Humanism "implies the dialectics of self and other, and the binary logic of identity and otherness as respectively the motor for and the cultural logic of universal Humanism."

Braidotti continues, "This universalistic posture and its binary logic" is animated by understanding difference as a pejorative.[26] In this Humanist logic—a logic animated by hierarchical thinking—difference becomes a mark of "inferiority." People who are marked as other become "reduced to the less than human status of disposable bodies."[27] In the first narrative arc, the trench are ideologically constructed as others; and tellingly, the second narrative arc in the series is titled "The Others" (issues 7–13, March/May 2012–October/December 2012). The New 52 *Aquaman* critiques the destructive logic of otherness that animates Humanism and underpins the Anthropocene.

At the end of issue 1, the trench breach the water's surface; and in issue 2, they attack the seaside town of Beachrock. Aquaman rushes to Beachrock, where he learns that "half the town" is "missing" and that the U.S. Navy and Coast Guard have secured the scene of destruction.[28] In a double splash page, we see the full force of the U.S. military-industrial complex, replete with large U.S. Navy ships, rescue boats, scuba divers, and helicopters circling the surrounding waters, searching for survivors and victims. In the foreground, a U.S. military man in full fatigues stands with an automatic weapon in his hand. Although it's night, the U.S. military apparatus overcomes nature's setting with powerful illumination coming from all sources, including the militarized ships and helicopters patrolling the Ocean.[29]

Aquaman rushes to the scene of violence with Mera, a marine-centered superhero who is also Aquaman's intimate partner. (Chapter 2 will center on Mera and chart how she learns to see the surface world as a patriarchal kingdom.) When Aquaman and Mera arrive at this scene of mass death in order to help, the Human community does not express gratitude. Rather, authorities dismiss and degrade the two marine superheroes. The town's sheriff, for example, is annoyed at the presence of Aquaman and Mera, the latter of whom he calls, against

Mera's wishes, "Aquawoman."[30] After the sheriff makes it clear that Aquaman and Mera's presence is unwelcome, Mera tells Aquaman, out of Human earshot, "They should be bowing before you." Aquaman replies, "I'm not a king to them, Mera." Mera has the last words on the page, words that we should read as having a pedagogical charge: "They need to be educated."[31] In the following pages, I read Aquaman as a pedagogical figure who helps teach an accessible form of Ocean literacy. Using the grammar of popular culture and the medium of comic books, The New 52 Aquaman teaches surface-world subjects that the Global Ocean is a sovereign space worthy of respect, reverence, appreciation, and study. Moreover, the series also teaches that the Oceans are an all-too-Human space that is shaped by the interlocking, hierarchical structures of capitalism, racism, and genderism.

Learning to see Aquaman as a pedagogical figure is an activist gesture. However, as the opening narrative arc foregrounds, wherever Aquaman goes on the surface world, he is mocked, marginalized, and alienated. When The New 52 Aquaman opens, both Arthur and Mera have abdicated the Ocean and, instead, have committed to living on the surface world, trying to pass as Human. However, this effort proves futile. Arthur's backstory, one alluded to in The New 52's opening arc, is that he used to be King of Atlantis. However, he abdicated his throne, because the citizens of this underwater nation refuse to accept him into their political community, because he is not a pure Atlantean. Arthur is half-Atlantean and half-human, a mixed superhero who is rejected and disavowed in both the surface and water worlds. Arthur's status as being of two worlds, but belonging to neither, highlights the complex social construction of identity, belonging, and community, themes that will become more prominent as this book unfurls. This theme of not belonging due to one's mixed status is a thinly veiled allegory for race and racism. Arthur is not just a superhero; he is an allegory of a mixed-race superhero.[32]

In the second narrative arc, "The Others," Arthur has a hallucinatory episode due to extreme water deprivation during which his human father appears. Aquaman is in a desert, on the verge of death, when his father, Tom Curry, manifests. Leaning down, Tom tells his son that he will never be embraced by the Human community. In what could be Aquaman's dying moments, he imagines his father admonishing him: "You're not like anyone up here. Up here they laugh at you."[33] As Tom rehearses, his son left the Ocean because he wanted to find a community that would accept and welcome him, but this desire proved futile: "You'll never belong anywhere. You'll always be lost."[34] This is not a father being cruel; rather, Tom is articulating a form of social realism. Humanism, it is implied, is a form of racism.[35] Despite his Aryan appearance, Aquaman is marked as a mixed-race superhero, a theme that will become more explicit as Johns's three-year run nears its conclusion (see chapter 4).

The dominant, terrestrial culture needs to be "educated," as Mera suggests, to respect Aquaman and, by extension, the Ocean. Just as Aquaman defies and transgresses Human categories, so too does the Ocean. Literature and environmental scholar Steve Mentz argues that turning to the Ocean requires a new vocabulary, one that is fluid and dynamic, not stable and fixed. For example, Mentz writes, turning to the Ocean, the organizing category of "field" becomes displaced and replaced by a new keyword: "current."[36] Mentz elaborates, "For a long time thinking has happened in fields, areas of expertise imagined to be as stable and reliable as pastures. What if instead we redescribe the adventures of thinking as currents, as rates of flow and change?"[37] The Ocean upsets Human frames of understanding. Learning to see how the Ocean dissolves dominant paradigms is the comics activism practiced in The New 52 *Aquaman*. This is not a didactic activism but, rather, one that assumes allegorical forms. In the series' opening narrative arc, one of the most prominent activist missions is to teach readers how to see the Ocean as a complex, layered ecology with an awesome array of diverse, interlocking species that defy Humanistic categories such as "others" and "monsters."

In the opening narrative arc, there are two competing ways to frame and understand the trench. The Human paradigm is symbolized by the military-industrial complex, which sees the world through scopes that frame all living beings as potential targets to be killed from a distance. In this paradigm, the trench exemplify otherness, Humanity's "negative and specular counterpart" that should be eliminated by any means necessary.[38] It is telling that Aquaman does not assist or abet this militarized effort. Instead, he breaks away from this militarized operation and engages in his own investigation. What guides Aquaman's action is not violence but a quest to understand why these marine creatures are attacking the surface world in the first place. Aquaman offers an alternative way to see the trench, a way of seeing that allegorizes ecological seeing.

Aquaman tears away from the military assemblage and goes to the end of the dock, where he stares into the distance. In the water, two military figures converse as if Aquaman is not within hearing distance: "What's he doing?" Although the question is not directly addressed to Aquaman, as if communication between Humans and the non-Human world is not possible, Aquaman answers in a panel that zooms in on his eyes: "I'm looking."[39] This explanation is both diegetic, existing within the story world, and nondiegetic, addressing the reader. The New 52 *Aquaman* urges us, in creative, innovative ways, to see the Ocean in all its layers and multitudes. Using echolocation to see into the Ocean—highlighting how different beings have evolved different ways of experiencing and processing the world—Aquaman tells Mera that the seas are shockingly empty: "There's nothing out there to respond. No fish. No anything."[40] Within a dominant, Human paradigm, this empty sea is the result of the monstrous sea creatures eating everything. But reading allegorically, this empty sea signifies a structural ecological crisis.

Throughout "The Trench" arc, multiple Humans allude to the ecological crises unfolding in the Ocean. At the end of issue 1, for example, several fishermen are surprised that they are not hauling in any fish. As one fisherman says, "We've been at it all day and not a single bite," to which another fisherman replies, "Something's up. These waters aren't overfished."[41] Although it's posited that the trench are responsible for eating a copious amount of food, this conversation casually indexes a crisis marking the Global Ocean: overfishing. These fishermen are surprised they are not catching fish only because this area is not overfished. The logic, of course, is that other areas are. Famed ecologist and conservationist Jeremy Jackson summarizes that the "threats to marine ecosystems" are myriad: "The synergistic effects of habitat destruction, overfishing, ocean warming, increasing acidification, and massive nutrient runoff" are "culprits in a grand transformation of once complex ocean ecosystems."[42] All these interlocking destructive processes are mentioned, suggested, or allegorized in The New 52 run.

As Aquaman investigates the coastal waters, he sees a dead zone. Dead zones are defined by having little oxygen (hypoxia) or no oxygen at all (anoxia).[43] Such areas with reduced or no oxygen mean that "most marine life either dies, or, if they are mobile such as fish, leave the area. Habitats that would normally be teeming with life become, essentially, biological deserts."[44] In the Anthropocene, such dead zones are proliferating in the Oceans, and their cause is Human economies and activities.

Roorda explains, "The causes for dead zone[s] lie far inland, and the culprit is chemical fertilizer." Roorda continues, "Fertilizers in many forms flow over the vast fields of corn, wheat, and soybeans . . . across the thousands of golf courses, sports fields, and landscaped areas of . . . towns . . . and onto innumerable grass lawns, the tidy icon of American suburbia. Rainstorms wash away much of it, which then flows into tributaries of every description on its way to the Ocean, where all water wants to go, if it ever gets the chance."[45] Chemical fertilizers contain exorbitantly high levels of nitrogen and phosphorus, which, when introduced into Oceanic ecosystems, strangle the oxygen to minimal and even zero levels.[46] Dead zones are now developing throughout the watery world. In a U.S. context, dead zones are primarily spreading in the Great Lakes and coastal regions. Tellingly, when Aquaman "looks" at the Ocean, he is looking at a coastal region. If Aquaman were to look south with his echo-location powers, he would see the second-largest dead zone in the world, located in the Gulf of Mexico, just off the U.S. coast.[47]

While Aquaman studies this dead zone, the trench attack again. Even though Aquaman's life is endangered, he remains curious about the creatures. "What are you?" he inquisitively asks.[48] Despite using the pronoun "what" rather than "who," Aquaman refuses to see the trench as categorical monsters that need to be destroyed. This refusal becomes the narrative engine of "The Trench" arc. While all the Humans around him insist that the trench are unintelligible monsters, Aquaman remains steadfast that these are forms of life worthy of respect and dignity. Aquaman refuses to see the trench as exemplifying monstrosity. Instead, he tries to understand what is ecologically catalyzing the trench to come to the surface in the first place. As Aquaman's actions signify throughout the narrative arc, to understand this unknown species, one must first find and study their home ecology.

Aquaman's ecological investigation is informed by an open mind, radical empathy, and a commitment to biodiversity. This quest for understanding is contrasted by the dominant surface attitude that sees the marine creatures as monsters beyond intelligibility and care. This dominant ideology is critically encapsulated by the cover of issue 3, whose title reads, "Cannibals of the Deep." Calling the trench "cannibals," like calling them monsters, legitimates their otherness and sanctions their mass destruction. After the trench's second attack, a military leader barks, "Get our guys out of the water and keep those choppers in the air. They see anything moving below the surface, they take it out."[49] An all-out war has been declared on a species. This war on the Ocean abounds with allegorical significance.

The militarization of the seas is a prominent development of modernity, a process that has enabled the expansion and perpetuation of empires.[50] Political scientist Nicholas J. Spykman wrote in 1944, when Aquaman comics were in their infancy, "Maritime mobility is the basis for a new type of geopolitical structure, the overseas empire. . . . The British, French, Japanese empires and the sea power of the United States have all contributed to the development of a modern world which is a single field for the interplay of political forces."[51] The militarization of the Ocean is explicit in "The Trench" narrative arc. But what The New 52 *Aquaman* suggests is a different form of empire, a capitalist empire that extends around the globe and wages constant war on the Global Ocean, a war that takes on a literal register in the third narrative arc, "Throne of Atlantis" (November 2012 / January 2013–February/April 2013), which will be the subject of chapter 3.

Humanity's military apparatus sanctions helicopters to shoot all living beings in the Ocean. Aquaman protests this militaristic paradigm: "You don't want to shoot into the water."[52] This

Human authorization to wantonly kill anything in the water that moves allegorizes the Human attitude toward marine life in modernity. As Aquaman explains, by shooting into the Ocean, the military will kill not just marine life (viewed as disposable life) but Human life as well. This is the message of Ocean activists around the world. This philosophy—that what kills marine life also kills Human life—echoes, for example, Sylvia Earle's message: "If the sea is sick, we'll feel it. If it dies, we die. Our future and the state of the ocean are one."[53] By killing the Ocean, we kill ourselves.

Against this militaristic logic, Aquaman understands that the trench are not monsters with a singular drive to kill. Rather, they are coming ashore in desperate search for food. Their appearance on the surface world signifies that something radically disruptive has occurred in their home ecology. If we learn to see beyond their "monstrous" appearance, we can see evidence of their political organization. The trench preserve select prey in cocoon-like structures and bring the preserved prey back home to other community members. In contrast to the Human projection of this species as monsters, the trench prove to be a complex, layered community that is engaging in activities that should be understood as both ethical and political. They are risking their lives to bring back food for their community, willing to sacrifice their lives for the benefit of a greater, collective good.

However, the Human world is ideologically blind to the ethical and political life of non-Human species, especially marine species. When the trench suddenly return to the Ocean's depths with their preserved prey, Aquaman wonders where they went. A military figure retorts, "Who cares where?" And another armed figure adds, "I saw them eating their dead."[54] This Human perspective to not care about marine life is buttressed by ideologies of barbarity projected onto this marine species. Here, a

military figure purports to have witnessed this unknown species engaging in acts of cannibalism, the same claim European colonialists projected onto Africans, ideologically justifying that Africans are ontologically unfit for Human civilization.[55]

The New 52 *Aquaman*'s attention to how monsters are socially constructed is made explicit in issue 3. In that issue, Aquaman and Mera visit marine biologist Dr. Stephen Shin. Before seeing the scientist, we see his messy abode in a page consisting of four horizontal panels, each stretching across the page (fig. 4). In all four panels, a television show discusses how popular culture irresponsibly misrepresents piranhas, marine creatures that the trench's facial design explicitly echoes.

In the first panel, the television show's narrator articulates the familiar trope that piranhas are monsters: "Their teeth are designed to shear meat from the bone. And they've been known to attack animals that wander into their rivers, including humans."[56] (The danger of piranhas to Humans harkens back to Aquaman's history. In *Aquaman* 2 [1994], penned by Peter David, piranhas graphically attack and sever the titular hero's left hand. After the attack, Aquaman calls piranhas "monsters.")[57] In the above panel, there is a contradiction between the verbal and visual content. Rather than the panel showing an image of piranhas demonstrating their ferocious powers and capabilities, taking down a large mammal, we instead get the interior of a Human space. The panel's arrangement—its rhetoric—disconnects the verbal content from the visual content, suggesting that the ideology of monstrosity disseminated through broadcast media can be applied to any species or group, including humans deemed outside of Humanity.[58] What is important to highlight is how mass media and popular

4. Mass-mediated representations of marine life. "The Trench, Part 3," Geoff Johns (writer), Ivan Reis (penciller), Joe Prado (inker), and Rod Reis (colorist), *Aquaman* 7, no. 3, The New 52 (New York: DC Comics, November 2011 / January 2012).

culture shape and perpetuate discourses that transform subjects into monsters. Tellingly, as we later learn, the home's owner, Dr. Shin, is an Asian American who struggles to be accepted and respected by the U.S. scientific community. While there is no explicit evidence that his marginalization is due to white racism, the specter of racism still haunts.

The first panel includes an icon that gestures beyond the violent logic of Humanism. In the panel's background is a framed map of Earth, which comes into better view in the second panel (fig. 4). While this icon is not prominent, due to its background position, it's still important to note that Ivan Reis places the map in the panel's center, a privileged position of significance. This positioning—in the center yet in the background and partially concealed behind a refrigerator—visualizes the contradictory position of the Ocean in the surface world. In the second panel, the framing shifts to the left so that the entirety of the map is now revealed. Even though it's a Human mapping, it shows how Earth is predominately water. Yet still, this map visually suggests Humanity's myopia regarding the Ocean. In the panel, a nearby lamp only partially illuminates the map; the rest is cloaked in shadows.

Metaphorically, the map's partial illumination symbolizes Humanity's myopic knowledge regime in relation to marine life, a reading reinforced by the accompanying speech bubble: "But there is an abundance of myth to the nature of these fish."[59] The third panel elaborates, "They cannot eat a cow down to the bone in a matter of minutes. They are not the monsters we think they are."[60] We can read this page as a metacommentary on the entire narrative arc. It begins by seemingly perpetuating the idea that a specific marine species is a monster that threatens Humans, yet by the page's end, this myth of monstrosity is critiqued and dissolved, a point made explicit by the television show's narrator: "They are not the monsters we think they are."

To change the public's perception is a form of activism, and this is a guiding ethos of The New 52 *Aquaman*'s run.

In the third panel, we see the television screen. While the now-visible show is a documentary, the presence of the popular medium suggests the role that mass media plays in perpetuating the myths that turn species—and other groups—into monsters. In the page's final panel, this messaging is made explicit: "Stories of their violent nature have permeated pop culture, but in reality . . . piranha are like every other species of fish."[61] As the page suggests, popular culture is an ideological battlefield that shapes popular opinion and structures what is ideologically recognized as common sense and reality. While mass media can be used for regressive purposes, it can also be used for progressive ones, such as popular texts that seek to challenge and change the dominant culture's perspective. In many ways, this page encapsulates The New 52 *Aquaman*'s activist project, intervening in dominant paradigms and opening our social imagination to our relation to the watery world.

Breaking the Humanistic Frame

In his attempt to understand this unknown species, Aquaman takes a dead trench to Dr. Shin. In this important sequence, Aquaman is revealed to be not an autonomous, self-reliant hero. Rather, he goes to a scientist for help in understanding this species and where it's from. (This sequence mirrors an early issue of Aquaman, *Adventure Comics* 120 [1947], in which Aquaman goes to college in order to study marine life. Although he lives in the Ocean, Aquaman needs to study this geography of immense diversity and complexity from the distance of a university.[62] This movement from sea to land in order to study the Ocean, we can say, allegorizes the method of "critical theory," which insists on the necessity of distance to critically understand social relations.) Before taking the specimen to Dr. Shin, Aquaman studies its features and observes, "They have bioluminescence like the benthic anglerfish on the Ocean floor. They're from somewhere deep."[63] Dr. Shin offers further insight, concluding that because the creature's "gills are crusted with sulfide minerals, the same kind that can be found in hydrothermal vents," they're most likely from the Mid-Atlantic Ridge.[64] In issue 3, we learn that this previously unknown species is from a specific Oceanic region, one bisected by the Romanche Trench.

Trenches are "long, narrow depressions on the seafloor . . . that harbor fantastic life forms" that have adapted to "thrive" in such extreme conditions.[65] Trenches exist in the hadopelagic zone, named after Hades, the Greek god of the underworld, and form one of the most alien ecologies to Human knowledge and understanding.[66] Science writer Carolyn Collins Petersen writes, "Some [trenches] are so deep that their bottoms are as far away from us as the upper reaches of our atmosphere. . . . These dark, once-mysterious canyons plunge down as far as 11,000 meters (36,000 feet) into our planet's crust. That's so deep that if Mount Everest were placed at the bottom of the deepest trench, its rocky peak would be 1.6 kilometers beneath the waves of the Pacific Ocean." Trenches contain "volcanoes and mountain peaks higher than any on the continents."[67] It's only recently that Humans have even begun to explore this deep, dark ecology. As of 2018 only three humans have ever explored the seafloor below six thousand meters.[68]

Comparing "The Trench" narrative to Aquaman's debut in 1941 is telling. In the first panel of *Aquaman*'s debut, the opening caption box informs readers that the marine superhero "dwells in the dim unknown depths of the Ocean, leaping forth to do battle with the evils and injustices of the world we know."[69] In Aquaman's debut, the Ocean is posited as a site of social injustice, but such injustices predominantly occur on the Ocean's surface. As the opening panel reads, Aquaman must emerge from the "unknown depths of the Ocean" and break the Ocean's surface ("leaping forth") to encounter evil. This epistemology is repeated throughout Aquaman's debut narrative. Later in the same issue, Aquaman reflects, "There is much evil in this upper world."[70] And the final panel reads, "Much to do—yes!— and Aquaman, sovereign of the sea, accepts the challenge of evil—from his lair in the deep he rises to face new dangers and win new triumphs!"[71] To confront "evil," to encounter social injustices, Aquaman must come to the surface. In the early comics' imagination, the Ocean's depths are posited as terra incognita, described as "dim" and "unknown."[72] In the 1940s, most of Aquaman's battles unfolded on the Ocean's surfaces— fighting Nazis, pirates, and sea monsters.[73] But as the series continued—as colonial capitalism continued to globalize— figures and scenes of injustice were no longer confined to the Ocean's surface. In the Anthropocene, social injustices extend from the Ocean's surface world to the Ocean floor's bottom and beyond.

When Arthur and Mera descend into the Atlantic Ocean's depths, they encounter a world that is alien even to them. As they descend, the artwork of Reis, Prado, and Reis challenges and changes the way we read the comic. As these superheroes descend, The New 52 *Aquaman* transforms from a surface-world text into an Ocean-world text, a sea change that occurs both in content and in form. The New 52 *Aquaman* has a relatively stable panel layout. Like many DC and Marvel comics, the series has a grid-like design. Grids are predictable, stable patterns of panels typically arranged on a horizontal plane that readers are supposed to read from left to right. In the first few issues of The New 52 *Aquaman*, the established pattern is a four-by-one grid. That is, on each page, there are four tiers (rows) and each tier is one full-width panel. The page analyzed above of Dr. Shin's apartment is an example of this layout (fig. 4). Like

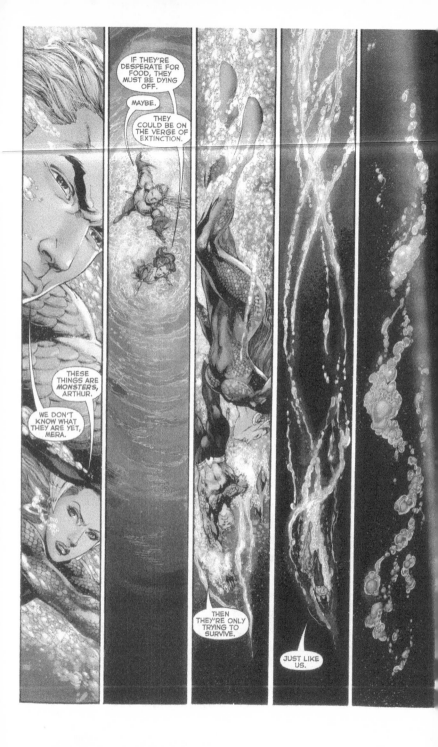

any pattern in any medium, such as music, there is variation throughout. In The New 52 *Aquaman*, this variation ranges from a three-by-one grid to a six-by-one grid. The one consistency is the repetition of full-width panels on nearly every page. In The New 52 *Aquaman*'s first issue, for example, out of a total of twenty-two pages, there are six pages with a three-by-one grid, three pages with a four-by-one grid, six pages with a five-by-one grid, and three pages with a six-by-one grid. In the second issue, this pattern becomes more explicit. Of the issue's twenty pages, more than 50 percent are either four-by-one grids (six pages) or five-by-one grids (five pages).

This pattern breaks, however, when Arthur and Mera dive into the Atlantic Ocean to learn more about the trench and their home ecology. When this happens, the grid transforms from tier-based panels (arranged horizontally) to column-based panels (arranged vertically). In Anglophone comics, the normative way to read comics is horizontally from left to right.[74] Vertical reading, reading from up to down, is unexpected.[75] When Arthur and Mera descend into the Ocean, the comic assumes a vertical layout, with full-height panels establishing a new paradigm, one that challenges and subverts a Western aesthetic norm (fig. 5). In issue 3, the penultimate page is a full-page panel of Arthur and Mera swimming down, their bodies vertical in orientation, swimming away from the shore and toward the trench (the bottom of the page). The issue's final page returns to a five-panel layout. However, now, the five panels are arranged vertically rather than horizontally. A tiered paradigm becomes a column paradigm (fig. 5). In the

5. As Arthur and Mera descend, the page layout assumes a vertical arrangement. "The Trench, Part 3," Geoff Johns (writer), Ivan Reis (penciller), Joe Prado (inker), and Rod Reis (colorist), *Aquaman* 7, no. 3, The New 52 (New York: DC Comics, November 2011 / January 2012).

fifth panel, the characters are out of view entirely, so far into the deep that we only see swirling air to signify their movement.

Rather than the panel stretching the width of the page, these panels are full-height panels that extend vertically down the entire page and insist on ~~vertical reading~~. ~~Reading vertically~~ mandates a new mode in which to see and engage with the story world; form, in other words, follows content. Instead of the expected horizontal panels, which insist on a horizontal reading, columns aesthetically mandate vertical reading. This aesthetic intervenes in the dominant Human way of seeing and experiencing the Ocean. Anthropologist John Mack writes in his "cultural history" of the Ocean, most Human narratives of life at sea, both fictional and nonfictional, typically take place aboard a ship and rarely consider the Ocean's depths.[76]

The collective art team of Reis, Prado, and Reis breaks from this normative, Human way of seeing the Ocean. Once Arthur and Mera dive into the Atlantic and the comic shifts from a horizontal to a vertical layout, we can retroactively go back and begin to see that the pattern of wide-length panels, reading left to right on the same horizontal plane, is a form of surface reading. But when Arthur and Mera dive and descend into the Atlantic, the comic's form insists that we read vertically. This is not the first time the comic has assumed a vertical orientation. In the first pages of The New 52 *Aquaman*, when we are first introduced to the trench, the page layout is also arranged vertically (fig. 3). Formally, the trench, Aquaman, and Mera all share the same underwater grammar.

Initially on this vertically organized page, Arthur and Mera are situated at the top of the panel. Below are deepening shades of blue that finally give way to various shades of blackness, representing the Ocean's various ecosystems stretching from the epipelagic zone (sunlight zone) to the hadopelagic zone (the trenches). The coloration mirrors how the zones become increasingly darker the farther one descends into the Ocean, beyond the reach of sunlight.

As Arthur and Mera descend into the Atlantic Ocean, Mera reiterates the trope that "these things are monsters," to which Aquaman replies, "We don't know what they are yet, Mera."[77] Arthur urges Mera and the reader to suspend normative classificatory schemes and to be open to ecological complexity. In the adjacent vertical column, Mera moves away from this monster classification and, instead, opens her ecological imagination: "If they're desperate for food, they must be dying off. . . . They could be on the verge of extinction."[78] For the first time in the series, the theme of extinction is broached, suggesting the sixth great extinction and the Anthropocene's violent legacy.

Although Arthur and Mera are at home in the Ocean, they swim toward an alien ecology. But how alien is it? Stacy Alaimo argues that in the age of the Anthropocene, the trope of the "alien Ocean" is both false and damaging, perpetuating the Humanist ideology that the Ocean is "radically disconnected from terrestrial environments, processes, and flows."[79] At the onset of issue 4, Aquaman articulates, "Normally I can see fine at the bottom of the Ocean but—my eyes are having a difficult time dealing with toxins in the water too."[80] The next panel reveals the presence of volcanic vents along the trench. While volcanoes do release toxins, the presence of overwhelming toxins should not necessarily be read as a natural occurrence. Rather, in the Anthropocene, Human toxins are everywhere. As Oceanographer Charles Moore informs, "the signs of human civilization are everywhere in the ocean," including in the trench.[81] One of the conspicuous signs of Human civilization are toxins.

The trench, which many consider the most "alien" ecology, is replete with Human-made toxins. Science journalist Jane Qiu reports, "Man-made pollutants" are "found in Earth's deepest ocean trenches."[82] Humanity has created more than 150 chemicals that did not exist prior to 1950, and these chemicals, these toxins, pervade the Ocean.[83] Perhaps the most pernicious and pervasive toxin in the Ocean is plastic. A 2016 World Economic Forum report predicted that by 2050 there will be more plastic in the Ocean than fish.[84] Moore explains that plastic is "affecting the entire marine food web" and that "the breakdown of plastics into microscopic, nanoparticle size-classes is carrying on an uncontrolled experiment in toxic drug delivery to every organism in the ocean with zero monitoring and zero controls."[85] Beginning in the mid-twentieth century, plastics have become constitutive of everyday capitalism. Repressed from the everyday economy, though, is that plastics are a form of poison for species everywhere, including for Humans. As Moore writes, the toxicity of plastics is "coming back to haunt us."[86] This return of the repressed animates "The Trench" narrative.

The deepest part of the Ocean is the bottom of the Mariana Trench, which is close to thirty-six thousand feet below sea level.[87] When Ocean explorer (and Hollywood director) James Cameron "used revolutionary technology to go deeper than any human in history," one of the biggest threats to his safety was "entanglement."[88] Jamie Condliffe explains, "Though you might not realize it, the sea bed—even the area surrounding the Mariana Trench—is littered with submarine communication cables. They're there to string together telecommunication systems around the globe, but also turn the bottom of the sea into an assault course for submariners."[89] Our digital modernity, so often discussed through romantic and idealistic discourses, is enabled because of a complex and extensive web of underwater cables crisscrossing the Ocean floors.

As Arthur and Mera descend into the geographic trench, they see how small and sickly the trench species has become, and they both conclude that the trench is a "dying race."[90] The trench are coming to the surface world because their food supply is "wiped out."[91] Arthur and Mera, in other words, bear witness to a collapsing ecology. Marine biologist Jeremy Jackson insists we should think of ecosystems "as if they were a species."[92] An important sign of an ecosystem's health is the presence of top predators.[93] Their presence signifies a healthy ecosystem in which a complex, diverse web of life thrives. Conversely, top predators dying off, or even absent, signals the deteriorating health of an ecosystem. Today, throughout the Ocean, regions that were once "intricate marine food webs with large animals" have become "simplistic ecosystems dominated by microbes, toxic algae blooms, jellyfish and disease."[94] Such devastating transformations are the result of the economies and industries that constitute the Anthropocene, and such transformations—highlighted by the dying off of top predators in an ecosystem—is one of the key allegories of "The Trench" narrative arc.

The trench ecosystem has been devastated, and myriad species have collapsed. The only way the trench species can survive is to come to the surface and feed off the Human world. Eventually, due to their increasing threat to the surface world, Arthur becomes convinced that the trench must be stopped. This is an anthropocentric framing that produces an anthropocentric solution: Arthur sets off an underwater volcano that collapses, imprisons, and kills the species. Before setting off the underground volcano, Arthur says to the trench, "I'm sorry."[95] The import of these words may initially be lost, though, as the reader turns the page and encounters a spectacular, two-page spread that shows the underwater volcano erupting with billows of smoke spreading everywhere, suggesting that the "monsters" and their ecology are destroyed.[96]

This spectacular destruction of monstrous others doesn't conclude the narrative arc, though. Rather, the arc ends on

6. Arthur haunted by the destruction of the trench. "Lost," Geoff Johns (writer), Ivan Reis (penciller), Joe Prado (inker), Eber Ferreira (inker), and Rod Reis (colorist), *Aquaman 7*, no. 5, The New 52 (New York: DC Comics, January/March 2012).

a quiet moment. Whereas Humanity celebrates the defeat of the trench, Arthur is haunted by his actions. At the narrative's end, Arthur sits with Mera in their surface-world home and looks crestfallen and despondent. Rather than acting as a hero who saved Humanity, Arthur mourns the lives he destroyed. Mera tries to comfort him: "You only did what you had to do, Arthur." And Arthur responds that he wishes there was another option that didn't include mass violence. Mera says in worry,

"I know you, Arthur. Don't let this haunt you." Arthur insists that he will "be fine," to which Mera retorts, "You always say that."[97] Silently, Arthur sinks into despair. His feelings and reflections place him at odds with Humanity. For Humans, killing monsters is not an ethical dilemma or a reason for mourning and trauma. Rather, such killing is expected and even constitutive of Human subjectivity and politics. Categorizing a being as a monster removes them from empathy and care and casts them as an object that can be killed without mourning. In contrast, Arthur is haunted and traumatized by what happened, by what he did.

The second narrative arc begins by visualizing how the past continues to haunt the present. In a quiet, interior scene, Mera sleeps cuddled in a blanket while Arthur stands at a bay window, staring at the sea. The next panel is a close-up of Arthur's face. His face is slack, his eyes, lost. We have no access to his interiority, nor do we know how much time has elapsed between the two panels of Arthur staring out the window. When Mera asks, "What are you doing?" Aquaman curtly answers, "Watching the storm. Just thinking." Mera queries, "About what?"[98] Arthur doesn't answer; his thoughts remain locked within his interiority. Artist Rod Reis, though, visualizes Arthur's haunted mind (fig. 6). Arthur turns to face Mera, refusing to disclose why he's staring blankly out the window in the middle of the night, but behind him, projected onto the window panels, is the image of a trench. From a Human perspective, the trench still looks like a monster, but from Arthur's posthuman perspective, this is a life lost, a life worth mourning.

Although we're in a new narrative arc, Arthur remains haunted. Reis visualizes this haunting by having the trench appear in a reflective form, in the window panels. This is not a reflection visible in the Human world, a world in which the trench remain illegible as anything other than monsters. This is a reflection only visible to those who develop a posthumanist perspective.

In contrast to the kingdom of the Human, Arthur feels empathy for the trench. Returning to the final issue in "The Trench" arc, before Arthur imprisons and kills the trench, we see him attempting to understand and communicate with them. When fighting the trench, Arthur says, "I wish we could talk. I wish I could make you understand, I can't allow you to use us as food."[99] In contrast to the stereotype that Aquaman talks to fish, this passage discloses the Ocean as a complex, multispecies ecology teeming with languages that are not translatable across all marine species. Aquaman knows the trench have a language, but he doesn't understand it. This failure to understand the language of others contrasts with the Human fantasy of perfect translatability of all languages.[100]

The New 52 *Aquaman* teaches readers to see and read ecologically. Rather than see the trench as monsters, as creatures beyond care and empathy, the series teaches us to see the trench as part of the web of life. Using a popular medium, *Aquaman* teaches a form of Ocean literacy. This literacy is a break from Humanism. From the perspective of Humanism, the trench may be ideologically cast as monsters, but the real monsters, the unrecognized monsters, are Humans, whose way of life is predicated on recklessly and endlessly plundering and polluting the Global Oceans. To reiterate a point made earlier, the term *Humans* does not mean all humans. Rather, the dominant "genre" of the Human, to use the language of Sylvia Wynter, is predicated on "slavery, conquest, and colonialism" and pertains to a specific, idealized version of the human.[101]

Foucault suggests, and the later field of "posthumanism" makes explicit, that the critique of Humanism is the critique of all hierarchical regimes of knowledge/power, including capitalism, genderism, sexism, racism, imperialism, ableism, and speciesism. Tony Davies avers, "All Humanisms, until now, have been imperial. They speak of the human in the accents and the interests of a class, a sex, a race, a genome. . . . It is almost impossible to think of a crime that has not been committed in the name of humanity."[102] As Davies stresses, Humanism is not a unified, coherent project. But regardless of the specific, material form it takes, the ideological project of the various Humanisms is predicated on the belief that life is organized not by an intricate web of relations but as a hierarchy with Humans on top. Moreover, within this violent ideology, not all people biologically born human are socially recognized as Human, which is to say, not all individuals and groups are afforded the rights, respect, dignity, and protection afforded to individuals and groups who are recognized as Human. The dominant form of Western Humanism was codified during the Enlightenment and attempts to pass as a form of universalism in such guises as "the Cartesian subject of the cogito, the Kantian 'community of reasonable beings,' or in more sociological terms, the subject as 'citizen' and 'rights-holder.'"[103] But the Human is a restricted, elitist, and policed category. *Human* and *Humanism* signify the violent, interlocking projects of whiteness, masculinity, heteronormativity, ableism, and nationalism. Humanism is one of the ideological faces of the Anthropocene, enabling and perpetuating mass extinctions to ecologies everywhere.

A commitment to posthumanism, which can assume many forms, is a break from hierarchical structures. In The New 52 *Aquaman* this posthumanism means, in part, extending the circle of care beyond Human life to include *all* life. This expansion of care to include all life is to break from the genocidal logic of the Anthropocene. But can this violent, monstrous order be countered nonviolently? Is the expansion of care enough to create a new world order of social and ecological justice? What happens when posthumanism assumes a violent form? These questions animate the most explicit allegory of The New 52 *Aquaman*: the war between the Ocean and Humans. However, before I turn, in chapter 3, to this allegorical war, I will first journey to the surface world with Mera to examine the violences of the Anthropocene as enacted on other human beings.

2

Waves of Feminism

The Anthropocene is enabled by hierarchical thinking and structures. At different junctures, from different perspectives, some hierarchies become more visible than others. Early in The New 52 *Aquaman*, Mera learns to see the kingdom of Humanity as a kingdom of patriarchy. Throughout "The Trench" narrative arc, the surface world continually disrespects and disparages Mera because of her gender. In issue 2, for example, when a police officer sees Mera, he calls her "Aquawoman."[1] This is the first of many panels in which Humans assume that Mera's name is a derivative of, and that her identity is tethered to, Aquaman. While Arthur embraces the moniker "Aquaman," Mera detests this projected name. In issue 6 (February/April 2012) a young woman says to Mera, "They call you Aquawoman," to which Mera responds, "I wish they would stop."[2] Mera doesn't want to be seen as dependent and contingent upon Aquaman. She wants to be seen with respect, dignity, and autonomy.

In this chapter, I explore how Mera emerges as an icon of ecofeminism. Initially, Mera seems trapped in a patriarchal network. Patriarchy defines the surface world in which Mera tries to be at home, and patriarchy, of course, also reigns outside the text. In fact, Mera's visualization throughout the series can be read as a product of patriarchy. Throughout The New

52 *Aquaman*, Mera is visualized with a skintight outfit that hugs her impossibly proportioned body. She has long legs, no waist, and no visible fat anywhere except in her ample breasts, which are bursting out of her low-cut top. Mera's visualization perpetuates a pervasive gendered trope in mass-market superhero comics. In her book *Superwomen: Gender, Power, and Representation*, Carolyn Cocca succinctly summarizes this trope as follows: "Large-breasted and small-waisted, long-haired and long-legged."[3] Mera's visualization highlights the complex politics of representation. As Peggy Phelan astutely observes, "If representational visibility equals power, then almost-naked young white women should be running Western culture. The ubiquity of their image, however, has hardly brought them political or economic power."[4] In a trend that began in the 1980s and was amplified by The New 52, mass-market superhero comics visualized "hypermuscular men and hypersexualized women."[5] Like many women superheroes in DC and Marvel, Mera is visualized with "anatomically impossible proportions" in "anatomically impossible poses."[6] Throughout the series, Mera is positioned in what has been called the "brokeback pose" (fig. 7). As Cocca summarizes, women superheroes are "often posed" as "unnaturally twisted and arched to display all of their curves in front and back simultaneously. One's back would have to be broken to contort in such a way, which is why it would come to be labeled the 'broke back' pose."[7] In The New 52 initiative, this trope of hypersexualized women, frequently in brokeback poses, is repeated and perpetuated by the visualization of Black Canary, Catwoman, Fahrenheit, Harley Quinn, Mera, Poison Ivy, Power Girl, Raven, Starfire, and Wonder Woman. This is not to say they are not complex characters, but visually, they seem to circulate in a patriarchal ecology. In conjunction with centering on Mera, The New 52 *Aquaman* also introduces a new female superhero, Ya'Wara;

7. Mera in a "brokeback pose." "The Others, Chapter 2," Geoff Johns (writer), Ivan Reis (penciller), Joe Prado and Ivan Reis (inkers), and Rod Reis (colorist), *Aquaman 7*, no. 8, The New 52 (New York: DC Comics, April/June 2012).

8. Ya'wara in a "brokeback pose." "Death of a King, Interlude: The Return of the Others," John Ostrander (writer), Manuel Garcia (penciller), Wayne Faucher, Sandra Hope, Ray McCarthy, and Rob Hunter (inkers), and Pete Pantazis (colorist), *Aquaman 7*, no. 20, The New 52 (New York: DC Comics, May/July 2013).

she, too, becomes a perpetuation of this hypersexualized trope and is visualized in brokeback poses (fig. 8).

At least initially, The New 52 *Aquaman* seems to reinforce the trope that Mera is a sexualized object within a patriarchal matrix. The series begins in medias res, with Arthur and Mera renouncing their ties to the Ocean and trying to pass as Human. As issue 1 makes clear, to become Human is to turn away from the Ocean, both literally and imaginatively. The decision to become Human, to pass as Human, seems to be Arthur's choice. In the first issue, Arthur stands on the shoreline, gazing at the Ocean when he tells Mera that he has "made" his "decision."[8] This decision is rooted in his adolescent past. Johns turns Arthur into a Batman-like figure whose origin story is linked to childhood trauma. Looking out into the Ocean, Arthur shares that he was raised on the surface world by his Human father, Thomas Curry, in the coastal Maine town where Arthur and Mera now live. When he was thirteen, three Atlanteans emerged from the Ocean to kill Arthur. The reason, Arthur explains to Mera, is "because of who my father was. Because of who I am."[9] This traumatic event occurs at the symbolic age of thirteen, an age that in many cultures is marked as a threshold age in which an individual passes from childhood to adulthood. However, Arthur is not at home in either community. Both Atlantean and Human communities reject him, because from both perspectives, Arthur doesn't pass the purity test. He is neither purely Atlantean nor purely Human. Arthur lives between two cultures—two identities—and initially, these two cultures seem irreconcilable.

From the outset, the series situates Arthur as the character with depth, history, and agency whose decisions drive the narrative. In contrast, at least initially, Mera is narratively marginal, an ideological position reinforced by the artwork, which shows Mera standing behind Arthur with her arms wrapped around him, visually signifying that she is there to support her partner, whatever decisions he makes. In the first issue, Arthur decides that he doesn't "want to be" Atlantean and that he doesn't "want the responsibility" of being a ruler.[10] This is Arthur's choice, not Mera's.

But Johns's three-year run as the series' sole author frequently upends expectations and subverts narrative trajectories. While the series begins by placing Arthur at the narrative center—and at the center of nearly all panels—this focus shifts. In issue 6, the narrative breaks away from Arthur's perspective and, instead, centers on Mera. This narrative shift helps disclose Arthur's relative privilege. Although Arthur is not accepted by Humanity due to his mixed heritage, he is still recognized as a man and, therefore, receives the privileges of masculine legibility. When the narrative shifts focus from Arthur to Mera, she is doubly oppressed, both as an alien other (a royal from an underwater kingdom) and as a woman.

Issue 6 is a Mera-centric issue that shifts the dynamics of how the surface world is represented. The issue begins with a flashback. Four years prior to the narrative's present, we learn that Mera was a princess of the underwater kingdom Xebel. In the complex political mythology of Xebel—a mythology whose enrichment began in the *Brightest Day* series (2010–11), also written by Johns—the underwater kingdom was previously used as a prison colony to confine criminals and political dissidents from Atlantis. In the modern iteration developed by Johns, Xebel is isolated from the rest of the Ocean, surrounded by an impenetrable barrier. To some extent, the relationship of Xebel to Atlantis is analogous to Cuba and the United States. While Cuba is an autonomous nation, Guantánamo Bay, which is within territorial Cuba, remains under the control of the United States as a penal colony outside the formal law. (Xebel is located under the Bermuda Triangle, invisible to the dominant surface and Atlantean world; in this sense, Xebel is also analogous to Guantánamo Bay, unfolding beyond normative Human vision.) Mera's father, the King of Xebel, sends Mera on a covert mission to assassinate Arthur. For Xebel, this political violence is justified because, from Xebel's perspective, Atlantis is a colonial kingdom and Arthur is a symbol of colonialism because his birthright is to be King of Atlantis. If Atlantis is read as a colonial nation, then Xebel becomes a postcolonial nation, and Mera, a postcolonial subject. If one dives deeply into Atlantis's political history and mythology—which I will do in chapter 4—one finds a complex, layered narrative that critically thinks about colonialism, racism, xenophobia, and nationalism.

On Mera's mission of political violence, the unexpected occurs. Mera falls in love with Arthur and abandons her assignment. In this modern iteration, Mera, like Arthur, is of royal blood from an underwater kingdom, and like Arthur, she turns her back on her watery home to build a life on the surface world in an attempt to become Human. Therefore, the choice to abandon the Ocean is both Arthur's and Mera's decision.

To appreciate how The New 52 *Aquaman* reimagines Mera, it's important to sketch the character's history. Mera debuted in *Aquaman* 11 (September/October 1963). In this issue, Mera is introduced as a queen from "a watery world in another dimension," initially called "Dimension Aqua." (The kingdom wasn't called Xebel until *Brightest Day*.) However, as Mera explains to Aquaman in several panels, an enemy usurped her throne and forced her to flee through a "dimensional warp" and enter a new world: Earth.[11] Mera explains this to Aquaman while bobbing in Earth's Ocean. Arthur promises Mera that he "will take good care of" her while she remains "a visitor in this dimension!"[12] A mere seven issues later, Aquaman and Mera marry in an underwater wedding attended by the Justice

League (*Aquaman* 18, November/December 1964). This is the first superhero wedding in DC history.[13] And five issues after their wedding, Mera and Arthur have a baby—Arthur Jr., or Aquababy (*Aquaman* 23, September/October 1965). Mera follows the normative trajectory of any properly gendered U.S. Cold War woman.

However, a decade later, Mera and Arthur experience perhaps the most shocking form of loss and trauma in DC history. In 1978, after a decade of marital bliss, Aquaman's archnemesis Black Manta kidnaps and murders their child. This shocking murder and subsequent trauma leads to Arthur and Mera's marriage collapsing. From this point forward, for decades, Mera suffers from post-traumatic stress disorder. I will return to this shocking scene of infanticide in chapter 4 and interrogate what it means that one of the few African American villains in DC Comics is responsible for this unprecedented comic violence and how The New 52 *Aquaman* engages with this troubling history.

The New 52 *Aquaman*, however, breaks from the comic's past. When the series opens, Arthur and Mera are not married, nor do they have any children. Initially, Mera seems enamored with the idea of living with Arthur and building their own private surface bubble, severed from the Ocean. By the end of issue 1, becoming Human is indexed, in part, by moving away from multispecies living and toward a narrow form of social life emblematized by romantic love and a heteronormative family. Arthur tells Mera, "I want a life up here. With you. I'm not going back to Atlantis."[14] Mera readily agrees with this plan and this desire to create "a new life," deracinated from the past and divorced from the Ocean. The possibility of a blue humanities—a posthumanist paradigm that thinks about and positions humans within a wider spectrum of life, including marine life—appears ideologically impossible in the

9. Mr. Rovner degrades and harasses Jennifer, an employee. "Deserted!," Geoff Johns (writer), Ivan Reis (breakdowns), Joe Prado (artist), and Rod Reis (colorist), *Aquaman 7*, no. 6, The New 52 (New York: DC Comics, February/April 2012).

early issues. To pass as Humans, Mera and Arthur must sever themselves completely from the Ocean.

But this promise of a new life of isolated romantic love—of a heteronormative family—proves to be an unsustainable fantasy. To be Human is to be thrust into a world of violent hierarchies, and one of the pronounced hierarchies of Humanity, as Mera learns as she steps away from their private home, is misogyny. While such misogyny wends throughout "The Trench" narrative arc, the narrative doesn't dwell on these violent gender dynamics. In issue 6, though, it does. Leading up to this seminal issue, issue 4 (December 2011 / February 2012) concludes with Mera and Arthur adopting a dog and continuing to follow a script of heteronormative Humanity. The issue's last panel features Arthur, Mera, and their newly acquired dog embracing in a pose that resembles a family portrait.[15] At the end of issue 5 (January/March 2012), Arthur comes home to an empty house and finds a note from Mera that reads, "Went to town for dog food."[16] What may seem like Mera and Arthur falling into a normative, gendered script, investing exclusively in their personal lives, becomes shattered when, in issue 6, we follow Mera into a store to complete the menial task of buying dog food. As the opening sequence visualizes, to enter any U.S. public space is to enter a geography of patriarchy.[17] In this issue, Mera experiences and learns that the Human world is not marked by specific villains; rather, the entire structure is villainous. Mera learns to see the entire surface landscape as marked and defined by myriad forms of gendered violences threatening women's dignities, capacities, and lives.

In the everyday ritual of buying dog food, Mera experiences a world of gendered hate. This sequence begins by visualizing the public sphere Mera will enter. Before we see Mera, we see an establishing shot of Rudy's Groceries. A speech bubble, emanating from the store, reprimands, "You're doing it wrong."[18] This berating voice, we learn from the next panel, belongs to the grocery store's manager, Mr. Rovner, speaking to a young employee, Jennifer, who incorrectly shelves commodities. From this mistake, we can assume Jennifer is a relatively new employee. Nevertheless, the boss berates, "Anyone with common sense would know" that the labels must face potential customers (fig. 9).[19] This verbal harassment is accompanied by physical harassment. In the same panel, Mr. Rovner invades Jennifer's personal space. From the outset of this Mera-centric issue, we see a social world defined by a grossly unequal power dynamic in which the hierarchies of class and gender are inextricable.

Jennifer is first visualized from behind. Read in isolation and uncritically, this frame can be read as encouraging audiences to participate in the dehumanizing, male gaze. However, this potential gaze is disrupted and critiqued in the page's penultimate panel. In a tight close-up, Mr. Rovner engages in a form of everyday sexual harassment: "You know, you'd look very pretty with a little more make-up, Jennifer."[20] Coming from an employer, this suggestion for Jennifer to aestheticize herself is a form of both gender and capitalist abuse. This unequal power dynamic between employer and employee renders Jennifer extremely vulnerable. Speaking out against this sexual harassment could potentially result in her termination, regardless of how many laws are on the books to protect women from workplace gender violence. Jennifer's response to this harassment makes clear that this abuse has been habitual. She retorts, "Please. I told you I'm not comfortable talking about stuff like that."[21] This has happened before, and it will likely happen again. Regardless of Jennifer's pleas to stop, that she feels unsafe and uncomfortable, her employer's harassment continues and escalates. In this panel, Mr. Rovner explicitly violates Jennifer's personal space. Yet in a space of capitalism—where employers and managers are vested with sovereign authority and employees are replaceable pawns with little agency—there is nowhere for Jennifer to go. While Arthur being King of Atlantis may seem foreign to U.S. sensibilities, this sequence suggests that capitalist relations replicate such monarchical relations. In the economic system of capitalism, the owning class and their managerial surrogates are sovereign.

In the page's final panel, the manager's open hand threatens to embrace Jennifer's face as he wagers, "I bet I can help you get comfortable."[22] This page shows that everyday genderism, harassment, and sexual assault exist on a spectrum, a spectrum we can call the surface world's normative "rape culture."[23]

At this moment, Mera enters the store. But we are left to wonder: What would have happened to Jennifer if Mera hadn't arrived at this moment? Other questions should be asked as well: What has already happened to Jennifer? How many times has Jennifer experienced this everyday harassment, and has this harassment escalated into assault? And if so, how many times? Who else has been victimized by this manager? In the page's final image, the manager's hand is about to touch Jennifer's body without her consent, when Mera interrupts this scene of escalating sexual violence. Mera's menial task of getting dog food leads to a crime scene that wouldn't register as such to most male superheroes. In this scene, Mera both witnesses and becomes the victim of a crime that men are culturally engendered to not see and engendered to participate in and perpetuate.

When Mera enters the store, the manager proclaims in a loud voice that she's "hot."[24] At the same time, Jennifer says, "They call you Aquawoman." Mera articulates (once again) her displeasure at this media-driven labeling: "I wish they would stop."[25] Both Mr. Rovner and Jennifer initially see Mera through the prism of mass media. This discourse seeks to negate Mera's subjectivity, history, and integrity and to, instead, posit her as an object that can be classified and commented on by those in power, by those who own the means of production, whether mass media or grocery stores. The discourse that insistently calls Mera "Aquawoman," a name she despises, and the discourse that calls her "hot" are both forms of objectification and forms of discursive violence that lead to more extreme forms of gendered violence.

After Mr. Rovner introduces himself to Mera by his first name, "Randy"—his sexual desires are inscribed into his name—he asks probing, personal questions that dive deeper into the waters of sexual harassment: "You're a normal woman outside of the water, right? Biologically speaking."[26] In the normative kingdom of man, it's permissible to ask about a woman's body, and it's normal to use aesthetics to assess and judge women. Mera's alien status—alien to Human normativity—disallows her from initially seeing Randy's questions as a form of gendered violence. She initially construes his questions as a form of inquisitiveness. When Randy states, "You're like us," Mera replies, "Yes. I suppose I am."[27] When Mera says this, only her face is framed. The panel renders invisible her full body, which Randy assesses as "hot." In the next panel, Randy's harassment escalates into assault. As with Jennifer, Randy enters Mera's personal space and, without her consent, starts touching her hair and calls her "exotic."[28] At this point, it is Jennifer who intervenes in this scene of gendered violence: "Mr. Rovner, you shouldn't . . ."[29] Even as this scene of violence escalates, Jennifer shows proper capitalist-patriarchal respect and uses Randy's formal name, "Mr. Rovner." At this moment, the art makes visible the power differential between Randy and Jennifer. While Jennifer tries to interrupt this ongoing scene of violence with the interjection "Mr. Rovner," her name tag is clearly visible, reading, "Jennifer." The power hierarchy—one that intertwines class and gender—is reinforced by the "proper" way to address each person in this space of commodities and consumption. The logic of commodities—of usable, disposable, fetishized objects—does not pertain exclusively to the items on the shelf whose "labels" are supposed to face the customers. Here, Jennifer's commodified label faces the customer and reader.

The assault progresses as Randy places his hand on Mera's back and asks, "Where's the zipper?" Mera now knows she is being violated. Her response, though, at least initially, follows the way that young women are enculturated to react to sexual harassment and violence. She says, "Please, take your hands off me."[30] In rape culture, which is an essential attribute of Humanity, women are enculturated to see sexual harassment and sexual violence as part of reality, as the way the world is. Constant street harassment, unwanted comments, groping in public spaces and on public transportation are ideologically presented as the fixed ways of the world. Girls and women are taught to see this everyday gendered violence as normal and to express their hurt and fear with polite reprimands, which is what Mera does initially: "Please, take your hands off me." Randy's act of gendered violence is met with a polite request.

In the next panel, though, Mera emerges as a feminist superhero. When Randy refuses to heed her pleas, she grabs him by the wrist, and her superstrength power causes his skin to break and his bones to shatter. Mera justifies her violent act with the words, "I said don't!"[31] Randy collapses to the floor in pain, spewing in shock, "Y-You . . . You broke my arm!" Mera explains to the forming and growing crowd, "Of course, I did. This man touched me. I asked him to stop. He did not."[32] From Mera's perspective, she engaged in a justified form of violence. Her reaction was a form of self-defense. In fact, as she says, "I could have done much worse."[33] At this moment, two policemen arrive. Human law is narrated and visualized as masculine. Immediately, these male officers aim their guns at Mera and demand that she surrenders. In the eyes of Human law, Mera is the perpetrator, and it is Mera who is arrested. Only Jennifer resists this law-enforcement logic. "Wait! She's a hero." Jennifer reminds everyone that Mera saved the community of Beachrock "from those monsters."[34] While Jennifer refers to the trench, she could equally refer to the monstrous order of patriarchy.

Mera explains to the growing crowd that she acted out of self-defense and that her violent response was justified because the store manager assaulted her. But when the police arrive, Mera is the one arrested, while the sexual predator is seen as the victim. The only person who tries to intervene on Mera's behalf is Jennifer, but she is silenced by a male employee. In the workings of Human law, sexual assault goes unseen and women's voices are muted.

Although she has the capability to escape, Mera capitulates to the police. She is trying to assimilate into the Human community, and that means uncritically obeying Human law. While detained and captive in the back of a police cruiser, Mera hears a dispatcher report of another instance of misogynist violence—this time, a case of domestic violence that had escalated into a man killing his wife and now posing an imminent threat to his daughter. This sequence undercuts the romanticism of the nuclear family. In the first narrative arc, the family unit seemed to be the most important vehicle to becoming Human. But here, the family is disclosed as an ideological, patriarchal form that enables a range of violences, including domestic abuse.

Mera recognizes that her experiences of sexual harassment and assault are not an isolated incident but, rather, a pattern and structure of Humanity. And what is more, Human law aids and abets this misogynist culture. When the police car arrives at this unfolding scene of violence, with Mera detained in the back, the male perpetrator aims a gun at his daughter's head and yells at the police officers, "This is family business! It ain't none of yours!"[35] Although a murderer, this man articulates a prominent form of patriarchal ideology that enables the proliferation of domestic violence, especially against women and children. The family home is posited and construed as a private space distinct and separate from the public sphere. What happens in the home is private and not the "business" of the law or the public. This ideological split allows domestic abuse to thrive and for such abuse to be invisible and illegible to the dominant, public culture. In this instance, the man training a gun on his daughter thinks he has a right to discipline and harm his daughter because he has been engendered to see himself as the king of his family, as the sovereign of his autonomous, personal kingdom.

Mera watches this scene of violence unfold while handcuffed, from the back of the police car. She witnesses how misogynistic violence becomes ideologically justified by its male perpetrators. The gun-wielding man says to his daughter, "Your mom pushed me, Rachel. You know how she was. And you're just like her."[36] In this distorted, misogynist logic, a woman is to blame for this scene of violence. A woman is the agent, and the man is simply reacting. At this moment, Mera breaks. She recognizes that Human law is part of the problem, not part of the solution. When the man threatens again to kill his daughter, Mera snaps the handcuffs in two, thrusts the door completely off its hinges, and takes charge. In this sequence, violence against women is not a plot device for a male superhero to save the day. Rather, a female superhero intervenes in this masculine-dominated space of law to subdue this masculine threat. We witness Mera developing a feminist consciousness in relation to the systemic and everyday violences of patriarchy.

I want to read this scene allegorically. Mera learning to recognize, read, and intervene in this patriarchal ecology is analogous to the material conditions of corporate, superhero comics, especially at the time this series was produced. It's important to look at the material production of DC's The New 52 and to think about the initiative's gender representations and gender politics.

Diversifying and Modernizing Superheroes: DC Comics' The New 52

The New 52 demarcates a new era in DC publishing. As one journalist describes, the launch of DC's New 52 was the "September Heard throughout the Industry."[37] Starting in September 2011, DC launched an unprecedented fifty-two new monthly series (hence the name The New 52). All series started anew with first issues. Even *Action Comics* and *Detective Comics*, which had both maintained their number continuity since their 1930s debut, started over with new number 1 issues. From a narrative perspective, all of DC's iconic superheroes were getting a fresh start, divorced from their storied and layered histories. The past was ostensibly dead, and a new canon was being born (again).

In the decades-long "slugfest" between DC and Marvel, "relaunches and reboots" of series were a common ploy at the time to increase market share.[38] However, as Reed Tucker writes, DC took this strategy to the "next level." Rather than rebooting an individual series, it rebooted the "entire universe."[39] This initiative officially began on August 31, 2011, with a heavily promoted "Midnight Madness event" marketed as a "historic launch."[40] The New 52 initiative offered an accessible entry point for a wide, diverse audience. No prior knowledge or homework was needed for readers to enter the world of superhero comics. As a business strategy, The New 52 was designed to radically expand DC's market share and reverse the trend of flagging sales. In conjunction with rebooting an entire universe, DC also transformed their distribution model, releasing both the print and digital comic versions on the same day, creating a more coherent and standardized schedule and allowing consumers more avenues in which to consume DC comics.[41]

The New 52 was DC's concerted attempt to make their superheroes relevant to the widest possible audience. As then DC coproducer Dan DiDio explained, "We really want to inject new life in our characters and line."[42] To connect with a new generation of readers and potential readers, the corporation made a concerted effort to create narratives that addressed "today's real-world themes and events."[43] This attempt to make DC superheroes resonate with younger audiences began by concentrating on diversity. To expand their fanbase, DC made diversity a defining attribute of The New 52 brand. DC spokespersons used the buzzword "diversity" throughout their PR campaigns leading up to the launch of The New 52. In May 2011 DC's senior vice president of sales Bob Wayne described The New 52 as "a more diverse DC Universe," with "variations in appearance, origin, and age."[44] Two months later, DiDio, in an interview with the *Advocate*, a magazine for the LGBTQ+ community, proclaimed, "What we really wanted to do was show the diversity of our audience across the line of our books. Right now we have such a wide fan base and we wanted to create characters and stories that really reflected [that] fan base."[45] Many sources and institutions helped legitimize DC's new branding. In an article titled "Up, Up and Out of the Closet" (July 18, 2011), published in the *Advocate*, Jase Peeples writes, "The company has . . . taken advantage of the relaunch to establish a wider range of diversity, introducing several LGBT characters in their own titles. Apollo and Midnighter, a gay superhero couple who previously existed in DC's alternate *Wildstorm* line of comics, have been incorporated into the company's main cast of characters. They will join lesbians Batwoman, The Question, and the bisexual African-American superhero Voodoo in DC's new universe."[46] But is this diversity a radical rethinking of the DC universe, or is it a form of tokenism, a crass corporate attempt to strategically incorporate diverse characters for the sole purpose of enlarging their market share?[47]

The practice of diversity should be transformative, challenging and even redefining all preexisting metrics, paradigms, and narratives. Diversity can be a corporate buzzword employed to expand market share, or it can be a deep practice that becomes transformative at all levels, including content, theme, and form. The presence of diversity is not the same as the practice of diversity.

To think more about the politics of diversity in comics representation—and to stay with the organizing theme of this chapter—I want to concentrate on how The New 52 practices gender diversity. When The New 52 launched, the initiative featured seven titles led by women: *Batgirl*, *Batwoman*, *Birds of Prey*, *Catwoman*, *Wonder Woman*, *Supergirl*, and *Voodoo*. For the superhero comic industry dominated by DC and Marvel, this counts as a significant improvement. When The New 52 began in September 2011, Marvel only had *one* superhero series led by a woman, x-23—a series that would be canceled two months later.[48]

However, The New 52 gender politics sparked tremendous controversy.[49] Many of the women superheroes are visualized in ways that seemed, to many, exploitative. Take, for example, *Catwoman* 1 (September/November 2011). Laura Hudson, then editor in chief of Comics Alliance, writes of the new series:

> The writer and artist have decided that out of all possible introductions to the character of Selina Kyle, the moment we're going to meet her is going to be the one where she happens to be half-dressed and sporting bright red lingerie. That is in fact all we see of her for two pages: shots of her breasts. Most problematically, we are shown her breasts and her body over and over for two pages, but NOT her face. No joke, we get a very clear and detailed shot of her butt in black latex before we ever see [what] her face looks like.[50]

This gendered representation is not an aberration but what many have argued is a defining feature of The New 52. Starfire, who appears in *Red Hood and the Outlaws*, is described by one critic as "drawn like a centerfold from the swimsuit issue of *Sports Illustrated* and has become a promiscuous amnesiac."[51] Sociologist Casey Brienza assesses that "the sexual objectification" of "heroines" in The New 52, and superhero comics more generally, reflects "the conditions of their production and consumption: they are made almost exclusively by and for men."[52]

Returning to *Catwoman* 1, the issue concludes with the titular superhero having sex with Batman on a rooftop. Sex can and should be liberating, but as Hudson argues, *Catwoman* 1 is a "male fantasy."[53] In this fantasy, Catwoman wears lacy lingerie underneath her already eroticized, skintight catsuit.

Moreover, Catwoman and Batman's act of transgressive, public sex is because of Catwoman's initiative. As Catwoman straddles Batman and undoes his belt, she narrates, "This isn't the first time." The next narration bubble elaborates, "Usually it's because I want him."[54] This narration bleeds into the next panel, in which Batman unzips Catwoman's suit, revealing her lacy bra. The accompanying narration reads, "Every time . . . he protests. Then . . . gives in."[55] Catwoman describes the sex as "angry," animalistic, and without foreplay, and throughout, Catwoman is the sexual aggressor.[56] While there is no singular way to read this hypersexualized scene, we should listen carefully to women who identify as avid comic book fans and who describe how deeply disappointed they were by such hypersexualized representations of women superheroes and supervillains. Hudson writes, for example, that The New 52 undermines women's sexuality as a source of liberation and autonomy.[57] After reading most of DC's new series, Hudson assesses, "When I . . . see the way the female characters are presented, I don't see heroes I would want to be. I don't see people I would want to hang out with or look up to. I don't feel like the comics are talking to me; I feel like they're talking about me."[58] Hudson concludes, "Nearly 20 years of reading superhero books, these may finally have been the comics that broke me."[59] In DC's corporate culture, we cannot assign blame and responsibility exclusively to a specific writer or artist. Rather, we need to look up the corporate ladder. To what extent was Catwoman's design and story line mandated from the top? Patriarchy and misogyny are not located in individuals; they are structures of power.

Despite the corporate claim that DC featured a wide range of women superheroes and supervillains, the editors and creators were almost entirely men. When The New 52 launched, only 1.9 percent of DC comic creators were women.[60] Of the fifty-two new series launched in 2011, only two were penned by women. And both series were penned by the same woman. Initially, Gail Simone was the *only* woman writer in DC's The New 52. Laura Sneddon, creator of the blog *Comicbookgrrrl*, writes, "Without knocking how awesome Gail is, the fact that at no point someone sat back and thought 'wait . . . two out of fifty-two? This might look kinda bad . . .' is quite remarkable. Or not, depending how much sexism rage you like to read about every day."[61]

DC planned to make the 2011 San Diego Comic-Con—the world's largest comics convention—all about The New 52 initiative. From July 21 through July 24, DC organized multiple panels to help generate momentum and excitement for its new branding. But the tenor of this corporate-led conversation changed when fans started asking questions pertaining to gender. At each of the organized panels for The New 52, a woman dressed as Batgirl asked about women characters and queried which characters her daughter should dress as.[62] During a panel led by DC copublisher DiDio, a fan asked, "Why did you go from 12% in women [creators] to 1% on your creative teams?"[63] DiDio was neither apologetic nor reflective. Rather, he aggressively answered, "What do those numbers mean to you? What do they mean to you? Who should we be hiring? Tell me right now. Who should we be hiring right now? Tell me."[64] The ideological assumption of DiDio's retort is that there were no women creators for DC to hire. DiDio's professed ignorance of women creators is a mark of "privilege."[65] In fact, to not see structural inequalities and injustices is the very definition of privilege. At the panel, several fans began shouting out the names of women creators who could be hired, including Alex de Campi, Nicola Scott, Carla Speed McNeill, and M. K. Reed.[66]

Leading up to the launch of The New 52, women organized to disrupt and change DC's patriarchal structure. Soon after the comics convention, fans started a petition that began, "As of May 25th, 2011, 16% of DC's creative staff, including editors, was female. This coming September, 2 women have been . . . [given] spots on two books out of the fifty-two new books DC will be publishing. The number of female editors is still unknown."[67] The petition lists more than one hundred women comics creators who could be hired, including

Adriana Ferguson (*S.T.O.P.* and *Minor Acts of Heroism*)
Adriana Blake (*Fall on Me*)
Adriana Melo (*Star Wars*)
Alex Singer (*Sfeer Theory*)
Aliena Shoemaker (*Honeydew Syndrome* and *Two Keys*)
Alina Urusov (*Birds of Prey* and *NYX: No Way Home*)
Alisa Kwitney (*Dreaming, Sandman: King of Dreams, Destiny: The Chronicle Foretold,* and *Vertigo Visions: Phantom Stranger*)
Alice Fox (*Two Rooks*)
Alice Hunt (*Goodbye Chains*)
Amanda Lafrenais (*Love Me Nice*)
Amber Benson (*Buffy the Vampire Slayer* and *Four Letter Worlds*)
Amy Wolfram (*Teen Titans: Year One*)
An Nguyen (*Open Spaces and Closed Places* and *Womanthology*)
Ann Nocenti (*Longshot* and *Daredevil*)
Ashley Cope (*Unsounded*)[68]

And that's just the *A*s.

The petition was addressed to the top six executives at DC: Diane Nelson, Dan DiDio, John Rood, Jim Lee, Bob Harras, and Geoff Johns. In 2011 Johns was both a head writer and the chief creative officer of DC Entertainment.[69]

To some extent, the petition worked. DiDio and his fellow copublisher, Jim Lee, responded and wrote a public letter of apology: "We hear you and take your concerns very seriously."[70] The copublishers then attempted to defend the corporation's image by naming women comic writers who have worked for DC and name dropped some of the corporation's many "remarkable, iconic women characters." But most importantly, DiDio and Lee promised change: "We're committed to telling diverse stories with a diverse point of view." DiDio and Lee promised "exciting news about new projects with women creators in the coming months," acknowledging that "we know there are dozens of other women creators and we welcome the opportunity to work with them."[71] Hudson called the response "incredibly heartening" and said that this public acknowledgment made her feel "more optimistic than I have in some time, or maybe ever."[72]

How warranted, though, is this optimism? In a 2017 article, Amanda Shendruk studied 34,476 DC and Marvel comic book characters in order to analyze women superheroes. As Shendruk discovered, only 12 percent of DC and Marvel superhero comics had women protagonists and only 26.7 percent of all characters were women.[73] U.S. superhero comics, dominated by DC and Marvel, remain largely a male-driven and masculine genre. When women are present, Shendruk writes, they are "often hyper-sexualized, unnecessarily brutalized, stereotyped, and used as tokens."[74] The radical gender imbalance and power dynamics are even inscribed into characters' names. Of the male superheroes Shendruk studied, 30 percent have the word "man" in their name. In contrast, only 5.7 percent of women superheroes have the word "woman" in their name.[75] For male-identified superheroes, 20 percent of names use the word "Mr.," and close to 10 percent use the word "King." Only 5 percent of male-identified superheroes have the word "boy" in their name. Conversely, the top gender identifiers for women are "girl," "lady," and "Mrs." All these labels appear twice as often as "woman."[76] Shendruk's analysis reveals that women "are more than twice as likely to be given a name that may make her seem weak, less dangerous, less aggressive and not on equal footing with male characters."[77] In this context, Mera insistently refusing the moniker "Aquawoman" reads as a feminist intervention. Names are an important ideological battleground. In a patriarchal society that seeks to label and identify women by dominant gender signifiers, Mera refuses to participate.

In a fundamental way, mass-market superhero comics are more than the exclusive property of authors, or publishers, or corporations. Iconic characters also belong to the public. Everyone who spoke up and out against DC's hiring practices did so because they care about the characters, they care about the narratives, and they care about the DC Universe. They spoke, in other words, from a position of love and engaged in a form of immanent critique. Mera is not exclusively defined by DC Comics. All superheroes, to some extent, resist their identity as intellectual property. Superheroes are a shared, accessible social grammar that millions of readers connect with, learn from, learn with, and, in the process, resignify. People from all genders, sexes, races, ethnicities, religions, and nationalities develop political sensibilities and social imaginations through their creative engagement with superheroes, and popular culture more generally. Regardless of DC's intentions and strategies, for many, Mera is a figure of feminism. Media scholar Suzanne Scott writes, "Comic book culture is currently witnessing a potentially transformative feminist intervention in which the 'how' and the 'what' of comics are being placed in meaningful conversation."[78] Scott made this assessment, in part, because of the surge in political activity galvanized by The New 52. Scott contextualizes, "The years 2011 and 2012 were marked by increased attention to the place and perception of women within comic book culture, from the pointed questions of the 'Batgirl of San Diego' at Comic-Con in July 2011 to the publication of *Womanthology* in March 2012."[79] Representation matters. As does seeing women kick patriarchy's ass.

Mera and Ecofeminism

On the surface world, Mera witnesses and experiences a geography in which violence against women is normative. Looping back to the first issue of The New 52 *Aquaman*, everyday patriarchy is made visible even before Mera is introduced. In the first issue, Arthur Curry goes to a local diner to eat. As discussed in the introduction, at this diner, Arthur is ridiculed and mocked by surrounding patrons. This discourse momentarily stops, however, when a waitress approaches to take Arthur's order. Before doing so, though, this unnamed waitress apologizes for her appearance: "I'm sorry, I, uh . . . I must look terrible. This is my third consecutive shift."[80] This logic echoes Mr. Rovner's harassment of Jennifer for not properly aestheticizing herself. In the workplace—in every place within a patriarchal culture—women are enculturated that to be properly gendered, they must properly aestheticize themselves. Patriarchy is external (as exemplified by Mr. Rovner) and frequently becomes internalized by its victims (as exemplified by this waitress).

This policed and regulated performance of gender—the insistence on proper aestheticization—becomes more layered and intersectional as the exchange continues. As the waitress explains, she is not properly aestheticized because she has been working "three consecutive shifts" in order "to put two kids through college and it's . . . Oh, God. I'm sorry again."[81] The waitress begins to disclose her financial precarity but regulates herself, apologizing for breaking the facade of a service worker whose capitalist identity is to strictly serve the customer. This economic exploitation is inextricable from gender exploitation. In the U.S. restaurant industry in 2016, 70 percent of all servers were women, and the average annual salary was $18,137.[82] This gendered industry has normalized its poverty-level wages, expecting customers to subsidize workers' lives, which is an irregular, imbalanced form of financial gratitude that doesn't make ends meet for millions of U.S. servers. As the Economic Policy Institute reported in 2018—the same year Kelly Sue DeConnick became the first woman writer in *Aquaman*'s then seventy-eight-year history—one in nine full-time U.S. workers were paid wages that kept them in poverty, and according to the Department of Labor, in 2012, seven of the ten lowest-paid occupations in the United States were in the food industry.[83] Being in the food industry is not a young person's job, either. Too often, the capitalist stereotype circulates that low-paying jobs, such as in the service industry, are for young people, especially for students, getting their financial start in life. In contrast, the average age for waitresses is 30.1 years old.[84] This social fact is narrated and visualized in The New 52 *Aquaman*. To try to get her two children through college to hopefully escape the trap of poverty, this waitress, it is implied, needs to regularly work multiple consecutive shifts.

The waitress, though, does not recognize herself as a victim of an exploitative, patriarchal economic structure. Just as she starts to share her story, she polices herself and stops, silencing her voice. She apologizes twice, in two consecutive sentences, for beginning to share her story, and then says, "My problems are probably ridiculous compared to yours, huh?"[85] The waitress assumes that her narrative of financial struggle— one compounded by myriad other struggles, including trying to raise and pay for her children's education—is "ridiculous" compared to Aquaman's. She assumes that Aquaman's narratives and problems are more important than hers.

At this moment, the waitress capitulates to a discourse that, in its dominant form, should be critiqued: the discourse of heroes. Rather than give voice to her struggles, the waitress stops and allows Aquaman's heroic narrative to take precedence. This capitulation symbolizes a dominant trend in the surface world—narrating social reality through the paradigm of heroes. Ecofeminist scholar Marti Kheel argues that the dominant hero narrative offers a myopic framework for processing and understanding social relations. Kheel writes, "Western heroic ethics is designed to treat problems at an advanced stage of their history," running "counter to one of the most basic principles in ecology—namely, that everything is interconnected."[86] Hegemonic heroic narratives, in other words, narrowly focus on conspicuous "crises" and "conflicts" and posit the individual—typically white, hypermasculine, and heteronormative—as an autonomous actor whose choices can make him into a socially recognizable hero. But as Kheel writes, "Little if any thought is given to why the crisis or conflict arose to begin with."[87] In contrast, holistic narratives, which Kheel also identifies as ecofeminist narratives, eschew and critique such heroic narratives to explore the complex, intersectional social relations and structures that are the condition of possibility for crises and conflicts to emerge in the first place.

The New 52 *Aquaman*, I want to suggest, can be read as a challenge to the dominant hero narrative. As illustrated in "The Trench" narrative arc, while the dominant surface world may temporarily recognize and celebrate Aquaman as a hero, he is haunted by his supposed heroic actions and refuses to embrace his ostensible heroic status. Aquaman implicitly understands that the surface world's heroic framing enables a false and dangerous binary that positions heroes on the side of Human civilization and, conversely, projects anyone and anything not recognized as Human as unworthy of respect, dignity, and life. This is the dangerous framing that discursively transforms the trench into monsters. This framing is both myopic and antiecological. In questioning the dominant hero narrative, does The New 52 *Aquaman* practice a form of ecofeminism?

Ecofeminist scholar Greta Gaard defines ecofeminism as "an evolving praxis" that centers on "entangled empathy."[88] Entangled empathy is an intersectional paradigm and praxis that recognizes the inextricable connections between "human justice, interspecies justice, and human-environment justice."[89] In contrast, empathy as policed and practiced by Humanism only extends to others recognized as Humans. This narrow form of empathy not only excludes nearly all nonhuman animals (with exceptions for select species enfolded into the Human everyday, like dogs), but moreover, such empathy also excludes most humans. Humanism excludes individuals not raced as white, not gendered as masculine, and not able-bodied.

Looking back at the opening narrative arc, two of the central concepts animating "The Trench" are entangled empathy and ecological interconnectedness. A central allegory of The New 52 *Aquaman* is the need to ever expand our circle of care and empathy to recognize that all species, all beings, are part of the web of life and should be seen with inherent worth and intrinsic value. In contrast, Human-produced and Human-projected categories such as monsters are antiecological and enable social injustices across all species.

This web-of-life paradigm—a paradigm central to ecological and ecofeminist thinking—is made even more explicit later in the series. In the fourth and final narrative arc of Johns's run (issues 18–25, March/May 2013–November 2013 / January 2014), we learn that the trench were once members of the Kingdom of Atlantis. Arthur and the trench, in other words, come from the same kingdom, from the same political community. The trench, a species deemed other by Humans and foreign by Arthur, prove to be Arthur's kin. This discovery, at the end of Johns's run (although hinted at earlier in the series), underscores the point that all living beings are interconnected, challenging the logic of hypersegregation and hierarchical classification practiced and perpetuated by Humanity.[90] In narrative form, can we claim that The New 52 *Aquaman* practices a form of ecofeminism?

Ecofeminism centers gender in understanding and narrating the violences of the Anthropocene. In their foundational book *Ecofeminism*, Maria Mies and Vandana Shiva focus on how genderism and speciesism are conjoined hierarchical structures. In her introduction to the coauthored book, Shiva writes, "I have repeatedly stressed that the rape of the Earth and rape of women are intimately linked—both metaphorically, in shaping world-views, and materially, in shaping women's everyday lives."[91] These linked violences become visible in Mera's narrative. Mera bears witness to how rape culture is normative in the surface world, and she bears witness to how Humanity wages war against the Global Oceans.

But Mera is more than a witness; she helps fight for a more socially just future for all species, as we shall see in the next chapter. Moreover, we can read her superpowers allegorically. Mera has the power of hydrokinesis, the ability to manipulate water with her mind. This power can be read allegorically for the pantheon of progressive ecological feminists who developed disruptive, paradigm-shifting perspectives for how we see and relate to the Ocean. In a U.S. context alone, the context of Arthur and Mera's surface home, this includes the following marine biologists, oceanographers, explorers, and activists: Maria Mitchell, Marie Tharp, Rachel Carson, Sylvia Earle, Cindy Lee Van Dover, Katy Payne, and Ayana Elizabeth Johnson. Moreover, multiple women artists have changed the way we see and understand the Global Ocean, including one of the great and prolific *Aquaman* artists, Ramona Fradon, who helped give form to the Silver Age version of the marine superhero.

While stereotypical visualizations of gender persist in The New 52 *Aquaman*, hegemonic narratives "can be and have been read, recognized, reworked, reformed, and/or resisted by readers in variable and unpredictable ways."[92] Despite the myth that superhero comics are predominately read by white, heteronormative men, all genders, races, ethnicities, and ages engage with and interpret superhero comics in ways that far exceed a panel's borders.[93] Reading through the prism of allegoresis—a political mode of reading that is willing to be unfaithful to corporate and authorial intentions—The New 52 *Aquaman* can be recognized as a form of ecofeminism, and Mera can be recognized as a superwoman who kicks ass both physically and ideologically.

In the comic, Mera learns that she is not a hero in the dominant sense—a single individual who can defeat injustice. Rather, she learns to see that the surface world is an ecology of violence, especially against women. As she learns, no one individual can change these material conditions. To change this patriarchal structure requires deep, structural change. And in the next narrative arc of the series, "Throne of Atlantis" (November 2012 / January 2013–February/April 2013), such a structural change becomes allegorized.

3

The Apocalyptic Ocean

Perhaps the central allegory of The New 52 *Aquaman* occurs in the third narrative arc "Throne of Atlantis" (November 2012 / January 2013–February/April 2013). In this arc, the Ocean wages war against the surface world, striking multiple cities with tsunamic waves and threatening to drown iconic DC cities such as Metropolis and Gotham. The enormity of this attack, which includes the drowning of perhaps millions of people and the destruction of countless buildings, threatens to swallow all signs of civilization. As the artists visualize, the apocalypse has arrived.

The New 52 *Aquaman* makes visible that the relationship between Humanity and the Ocean is one of war—a spectacular war. The Ocean's coordinated multicity attack on the surface world may be experienced as a shock for surface dwellers, but as various marine-based characters articulate throughout the series, Humanity has waged a continual, constant war on the Oceans for generations. Another name of this unending war is the Anthropocene.

In an obvious sense, the Ocean's attack on the surface world allegorizes the imminent threat of extreme weather, and climate change more generally, both hallmarks of the Anthropocene. The Ocean's attack does not come out of the blue. Rather, the war between Humans and the Ocean is hinted at throughout *The New 52* run. In *Aquaman* 7 (March/May 2012), for example, Arthur and Mera rescue ships from an incoming superstorm, which are described as becoming more frequent and ferocious. After the storm subsides, a journalist reports that the storm is "one of the worst storms to ever attack the New England Coast."[1] This journalistic discourse figures the storms as attacking, granting the weather both agency and autonomy. Moreover, the journalist calls it a "superstorm," which, in this context, suggests how storms are becoming analogous to superheroes in their power and strength. While journalists recognize a pattern of more extreme, increasingly violent weather, what is missing is a more holistic narrative framework. To use the language of ecofeminist Kheel, the news focuses on the immediate conflict—here the superstorm attacking the shore—and not the causes of this conflict.

Although the journalist reports that the superstorm was the most extreme weather in recorded New England history, it is telling how this mass-mediated news does not stay focused and reflect on the recent pattern of extreme weather. The narrative fails to frame this storm in terms of the structures that enable such superstorms; the narrative fails to broaden its scope to consider the pattern of climate change. After the lone panel in which the journalist reports the story of extreme weather that has shattered records, the very next panel abruptly shifts topics to update the status of Mera. In the previous issue, Mera was arrested, but she soon escaped. The journalist reports, "Aquawoman is still wanted in the questioning of a brutal attack against the manager of a grocery store and the assaulting of several police officers."[2] The mass media generates and sustains interest by selling stories of spectacular violence. The pace and frame of the news, in its dominant form, is antithetical to stories that make visible and legible structural violence. In the above example, the news only focuses on the immediate aftermath of the conflict, rather than the longer story that led to Mera breaking the store manager's arm. In the mass media's myopic framing, Mera is cast as the perpetrator; and the store manager, as the victim. The mass media only frames and shows the conflict and its aftermath—the storm "attacking" New England and Mera "attacking" the store manager—and fails to tell narratives with a wider scale and scope. The mass media, in other words, fails to tell ecofeminist narratives.

The New 52 *Aquaman* suggests how the dominant culture of global capitalism attempts to obscure, deny, and render illegible violences that are sustained and structural. To better understand the political and aesthetic challenges of representing structural violence, I want to briefly turn to the important distinction postcolonial and environmental scholar Rob Nixon makes between spectacular and "slow violence." Spectacular violence is hypervisible violence—the word *spectacular* is etymologically rooted in "sight"—and such permeates mass-mediated culture, from televisual news to blockbuster movies. Everywhere in mass-mediated culture, there are explosions, assaults, gunfire, and carnage. The dominant culture of the Anthropocene only recognizes spectacular violence and, conversely, is ideologically blind to slow violence. As Nixon explains, slow violence "occurs gradually and out of sight, a violence of delayed destruction that is dispersed across time and space, an attritional violence that is typically not viewed as violence at all."[3] Slow violence, in many ways, is synonymous with ecological violence. In fact, one of the examples Nixon offers to make the concept of slow violence more concrete is "acidifying oceans."[4]

Nixon argues that progressive cultural producers must innovate aesthetically in order to make slow violence visible and legible. Counterintuitively, Johns, Reis, Prado, and Reis use the popular grammar of spectacular violence to make visible the long and slow violence devastating the Global Oceans. In the narrative arc "Throne of Atlantis," the Ocean becomes allegorized in the figure of Orm, whom the surface world calls the Ocean Master. When The New 52 *Aquaman* begins, Orm is the King of Atlantis and Protector of the Seven Seas. He is a figure explicitly invested with agency, and in his symbolic identity as the Ocean's representative, he decides to launch an all-out assault on the surface world. Rather than the war between the surface world and the Ocean world being figurative, The New 52 *Aquaman* makes such a war literal and, moreover, sensational.

Structures of Capitalist Hate

Corporate superheroes are defined, in large part, by supervillains. Without Joker, there's no Batman. Without Lex Luthor, no Superman. Without Magneto, no Professor X. Yet this formula becomes complicated in The New 52 *Aquaman*. As analyzed in chapter 1, the trench prove not to be an "enemy," and similarly, in the narrative arc "Throne of Atlantis," Orm, the King of Atlantis, who leads the Ocean's assault on the surface world, also defies the categorization of "villain."[5] In fact, in The New 52 iteration, Orm can be read as an ecological hero.

Like many characters, Orm has been reimagined several times since he was first introduced in *Aquaman* 29 (1966). Created by Bob Haney and Nick Cardy, Orm was defined, in large part, by his intense jealousy of Arthur's birthright to the Atlantean throne. Orm and Arthur are half-brothers, sharing the same human father. The rivalry between Arthur and Orm is a sibling rivalry for political power. For decades, Orm has been one of Aquaman's long-standing and steadfast nemeses. The New 52 makes several important changes to Orm's identity and history. To begin with, Orm is switched from Arthur's paternal to maternal half-brother. That is, both brothers share the same mother, Atlanna, Queen of Atlantis. But more importantly,

Johns refigures Orm from being half-Atlantean into being full-blooded Atlantean. This transformation sets up a racial allegory that will become pronounced and prominent in Johns's fourth and final narrative arc, which I will analyze in chapter 4.

In conjunction with making Orm fully Atlantean, Johns also establishes that Orm is not a villain. In contrast to previous iterations, where Orm was envious of Arthur's political power, in The New 52, Orm initially harbors no resentment or animosity toward his half-brother. Rather, when the series begins, Arthur has already abdicated the throne because he wants to build a life on the surface world with Mera. Orm rules Atlantis because his half-brother, the heir to the throne, didn't want the responsibilities.

Orm's decision to attack the surface world is explored in *Aquaman* 23.2 (September/November 2013), an issue that centers on Orm, similar to how *Aquaman* 6 (analyzed in the previous chapter) centers on Mera. The issue begins with Orm sitting on the throne and informing his royal army that "it's time that the surface world learned they cannot attack us without being repaid in kind."[6] Orm frames the Ocean's proposed attack on the surface world as justified, balanced, and moreover, as a counterattack. The surface is "being repaid in kind." In The New 52, Orm is guided by a strong sense of justice. As Orm tells the legions surrounding him, he wears the crown of Atlantis "for the sake of our people," and he acts as their representative and on their behalf.[7] His decision to strike the surface world is not about a personal vendetta against his half-brother. Rather, it's about trying to halt and reverse the Anthropocene's wanton march of ecological destruction.

As King of Atlantis, Orm historicizes the Anthropocene to his subjects as follows: "For as long as Atlantis has existed, the surface world has hated us." Orm then offers a new path into the future: "But today they will learn to fear us!"[8] In this allegory, Johns and cowriter Tony Bedard offer an important political critique of the Anthropocene's libidinal economy. In this section, I take seriously Orm's insights that the surface world, the world of capitalism, *hates* the Ocean.

From the perspective of the surface world, Orm's charge of hate likely comes as a surprise. While thalassophobia—the fear of the Ocean—is a real condition, most people would not say they hate the Ocean, the way many hate, for example, bullies. But as Orm suggests, hate is not located inside Humans. Rather, it is located in Human institutions and the behaviors such institutions encourage and regularize. For more than a century, such institutions have proven hateful and harmful toward the Ocean.

This history of hate is evident if we return to Mera's narrative. When Mera enters the grocery store, prior to her sexual harassment and assault, she is overwhelmed by the abundance of commodities that define late capitalism. Even when purchasing dog food, Mera is surprised by the plethora of consumer choices available.[9] From an alien perspective, from Mera's perspective, this world of commodity abundance is shocking. Because of her home ecology, Mera knows that this world of abundance has a cost not reflected in the price of commodities—the cost of mass garbage and mass pollution, a significant portion of which ends up in the Global Ocean. As Mera sees this world of commodities, she knows—or she should know—that a "debris field the size of Texas has formed in the center of the North Pacific Ocean . . . composed mainly of microscopic Styrofoam particles and tiny pieces of degraded plastic."[10] The Oceans transforming into a giant Human garbage dump can be traced to the everyday practices of global capitalism. In the grocery store, before Mera sees the violence of sexism, she sees the violence of capitalism. As she sees, the Human way of life is a capitalist way of life that is driving the Anthropocene and the sixth great extinction.

Surrounding Mera is an endless array of plastics, one of the most prominent forms of modern hate. Political scientist Michiel Roscam Abbing writes, "Plastics have become enormously popular over the last seventy years, thanks to their particular properties and extremely low production costs."[11] The history of plastics overlaps with the history of *Aquaman* comics. Plastics are a central symbol and index of late capitalism. They are inexpensive to produce; they are pliable for myriad uses, from wrappers and bottles to containers and straws; and they last forever. From the perspective of capitalism, plastic is a "miracle" commodity.[12] From the perspective of Earth, however, plastics are toxic. Unlike all organic beings, plastics are nonbiodegradable. They do not decay or dissolve in water.[13] This means that "all the plastic that has ever ended up in the environment is still present in some form or other."[14] Plastic is an inorganic, immortal product and poison that is "designed to be waste," and it is choking the Global Ocean.[15] The World Economic Forum predicts that by the year 2050, there is estimated to be more plastic than fish in the world's Ocean.[16]

One would think that this widely disseminated knowledge would give Humans pause. However, the opposite has happened. Humans have created a plastic world. Oceanographer and boat captain Charles J. Moore, who helped spread awareness of the Great Pacific Garbage Patch, expresses in exasperation, "Every single thing is [now] wrapped in plastic. . . . Each toothpick is wrapped in plastic."[17] As the toothpick exemplifies, plastics are predominantly produced for single-use purposes. That is, plastics are designed to be used once and thrown away thoughtlessly: straws, spoons, wrapping, containers, everything. Abbing writes, "Plastic waste is a mirror that reflects the throw-away society that quickly emerged after the Second World War. . . . Never in our history have so many products been available so cheaply. These products are overwhelmingly made of plastic.

Consumers are awash with products that do not last long and that they often don't even need."[18] Mass production mandates mass consumption, and late capitalism enculturates Humans to live in a world of plastic and to participate in the ritual of buying and throwing away "cheap" plastic things. The capitalist category "cheap" occludes how a world of "cheap" is anything but cheap, from an ecological perspective. To use the affectively charged rhetoric of Orm, pervasive plastic use is a form of hate.

This everyday hate is a form of slow violence that accumulates over time and across geographies and that is largely invisible to Humanity. Plastics are now replete throughout the food chain, including in humans. In fact, today, "most people have plastic inside their bodies."[19] Humans are addicted to and daily participate in a plastic world and are enculturated to not see the toxins flowing in all organic fluids from the Global Ocean to the Great Lakes to the blood of all species.

There are multiple ways that Humans show and practice hate toward the Oceans. Peter Neill, founding director of the World Ocean Observatory, writes, "There is this notion that the ocean is so vast that it can encompass and dilute such poisons. Therefore, it's fine that we dump sewage there, or fracking residue, or obsolete ships, or nuclear waste, or plastic, plastic, plastic. That has been proven wrong and wrong-headed. The plume of radioactive water from a tsunami accident in Japan extended to the west coast of the United States in a few short weeks. The toxic dust from mining in Australia finds its way to deposit so remotely away on Antarctic ice in just a few weeks more."[20] In conjunction with treating the Ocean as a giant garbage dump, another prominent form of Human hate is to only see the Ocean as a source of wealth production. From the perspective of capitalism, the Ocean is "valued as mineral stockpile, oil reserve, fish tank and food pantry, cabinet of potential pharmaceuticals, and endless supplier of materials in the service of the human project."[21] Seeing the Ocean as a resource to be endlessly exploited is a form of hate. However, from the perspective of the surface world, seeing the Ocean—and nature more generally—as a limitless resource for Human wealth is constitutive of the capitalist everyday.

Capitalism imagines nature as a source of infinite resources that can be endlessly extracted and accumulated for endless profit. According to this logic, nature can be plundered and exploited without consideration of ecological ramifications and consequences. This ideology buttresses the most violent, destructive, and hateful practices. In this system, for example, fishing has transformed into a large-scale industrial process. In an economy now predicated on mass production and mass consumption that ignores ecological limits and boundaries, practices such as "bottom trawling" have become normative, a method that now brings in roughly nineteen million tons of fish annually, which is roughly a quarter of all wild-caught seafood.[22] While such fishing methods are highly effective and efficient from a capitalist perspective, from an ecological perspective, bottom trawling causes devastating, irreparable damage. Bottom trawling "reduces the complexity, productivity, and biodiversity of benthic habitats. . . . When disturbed by bottom trawling, as much as 90 percent of a coral colony perishes, and up to two-thirds of sponges are damaged."[23] While capitalism may see bottom trawling's yield as a resounding success, these industrial practices, according to the National Academy of Sciences, "permanently impact . . . the biological function and composition of . . . ecosystems."[24]

From a Human perspective, the violence of bottom trawling is a form of slow violence. Over a long period of time, species' populations plummet beyond levels of sustainability. However, from the perspective of the Ocean, such industrial fishing practices are a form of spectacular violence. In his book *The End of the Line: How Overfishing Is Changing the World and What We Eat*, Charles Clover helps us understand the massive, reckless, and irresponsible violence of bottom trawling by offering the following comparison:

> Imagine what people would say if a band of hunters strung a mile of net between two immense all-terrain vehicles and dragged it at speed across the plains of Africa. The fantastical assemblage, like something from a *Mad Max* movie, would scoop up everything in its way: predators such as lions and cheetahs, lumbering endangered herbivores such as rhinos and elephants, herds of impala and wildebeest, family groups of warthogs and wild dogs. . . . Picture how the net is constructed, with a huge metal roller attached to the leading edge. This rolling beam smashes and flattens obstructions, flushing creatures into the approaching filaments. The effects of dragging a huge iron bar across the savannah is to break off every outcrop and uproot every tree, bush, and flowering plant, stirring columns of birds into the air. Left behind is a strangely bedraggled landscape resembling a harrowed field. . . . There are no markets for about a third of the animals they have caught because they don't taste good, or because they are simply too small or too squashed. The pile of corpses is dumped on the plain to be consumed by scavengers.[25]

Industrial fishing indiscriminately kills all life-forms and entire ecosystems. This form of mass violence is "justified" because of Humanity's hierarchical mode of organization and terrestrial bias that fish are of lesser value than non-Human animals found on land. Because Humans can't "cuddle" fish and because fish are cold-blooded, a surface ideology reigns that marine life is at the bottom of the hierarchical structure.[26] Today, many vegetarians make an exception for seafood.

10. The first visualization of the Ocean from a surface perspective. "The Trench, Part 1," Geoff Johns (writer), Ivan Reis (penciller), Joe Prado (inker), and Rod Reis (colorist), *Aquaman 7*, no. 1, The New 52 (New York: DC Comics, September/ November 2011).

As The New 52 *Aquaman* allegorizes, the Anthropocene is a way of seeing and not seeing. In issue 1, after a battle sequence establishing Arthur's awesome powers, he goes to a restaurant to enjoy a meal at Sam's Seafood (fig. 10). Before Arthur enters, a full-width panel establishes the restaurant as a communal center, an identity indicated by a parking lot crowded with cars and a speech bubble that suggests a bustling crowd and an overtaxed kitchen. This is the first time in the series that we see the Ocean in a Human context. And tellingly, the Ocean is literally marginal.

In this panel, the Ocean is decentered, minimized, and shoved to the lower right-hand corner. In contrast, the restaurant and parking lot, packed with cars, dominate the panel. While this restaurant is on the waterfront, the Atlantic Ocean occupies a sliver of the panel, situated at the bottom right. In fact, if this comic were being taught in a classroom, a teacher would probably have to point out that the Ocean is even present in the panel. The Ocean's absence/presence is emblematic and allegorical of the Anthropocene. To not see the Ocean, even when it's right in front of us, is a form of hate.

When Arthur enters the restaurant, he is visualized as alienated from this Human community. Before Arthur enters, the panels show a vibrant community with crowded tables. However, when Arthur comes into the frame, he is visualized from a distance and as physically isolated. This alienation is visually registered throughout the scene, as Arthur is the only character who is framed in isolation and the only customer who dines alone. Arthur's alienation is because he is a symbol of the Ocean, a geography that is allegorically projected as outside of the Human.

In myriad ways, as Orm deeply understands, the surface world's relation to the Ocean is one of persistent and structural hate. Orm explains to Arthur that he is leading the Ocean into war against the surface world because, "for centuries," the surface world has engaged in a one-sided war against the Ocean. Orm asserts, the surface world "has done nothing but attack and poison us for centuries."[27] This sentiment is repeated multiple times throughout and beyond the narrative arc. Orm explains to his brother that the Ocean's counterattack was a long time coming and centuries in the making: "We are done fearing the surface. We are done living in terror."[28] Orm radically reframes the narrative of modernity. As Orm narrates, Humans are agents of terror, and the Oceans striking back is a counterattack on a structure that normalizes cruelty and mass violence against all living communities considered external to the kingdom of man.

Before turning to the Ocean's spectacular attack, I want to broach a notable absence. The New 52 *Aquaman* never directly visualizes the surface's violence against the Ocean. One can imagine the power, for example, of a two-page spread showing heaps of plastic accumulating in the Ocean. But instead, the comic just shows Orm's speech bubbles explaining the surface world's continual war on the seas. In a medium where images are foundational, The New 52 *Aquaman* does not visualize how capitalism systemically destroys the Ocean's ecosystems. The comic does not directly represent plastic pollution, acidification, garbage dumping, or overfishing.

Rather than read this absence as a failure, though, I want to suggest we should read such an absence as generative, signifying the challenges of representing this ecological war. In the superhero genre, where the expected aesthetic is spectacle, the absence of such an aesthetic is conspicuous and aligns with the tragedy unfolding in the Ocean. Acidification, for example, does not lend itself to an aesthetic of spectacle. Nor for that matter do plastics. While some activists use images of large pieces of plastic floating on the Ocean's surface to signify plastic pollution, most plastics are imperceptible to Human sight. While plastic pollution is visible—"every wave that breaks on shore leaves some plastic behind, and beaches all over the world have to be cleaned up constantly"—plastics continually break down into smaller and smaller parts, becoming what is known as microplastics, which are "so small that they are no longer visible to the naked eye and can easily get into food chains."[29] From within the bubble of Humanity, the Anthropocene is largely an invisible war.

When Orm is on land, he makes explicit that the poisons that pervade modernity are not legible through visuality: "I can smell the poisons you [Humanity] have tainted the ground and sea with. I can taste the toxins in the air you breathe. You kill the environment that provides for you."[30] In this articulation, the violences that mark modernity are sensible through smell and taste, not visibility. This insight is reinforced by the visuals.

11. Orm describes the poisons saturating the surface world. "New Fish," Geoff Johns and Tony Bedard (plot), Tony Bedard (words), Geraldo Borges (penciller), Ruy José (inker), and Rod Reis (colorist), *Aquaman* 7, no. 23.2, The New 52 (New York: DC Comics, September/November 2013).

When Orm observes that pervasive poisons saturate the land, his speech is not contained by panels. Rather, it disseminates across the page, similar to the movement of the poisons Orm describes (fig. 11). The dialogue is outside the panel, outside the normative space and grammar of standard comics. As this page suggests, to understand the systemic and everyday violence of the Anthropocene requires new ways of sensing and narrating.

The invisibility of the sixth great extinction is similarly addressed in issue 22 (July/September 2013). The issue opens with two Atlanteans on the surface world for the first time, and both are perplexed by the presence of automobiles. One of the Atlanteans asks, "What is that terrible smell?" An Atlantean who frequently travels between the Ocean and the surface world explains that it's a "machine" that "runs on processed fossil fuels." A different Atlantean replies, "And the air breathers wonder why we want them dead." From the dominant paradigm of the surface world, the everyday violences of global capitalism are ideologically rendered invisible.

The closest the artwork comes to visualizing the Anthropocene's violence is what catalyzes Atlantis to finally attack the surface world. At the beginning of the "Throne of Atlantis" arc, a large U.S. warship tests missiles by firing them into the Ocean, inadvertently striking Atlantis.[31] Allegorically, the missiles firing down into the Ocean mirrors the logic of modern aircrafts and drones firing down onto African, Latin American, and Middle Eastern regions. Yet even this act, one that lends itself to spectacle, is not visualized. We see multiple missiles firing into the Ocean; in the panel below this visualization, we see diverse aquatic life; and the final image on the page is a small panel at the bottom showing billows of clouds. Rather than a splash page visualizing the horrific violence wrought by multiple missiles, the violence is decentered and marginalized (existing at the bottom of the page)—and, moreover, not directly represented—once again suggesting that the violence against the Ocean exceeds the dominant grammar of our visual modernity.

What unfolds in the Ocean are forms of slow *and* spectacular violence. But these violences are largely illegible to Humanity. At the heart of the "Throne of Atlantis" story line is Orm's spectacular effort to make Humanity's centuries-long war on the Oceans conspicuously visible.

Allegories of Nationalism

As The New 52 *Aquaman* recognizes and allegorizes, the surface world and Ocean world are at war with each other. Yet Humanity fails to see this intergenerational, capitalist-fueled war. Orm's objective is to make Humanity see. His strategic, multicity attack on the surface world was the first big crossover event of The New 52. In the four-month arc that unfolds across *Aquaman* issues 14–17 and *Justice League* issues 15–17 (November 2012 / January 2013–February/April 2013), Arthur and Mera lead the Justice League to stop the Ocean's apocalyptic attack.

The "Throne of Atlantis" arc is centered on war and dominated by an aesthetic of spectacle. Yet in between panels of combat and carnage, a quiet narrative thread contemplates and questions the parameters and meanings of justice. This thread considers how non-Human animals and geographies can have access to justice in the Anthropocene, a period whose dominant conception of justice is limited to Humans and predominantly mediated by nation-states. More specifically, the series asks: How does the Ocean become recognized as a political geography whose inhabitants are recognized as having inherent rights and dignity? How can considerations of justice be extended to the Ocean? In The New 52 *Aquaman*, this philosophical challenge becomes concretized and allegorized by the underwater Kingdom of Atlantis.

A comic series centered on kingdoms, rulers, and warring worlds is intrinsically political, and The New 52 foregrounds these political dimensions. Central to The New 52 *Aquaman*'s political allegory is that the surface world is constituted, in part, by its collective refusal to recognize Atlantis—and the Ocean more generally—as a political space. Whereas the surface world views the Ocean as a geography outside the political, as a resource that can be endlessly exploited and a space where garbage can be endlessly dumped, the series recognizes the Ocean as a political geography and marine lives as political agents with "intrinsic value" and "inherent worth."[32] (This politicization of the Ocean is central to Aquaman's long and storied comic book history.) Whereas the surface world laughs at and mocks Aquaman's ability to talk to fish, the series visualizes the complex languages, ethics, and politics of multiple marine species—modes of community largely illegible to Humanity. To help make the Ocean visible as a political space, The New 52 *Aquaman* figures Oceanic species as citizens and Oceanic ecologies as political geographies. More specifically, the comic translates the Ocean into Human terms, as a geography replete with kingdoms and kings. This act of translation is most explicit in the Kingdom of Atlantis.

Atlantis has been a salient allegory for centuries. The first extant references to the mythical, island kingdom are Plato's dialogues *Timaeus* and *Critias*, written about 330 BCE. For Plato, the Kingdom of Atlantis was a political-ecological allegory about what happens when Humans imagine themselves as divorced from and superior to the web of life. Instead of living in balance with other species, geographies, and human societies, Atlantis became an empire committed to colonial expansion, with an unsatiated desire for material wealth. According to legend, the Kingdom of Atlantis was the wealthiest and the most militarily advanced kingdom of the ancient world.[33] In the dialogue that bears his name, Critias explains, "They said, too, that the kings of the island of Atlantis were the rulers of the other peoples. This island . . . was at one time greater than both Libya and Asia combined. But now because of earthquakes it has subsided into the great Ocean."[34] Plato's dialogue figures Atlantis's downfall as a political allegory. The kingdom was swept into the Ocean not because of arbitrary earthquakes but because of its political actions. Plato writes, "Inwardly they were filled with an unjust lust for possessions and power. But as Zeus, god of the gods, reigning as king according to law, could clearly see this state of affairs, he . . . resolved to punish them and to make them more careful and harmonious as a result of their chastisement."[35] As Plato allegorizes, Atlantis sank into the sea because of its colonial drive, a drive incompatible with healthy, "harmonious" ecological living. Such harmony means, in part, living within limits that allow other species and geographies to flourish. Instead, Atlantis established and practiced a hierarchical mode of organization with Atlanteans hubristically placed at the top.

Since Plato introduced this ecological allegory, "the story of Atlantis . . . has captured the imagination of readers for over two millennia."[36] In The New 52 *Aquaman*, Atlantis remains an ecological allegory, but the series uses the mythical kingdom for additional allegorical purposes. As I will explore in chapter 4, in Johns's final narrative arc of The New 52 *Aquaman*, Atlantis also becomes an allegory about racism. But for this chapter, I want to focus on how Johns makes Atlantis into an allegory about nationalism.

One of The New 52 *Aquaman*'s allegorical innovations is figuring Atlantis as a nation.[37] In the modern world, the nation has become the primary form of political organization through which recognition and rights are secured and, moreover, the form through which justice is mediated.[38] In a world in which political imaginations are tethered to and mediated by the nation-state, the series posits Atlantis—and the Ocean more generally—as a nation that should be afforded the same rights, respect, recognition, and access to justice as any other nation. What drives the political narrative of the "Throne of Atlantis" arc, though, is that the surface world refuses to recognize Atlantis as a nation. This refusal, as the series suggests, is one of the main catalysts of the Ocean's war with the surface world.

Aquaman is committed to stopping the Ocean's attack on the surface world, a political imaginary that, in the series, is synonymous with the United States. To stop the Ocean's attack, Aquaman joins forces with the Justice League, a collective organized, as its name highlights, by a shared commitment to justice. However, justice is not a fixed concept. Justice to the superhero collective means something other than what it means for Orm and the Ocean. Whereas the vast majority of the Justice League view the Ocean's attack as evil incarnate, Aquaman tries to reason with the collective of superheroes that Atlantis has a legitimate and justifiable reason for attacking the surface world. Aquaman tries to explain to Batman, for example, "You need to understand . . . Atlantis's interactions with the surface world have been sailors slaughtering its people and nuclear tests and environmental disasters poisoning their oceans."[39] Batman, however, refuses to empathize with the Ocean's perspective, asserting unequivocally, "There is no rationalizing an attack like this. Whatever the catalyst."[40] As this narrative arc foregrounds, the Justice League conceptualizes justice predominately in relation to Human concerns; it is Aquaman who tries to broaden and diversify their perspective.

While the Justice League is uncritically committed to violence as an appropriate response to Atlantis's attack, Aquaman desperately goes to different members of the collective to explain that a nonviolent resolution is still possible and preferable.

Aquaman tells Superman, for example, that this situation is "more complicated" than the reductive paradigm of good vs. evil.[41] As Arthur explains, Orm is "not a super-villain. He's the leader of an underwater nation."[42] This political figuration is key to The New 52 Aquaman's allegory. Atlantis is not just a kingdom, a largely arcane political organization in the modern world; rather, it's a "nation." In modernity, nationalism has become one of the most powerful ideologies and a central organizing principle of the political-juridical imagination. As Arthur explains repeatedly, Atlantis is a nation-state with the same rights as any other nation-state. Like any other nation, Atlantis has the right to protect its borders and engage in just and justifiable wars.

However, the surface world refuses to recognize Atlantis as a nation. In Aquaman 17 (February/April 2013), the final issue in the "Throne of Atlantis" arc, Director Amanda Waller, the founder and director of Task Force X (better known as Suicide Squad), tells Aquaman, "The world is refusing to recognize it [Atlantis] as a nation, and you as its king."[43] This refusal to recognize Atlantis as a nation with inherent rights and dignity becomes an allegory for how Humanity refuses to recognize the Ocean as anything other than an apolitical geography for Human exploitation, from extraction to dumping. The refusal to recognize the Ocean as a political geography justifies the Ocean's abject status in modernity. Legal scholar Irus Braverman and geographer Elizabeth R. Johnson write in their introduction to Blue Legalities: The Life and Laws of the Sea that even "as evidence mounts that marine ecologies are facing collapse, the ocean is also becoming a new frontier for resource extraction and economic expansion."[44] This new frontier of capitalism is an expansion of what is known as the "blue economy." The authors continue, "Growing the 'blue economy' has become a central component of national and regional strategies in coastal states around the world."[45] Beginning in the twentieth century, nation-states everywhere have been vying to extend their claim and ownership of the Ocean as natural expansions of their territories. This is a radically new ideology. Philip Steinberg writes that prior to the twentieth century, the Ocean was never seen as a geography that could be claimed and owned.[46] In a central text to modern juridical thought, Dutch jurist Hugo Grotius wrote the pamphlet *Mare liberum* (*The Freedom of the Seas*) in 1609 to argue that the Oceans could not be claimed as territory. Grotius writes, "The sea is common to all, because it is so limitless that it cannot become a possession of any one and because it is adapted for the use of all, whether we consider it from the point of view of navigation or of fisheries."[47] The Oceans were widely understood as a shared commons. That is, until the twentieth century and the development of late capitalism, a history that overlaps with the publishing history of *Aquaman*.

Only in the twentieth century did a new social construction of the Ocean emerge—the concept that the Ocean, in all its depth and volume, could be claimed and owned by nation states. The 1982 United Nations Convention on the Law of the Sea (UNCLOS) is "undoubtedly the most comprehensive contemporary inscription of ocean sovereignty, jurisdiction, and use."[48] This treaty created and solidified new norms that constructed the Ocean as a territory that could be mapped and divided, just as territorial geography could, and moreover, this treaty established new norms of marine ownership.[49] Most importantly, for our purposes, is that this international treatise, created and ratified by "territorial nation-states," granted coastal states sovereignty over two hundred miles extending from the state's shore. In this new ideological mapping of social relations, this two-hundred-mile area became economically recognized as a nation-state's "exclusive economic zone (EEZ)."[50] Today, "coastal states have sovereign rights to all living and non-living resources in their EEZS,"[51] ranging from the surface to the seafloor and even extending beneath that floor. To use the language of geographer Kathryn Yusoff, the Anthropocene turns "matter" into "property."[52] In this context, this means transforming the Ocean from a shared commons into national property that can be exploited however the nation wishes. Put differently, the Ocean becomes a privatized means to enrich the nation's wealth—a wealth narrowly conceived in racial, capitalist, and Humanist terms.

This radical remaking of the world began with the United States, the nation-state that *Aquaman*'s Atlantis sees as synonymous with the surface world and, hence, the nation-state that Atlantis exclusively targets and attacks. DeLoughrey writes that the "1945 Truman Proclamation"—an executive order made four years after *Aquaman*'s debut—is "the most significant, and yet largely unremarked, twentieth-century remapping of the globe."[53] For the first time in history, "a coastal state had asserted its right to a specific offshore resources area."[54] It was the United States that "created a scramble for the oceans, catalyzing EEZ declarations by nations all over the world and a U.N. Convention on the Law of the Sea that effectively remapped seventy percent of the planet."[55]

While different imperial powers have attempted to patrol and control the Ocean's surface for centuries, never before had a nation-state declared the Ocean, in all its depths and species and resources, as something that was claimable. In the journal *Diplomatic History*, historian Daniel Margolies writes, "The scale of the submerged land claims should not be underestimated. This offshore territory now declared to be 'appertaining to the United States' covered an area nearly the size of the Louisiana Purchase and contained mineral wealth of potentially even greater value."[56] In this new U.S. policy, "the equivalent of a new continent was thrown open for geological exploration and mineral exploitation. The continental shelves of the United States and its possessions comprise roughly a million square miles—four times the area of Texas, or one-third of the area of continental United States."[57] The Truman Proclamation led to a new international order that was codified by the 1982 United Nations Convention on the Law of the Sea. The first paragraph of Article 77 of the UNCLOS reads, "The coastal State exercises over the continental shelf sovereign rights for the purpose of exploring it and exploiting its natural resources."[58]

This is a new frontier of capitalist enclosures, enacted by nation-states, and one that is becoming normative in dominant discourses. The *Economist*, for example, claims that the Ocean "is a resource that must be preserved and harvested. To enhance its uses, the water must become ever more like the land, with owners, laws and limits. Fishermen must behave more like ranchers than hunters."[59] The way forward, in other words, is for nation-states to enclose even more of the Ocean. This is not a new idea. The conception of nature as something that can and should be enclosed for the purposes of economic development is intrinsic and necessary to capitalism. This logic now extends to the Ocean, and what was once a marginal position has now taken center stage.

From the perspective of capitalism, John Selden, not Grotius, is correct in his early modern theory. In contrast to Grotius's conception of the Oceans as free, John Selden coined the phrase *mare clausum* ("closed sea") in 1635 to signify that the Ocean could be appropriated, similar to how land was appropriated.[60] But Selden was making the case for "neighboring waters," visible from the shore, to be enclosed.[61] Selden could not anticipate what Steinberg calls "the international seabed regime."[62] The Oceanic future, according to colonial capitalism, is privatization, and this expansion of privatization is achieved through the mechanism of the nation-state. This is why, in The New 52 *Aquaman*, it is salient for Atlantis to achieve the recognized status of a nation-state.

As a nation-state that has the right to defend its borders and territory, Atlantis is justified in attacking the surface world, and the United States in particular. Near the beginning of the "Throne of Atlantis" arc, we learn that Orm is not acting impulsively to engage in a multicity attack. Rather, he is following what is known as the "Atlantean War Plans." This codified document offers a detailed, rational plan in case the nation of Atlantis needs to go to war with another nation—or, rather, what perhaps should be recognized as the global economy. As Aquaman informs the Justice League, he is the coauthor of these war plans.[63] A founding member of the Justice League, a collective that symbolizes universal justice, recognizes that the Ocean has a right to defend its borders and ecological integrity.

As Orm leads the attack on the surface world, he makes explicit that this is indeed a justified war—more than justified. In *Aquaman* 16 (January/March 2013), Orm declares that the attack is "retribution for all those tortured, poisoned and murdered over the centuries by the surface world." This war has been "centuries" in the making. From the Ocean's perspective, capitalism's continual assault has been brutal and vicious, and as capitalism develops, the intertwined processes of extraction, colonization, destruction, waste, and toxin dumping have only exacerbated the scope and scale of this assault. However, as the series suggests, what is hypervisible from the Ocean's perspective is imperceptible from the surface's perspective. When Orm attacks the surface world, he expects to find an enemy seething with hatred. Instead, what he finds is an enemy indifferent to and ignorant of the attacks decimating the Oceans.

Orm explains to Arthur why he initiated the Atlantean War Plans, saying that Humans "broke our agreement, Arthur."[64]

Orm believes that there is a mutually agreed upon social contract between the surface and the Ocean to respect each other's sovereignty, rights, and dignity. But as Orm learns, perhaps worse than being seen as an enemy by foreign states is to not be seen at all. Arthur tries to explain: "Orm, listen. There was no agreement. None that the surface world knew anything about. They don't even think Atlantis exists."[65] This structural ignorance—what historians Robert N. Proctor and Londa Schiebinger call "agnotology"—is central to the Anthropocene's relation to the Oceans.[66] Another term for this structural ignorance, to use Orm's language, is "hate." Humanity, in its dominant form, doesn't even recognize that it's in the midst of a centuries-old, unilateral war; it doesn't even recognize the Ocean as a political geography.

Analyzing Orm's attack, it is clear that the goal is not to destroy the entire surface world but, rather, to make a political point—a spectacular one. As stated above, Orm attacks multiple cities, and tellingly, they are all located in the United States. In these attacks, Boston in particular plays a seminal and symbolic role. Orm personally leads the attack on Boston, and as he explains to Arthur, his objective is to sink the city into the Ocean. Orm's decision to personally lead this charge is both to demonstrate the Ocean's powers in spectacular form—giving global capitalism a taste of its own aesthetics—and, moreover, to make a political point. Boston is the mythical heart of the United States, the American colony at the center of the revolution against imperial England. As historian Mark Boonshoft writes, "The *American* Revolution is usually told as a very *Boston*-centric story."[67] To destroy Boston is to destroy the symbolic and imaginative heart of the United States in its dominant, white, capitalist, patriarchal form.

Orm intuits that nations are imagined forms that can be dissolved. As Orm speculates, anticipating the sinking of Boston,

"Who knows? Perhaps one day these foolish surface dwellers will refuse to believe Boston ever existed either."[68] Orm's political, dialectical imagination posits two things: (1) a future in which the United States is a faded memory whose existence is the realm of myth rather than history and (2) a future in which Atlantis—and by extension, the Ocean—is recognized as a nation, as a political geography. However, as Arthur tries to explain to Orm, the challenge is that Humans see the Ocean as "nothing but waves."[69] As Braverman and Johnson write, "In the popular imaginary, the oceans continue to be seen as a place outside of conventional politics."[70] When Orm is captured and his plans to drown Boston and other strategic cities are thwarted, he challenges the dominant sense of justice that prevails in the United States and the surface world more generally. While subjects of Human law brand Orm a monster and terrorist, Orm retorts, "Atlanteans were killed too. And yet in all of these days of endless discussion, no one has asked about them. Not how many died or if any were children. It seems to me if the lives lost weren't 'Americans,' they are not worth mentioning."[71] This is an explicit critique of American exceptionalism in particular, and nation-states more generally. In their dominant form, nations are imaginative and affective communities, and in the age of nationalism, the people whose lives matter most are those considered citizens.[72] Conversely, anyone outside the nation-state is a life that doesn't matter, a life that is not, in Orm's language, "worth mentioning," a life that is not grieved. As I will discuss in the following sections, to be outside the nation-state is not just to be on the other side of a territorial border. Rather, the project of nationalism renders many subjects living within a nation-state's territories as external to the nation due to a variety of factors including race, ethnicity, religion, and sexuality.

As suggested by The New 52 *Aquaman*, if we are going to recognize the Ocean as a geography central to the web of life, we need to move beyond the political imaginary of nation-states. Even though Atlantis initially fights for national recognition, the nation-state proves a myopic and pernicious paradigm for framing social relations. Thinking beyond the nation-state has been central to what DeLoughrey calls "critical ocean studies," exemplified by the work of—to name a few such scholars and creative thinkers—Stacy Alaimo, Paul Gilroy, Melody Jue, Marcus Rediker, and Craig Santos Perez.[73] Imagining beyond the nation-state is also imagining beyond Humanism. Ecofeminist scholar Astrid Schrader writes, we need a radical "decentering of the human and the formulation of a more-than-human biopolitics."[74] What is at stake in thinking of new formations of biopolitics is nothing less than a "reconceptualization of political subjectivity that builds on neither freedom nor autonomy but reconfigures the relation between selfhood and living."[75] That is, we need to move away from the model of politics as a Human-only practice that is predicated on the conception "of the autonomous liberal human subject" and, instead, recognize that politics is enabled by a web of relations of all living things, both human and nonhuman.[76] In this extending sense of the political, the Ocean can be recognized as a political geography whose health and flourishing is not adjacent to humanity but, rather, essential to humanity's health and flourishing. As Sylvia Earle stresses, "Now we know: If the ocean is in trouble, so are we. It is time to take care of the ocean as if our lives depend on it, because they do."[77]

The challenge, though, as Carl Schmitt writes, is that the dominant Western perspective posits the Ocean is "nothing but waves."[78] During World War II, Schmitt published *Land and Sea: A World-Historical Meditation* (1942), a work that situates the Ocean at the center of world history. According to Schmitt, "World history is a history of the battle of sea powers against land powers and of land powers against sea powers."[79]

Schmitt's narrative is largely about empires expanding through their dominance over the Ocean. For Schmitt, the Ocean is a surface to be controlled and patrolled by imperial powers.

Schmitt is more than an academic theorist of the Ocean. Rather, he was an influential and prominent member of the Nazi Party. Schmitt's theories were central to promoting and disseminating fascism. In fact, his book *Land and Sea* seeks to justify the rising empire of the Third Reich. I want to suggest that Schmitt's work is also central to the dominant culture of the Anthropocene. In Schmitt's theory, the Ocean is a surface to be conquered by empires, not a living ecology that deserves recognition, respect, and care. This is the same structure of thought at the center of Anthropocene culture.

I bring up Schmitt intentionally, not only because he is a prominent theorist of the Ocean, the nation-state, and politics more generally, but because he is obliquely referenced in the "Throne of Atlantis" arc. The subtitle of "Throne of Atlantis, Chapter 3" (January/March 2013) is "Friends and Enemies."[80] This is the infamous definition of politics offered by Schmitt in *The Concept of the Political*. As Schmitt theorizes, the most important distinction organizing and animating a political state is "between friend and enemy."[81] Schmitt theorizes the nation-state as an affective form united by a shared, collective hate.

The nation-state is organized, enabled, and perpetuated by having a clear and distinct enemy, even if such an enemy needs to be fabricated. According to Schmitt, enemies of the state must be specific and material, and the threat of state violence must always be palpable and realizable. What is at stake in this concept of politics is exemplified by Schmitt's political career—a political order predicated on enemies is a fascist order.

As allegorized in The New 52 *Aquaman*, from the perspective of Atlantis, the United States treats the Ocean as an enemy. In this chapter's final sections, though, I want to analyze Atlantis's attack on the United States to suggest a different enemy of the state—one that is internal, gendered, and racialized.

Enemies of the State

Eventually, the Ocean's attack is halted and Orm is arrested. When Orm is apprehended, the United States does not treat him as the head of a nation-state who lost a legitimate and justifiable war. Instead, the United States charges Orm as a terrorist.[82] Whereas nation-states have legitimate claims to violence and have the right to declare and fight justifiable wars, Orm is denied this political recognition and, hence, refused these rights. The Ocean responding to the Anthropocene's centuries of accumulative violence is judged an act of terrorism, a charge that brands the actors outside any normative and sanctioned frame of justice. This charge negates the Ocean's legitimacy, its perspective, its narrative, and its access to social justice. As the comic critically narrates, in the Anthropocene, justice remains bounded by and limited to Humans.

Eventually, Orm breaks free from a Louisiana jail, and upon escaping, he articulates, once again, that the surface world is a culture of toxicity. The American way of life, the Anthropocene's way of life, is one of death. In the free air beyond incarceration, Orm says, "I can smell the poisons you have tainted the ground and sea with. I can taste the toxins in the air you breathe."[83] The politics of the surface world, as Orm intimates, is one of necropolitics.[84]

At this juncture, Orm still believes that Humanity is an objective, biological category that includes all members of the species. Orm believes that every human he meets, regardless of their raced, gendered, and classed body, is a synecdoche for Humanity. However, as Orm learns, the Human is an ideological category that excludes most biological humans. Judith Butler exhorts that we must continually ask, "Who counts as human? Whose

12. Orm hears a cry for help as he is about to return to the Ocean. "New Fish," Geoff Johns and Tony Bedard (plot), Tony Bedard (words), Geraldo Borges (penciller), Ruy José (inker), and Rod Reis (colorist), *Aquaman 7*, no. 23.2, The New 52 (New York: DC Comics, September/November 2013).

lives count as lives? And finally, What *makes for a grievable life*?[85] In *Habeas Viscus* African American studies scholar Alexander G. Weheliye writes, "The western configuration of the human" is "synonymous with the heteromasculine, white, propertied, and liberal subject that renders all those who do not conform to these characteristics as exploitable nonhumans, literal legal no-bodies."[86] This dominant ideological formation of the Human is inextricable from the rise and dominance of capitalism. Sociologist Jason W. Moore writes, "From the beginning of capitalism . . . most humans were either excluded from Humanity—Indigenous Americans, for example—or were designated as *only partly* Human, as were virtually all European women."[87] Moore continues, "As with property, the symbolic boundaries between who was—and who was not—part of Nature (or Society) tended to shift and vary; they were often blurry; and they were flexible. But a boundary there was, and much of the early history of modern race and gender turns on the struggles over that line."[88] As an ideological construct, the dominant Human tries to pass as a universal category, but this universalist posture masks its fundamental hierarchical structure, which manifests itself in a variety of forms, from racism to ableism. Bodies who do not conform to the dominant form of the Human are cast outside the kingdom of man.

Orm begins to understand the Human as a hierarchical, ideological category by witnessing the everyday, normative practices of patriarchy. When Orm escapes, he encounters a woman whom he initially treats as a symbol of Humanity. This woman mirrors the woman Arthur converses and empathizes with in *Aquaman* 1 (see chapter 2). Both are waitresses and single mothers who are drowning in debt and trying to navigate a world of normative sexism and genderism. In *Aquaman* 23.2 (September/November 2013), Orm initially comes to the defense of the waitress when two male customers threaten her at the diner where she works. But Orm's help only goes so far. Later in the same issue, this waitress, her eight-year-old son, and a babysitter are being assaulted by two different men. Although Orm witnesses this second attack, he refuses to intervene. Or so it seems. For Orm, the woman remains a symbol of Humanity, a symbol of the species who has perpetuated a centuries-long assault on the Ocean. While the two men are on the verge of assaulting the waitress, Orm walks away from this scene of mounting violence, sensing that he is close to the coast and, hence, close to home. The waitress yells in desperation, "What kind of man are you?" And Orm retorts, "I am not a man. I am an Atlantean."[89] Orm walks away from Humans and their pervasive necropolitics.

When the waitress tries to save her son from the two men, this scene of generalizable violence becomes one of implied sexual violence. In a panel that stretches across the page, the waitress is thrust into the ground, face-first, and a man pins her in place. In the next panel, Orm is ankle-deep into the Ocean when the woman's voice intrudes into the panel. A speech bubble that reads, "Tommy, Run!" interrupts Orm's departure from the surface world. The woman wants her son to run to safety and not to see what these two men will do to her body. The final panel on the page is a close-up of Orm's face. Although he walks deeper into the water, his eyes turn toward the waitress's voice, which has become louder and more urgent, a tone established by the letters being bolded, jagged, and in a large font: "SOMEBODY, PLEASE, HELP!!!"[90] These letters are surrounded by a thickly inked, red speech bubble (fig. 12). Despite the desperate call for help, Orm dives into the Ocean, leaving the surface world behind.

Orm's departure, though, proves an aesthetic sleight of hand. In the "Epilogue" of Johns's run, we see that Orm didn't return to the Ocean. Instead, he stayed on the surface. In Johns's final issue of the series, *Aquaman* 25 (November 2013 / January 2014), the final three pages show Orm now living with the unnamed woman and her son, Tommy. At the conclusion of the run, Aquaman and Mera are now King and Queen of Atlantis, and Orm is in the same structural place as Arthur was in *Aquaman* 1 (September/November 2011), having abdicated the Ocean for the surface world. In the final pages, seven panels visualize a scene of domestic tranquility, in which the drama is getting Tommy to sleep.[91] Orm seems to have sympathized with some humans and seems to have turned into a normative American subject.

Orm staying on land is a grave risk. He remains a wanted fugitive, and he is branded a terrorist. If Orm returned to the Ocean, he would be celebrated as a hero by all marine life. His attack on the surface world would be understood as not only justified but, even more, as an act of social justice. Orm, though, stays on the surface and risks his life due to his expanding sense of care and empathy, which now extends to a single mother and her young son. Orm's care about select humans is galvanized by learning that Humanity is a hierarchical category that excludes the majority of humans. Orm learns this through the power dynamics of gender. More specifically, he witnesses how women are excluded from the kingdom of Humanity.

While Orm's political development is progressive, it remains incomplete. Gender and Humanity are also and always informed by a third social relation: race. It's not until the fourth and final narrative arc, "Death of a King," that race becomes explicitly addressed. However, reading allegorically, the "Throne of Atlantis" arc is about race, and as the arc visualizes, in the dominant U.S. nation-state, Humanity is coded not just as masculine but also as white.

Invisible Cities and Subnational Communities

Why is gender the central and sole dynamic that allows Orm to recognize the violent and exclusionary practices of Humanity? What about race? Why not an intersectional approach? What does it mean that the surface world, as depicted in The New 52 *Aquaman*, is a world awash in whiteness? In the final chapter, I will explore how the series addresses and complicates narratives of whiteness at a narrative level. But for now, I want to suggest, perhaps counterintuitively, that The New 52 *Aquaman* should be read, in large part, as a Latinx text.

This claim challenges DC Comics marketing. In 2018 DC Comics collected the first twenty-five issues of The New 52 *Aquaman* for an omnibus—the first omnibus edition devoted exclusively to the aquatic superhero. An omnibus edition denotes a large-format, high-quality, hardback publication that signifies prestige, collectability, and posterity. In the hierarchy of superhero comics publishing, an omnibus edition is at the top, conferring the status of art. On the credit page, inside the omnibus, Geoff Johns is recognized as the head writer; Ivan Reis, the head penciller; Joe Prado, the head inker; and Rod Reis, the head colorist. Moreover, Reis, Prado, and Reis are credited as the collection's cover artists. However, and tellingly, this first-ever Aquaman omnibus privileges Geoff Johns as the primary creator. The full title is *Aquaman by Geoff Johns Omnibus*. While Johns is important and the sole writer of the first twenty-five issues, the title perpetuates an aesthetic hierarchy that positions the writer above all other members of the art team. In this hierarchy, the writer alone becomes hypervisible. This aesthetic hierarchy, in this case, is also a racial hierarchy. Of the four primary creators of this run, only Johns is white. Ivan Reis, Joe Prado, and Rod Reis are all Latinx creators.[92]

Ivan Reis was born Rodrigo Ivan dos Reis outside of São Paulo, Brazil. He began his career in comics at the age of fourteen, and eventually worked at the prestigious Estúdios Maurício de Sousa.[93] Since then, Reis has worked for many major U.S. comic publishing houses, including Marvel and DC. In a September 2011 interview with *Comics Bulletin* to promote Reis's artwork for The New 52 *Aquaman*, interviewer Andre Lamar turned to the topic of Brazil. Lamar observes, "Over the past couple of years it seems like other Brazilian artists like Joe [Prado], Eddy [Barrows], Fábio Moon, and Gabriel Bá are turning heads with their impressive artwork." He then asks, "Is Brazil a goldmine for talent?"[94] As Lamar's question acknowledges, corporate superhero comics are enabled, now more than ever, by an international division of labor.

The first Brazilian artist to draw for DC Comics was Marcelo Campos, who worked on *Justice League America* in the 1980s.[95] A few decades later, Brazilian artists were drawing, inking, and coloring many mass-market superheroes, including Spider-Man, Superman, Hulk, X-Men, Wolverine, Green Lantern, and Captain America.[96] In response to the question about the international division of labor defining DC Comics and Marvel, Reis replied, "Today, what's the difference for DC, with offices in New York, to work with a guy from San Diego or another from Brazil? It doesn't matter."[97] As U.S.-based corporations become increasingly transnational, the labor market stretches far beyond U.S. borders, as do the possibilities of exploitation. Of the four primary creators of The New 52 *Aquaman*, three are Brazilian. While Reis's response above makes labor from San Diego and Brazil seem analogous, they are anything but, from a capitalist perspective. As Reis confesses, growing up in Brazil, "there weren't many options for artists."[98] While Brazil's labor laws offer tremendous benefits and protections to employees in the formal economy, Juliana Mello writes that in 2011, the year The New 52 launched, "only 46.3% of the Brazilian workforce" were in the formal market. The rest were freelance workers who labor in tremendous precarity without benefits.[99] Moreover, in 2011, when DC Comics inaugurated its then latest era, Brazil "skidded dangerously close to a recession."[100]

This international division of labor is a racialized division of labor. And as stressed above, this division is a hierarchy in which, during the twenty-first century, the writer is now privileged. The article "Comics and the Diminishing Role of Artists in a Visual Medium," published in 2014, the same year that the Johns-Reis-Prado-Reis run concluded, begins as follows:

> Brian Michael Bendis' "Avengers."
> Geoff Johns' "Green Lantern."
> Jason Aaron's "Wolverine and the X-Men."
> When you see people talk about some of today's greatest and most celebrated runs in comics, it's quite often only the writer who gets mentioned, even though each of those books wouldn't have been the same without people like David Finch, Ivan Reis and Nick Bradshaw. We're living in the Era of The Writer in comics, a time when the quality of comics . . . is at an all-time high, with art that astounds and thrills—yet there may never have been a time in comics where being an artist is more thankless or minimized.[101]

As comic journalist David Harper argues, the elevation of the writer and simultaneous devaluation of the artist is a recent phenomenon. "Looking back," Harper writes, "it wouldn't be outlandish to say you read 'Todd McFarlane's Spider-Man' or 'Jim Lee's X-Men,' because in that period, artists occupied the place writers do now."[102] This historical transformation coincides with the internationalization of the art labor market. The devaluation of artists coincides with Marvel and DC turning more intentionally to the international market for artistic labor. In this corporate logic, the writer becomes the recognized and respected creator, while artists are largely treated as replaceable, disposable cogs in the profit machine. This devaluation of artists is linked to the major publishing houses turning to populations whom the United States codes as nonwhite and, therefore, less valuable to racial capitalism.

The elevation of the writer over the artist extends across the superhero comics network, including comic book stores. In a widespread retailer poll published in 2015, only 4.8 percent of retailers order a comic based on the artist.[103] In her article "Does Anyone Care about the Artists on Comics Any More?" Heidi MacDonald writes that in "the Big Two [Marvel and DC] . . . even the finest artists have been cogs in an ever grinding machine."[104] In a 2018 essay, Augie De Blieck Jr.'s thesis is broadcast in his title: "Seriously, Don't Be a Comic Book Artist. Just Don't." De Blieck details how the desire to be a comic book artist is a form of "suicide."[105] Supporting this claim, cartoonist Philip Hester, who draws for Marvel and DC, writes, "Comic book creators are like musical ones. A vanishingly small number of us can fill arenas, a lucky few get a hit or two and can tour our whole careers, most are gigging at local venues, some just jamming in the garage."[106] As Hester intimates, comic book artists are mostly part of the gig economy. They are mostly freelance workers laboring in extreme precarity. While many artists love what they do, this passion is frequently exploited by the comic industry. Most comic artists have no financial stability and slim-to-zero social safety nets. Being in the gig economy, for example, means that employers do not offer health care insurance. Moreover, even if an artist does secure a contract with Marvel or DC, De Blieck advises prospective artists to "know upfront that the work you do will only get you paid once and that they owe you nothing past that. It's in your contract, even if it isn't rubber stamped on the back of your paycheck anymore. Don't expect anything in royalties. . . . Don't be upset when your name isn't in the credits and you don't get a royalty from the latest TV show or movie based on your work."[107]

Marvel and DC have become billion-dollar, multimedia empires, but these riches don't filter down to all creators. During The New 52, the writer was at the top of the aesthetic hierarchy, and the vast majority of writers for the so-called big two were white. In 2014, when Johns's run concluded, 78.9 percent of writers at the big two were white.[108] Moreover, at the time of his New 52 *Aquaman* run, Geoff Johns was also the chief creative officer (CCO) of DC Comics, and from 2016 to 2018, he was president and CCO.[109] In his executive position, Johns was also central to the development and production of DC Comics television and movies.[110] For the *Aquaman* movie (2018), Johns received credit for the story, and he served as executive producer. Ivan Reis, in contrast, only received thanks in the end credit.[111] This recognition disparity is also a financial disparity. *Aquaman* theatrically grossed more than $1.1 billion worldwide, making it the highest-grossing DCEU film. Being an executive producer, Johns profited handsomely. Conversely, although Reis was the "artist who inspired the movie," he was given an empty "thanks."[112]

As I will explore in my afterword, *Aquaman*—and DC Comics more generally—is becoming a site where diversity is flourishing in innovative ways, but in 2011, DC's story worlds were largely a white enterprise, a racial formation that The New 52 *Aquaman* both exemplifies and attempts to critique. While on the surface (and in its depths) *Aquaman* is awash in whiteness—Arthur, Mera, Orm, and nearly all the citizens of Atlantis are phenotypically white—I want to suggest that The New 52 *Aquaman* can and should be read, in large part, as a Latinx text. It's important to recognize, make visible, and honor the Latinx labor that is central to producing superhero comics. But if we read The New 52 *Aquaman* as a Latinx text because three of the four primary creators are from Brazil, how do we reconcile the contradiction of Reis, Prado, and Reis visualizing the Aquaman story world as being so white?

In his book *Latinx Superheroes in Mainstream Comics*, Frederick Luis Aldama writes that "we should be upset" about the paucity of Latinx superheroes and communities in "mainstream comics."[113] The so-called Golden Age of superhero comics began in 1938 with the introduction of Superman, but "it wasn't until 1975, almost 40 years later, that Marvel would debut its first Latinx superhero: White Tiger, cocreated by George Pérez."[114] Edgardo Miranda-Rodriguez, the creator of the Latinx superhero La Borinqueña, observed in 2019, "Combined there are possibly close to 30,000 characters, heroes, and villains, at both Marvel and DC. Of that, there probably are about 3% that are Latinx."[115] (La Borinqueña, first published in 2016, is the superhero identity of Marisol Ríos De La Luz, who was born in Brooklyn to an Afro–Puerto Rican father and a white Borícua mother and who discovers her superhero powers while visiting Puerto Rico. Marisol's chosen superhero name foregrounds her progressive nationalism; her chosen name is the same as Puerto Rico's official anthem. Tellingly, La Borinqueña is a superhero produced outside of the big two.) As Miranda-Rodriguez's quote makes explicit, the world of superhero comics, dominated by Marvel and DC, is a world of whiteness. In this world of whiteness, as Aldama observes, DC has historically been the more progressive of the two. Aldama writes that in DC Comics, "Latinos began to appear just after World War II with DC's Rodrigo 'Rodney' Elwood Gaynor, followed by Santiago Vargas as El Gaucho in the 1950s."[116] However, these were predominantly stereotypes, and "it wasn't until the 1990s, when Anglo-Mexican Axel Alonso took over as editor in chief of DC, that we began to see more interesting Latino characterizations."[117] Still, as Aldama stresses, there is no linear narrative of progress.

While there has been a paucity of Latinx representation in mainstream comics, behind the scenes, Latinx creators have been central. Marilyn La Jeunesse wrote in 2019, "Although there has historically been a lack of representation for Latinx people as nuanced comic book characters, Latinx creators are the basis for some of the most vibrant comic characters we know today. From Deadpool to Captain America, Latinx artists and writers behind the scenes have shaped the worlds we see today."[118] Although not always recognized, mainstream comics have become a Latinx genre.

So let's consider how Reis, Prado, and Reis use their limited creative autonomy to shape *Aquaman*'s story world and, more broadly, the shared world beyond the comic book pages. The artistic team was under the supervision and oversight of DC editors, so Reis, Prado, and Reis did not have the creative luxury to make Arthur, Mera, and Orm anything other than white. However, I want to think about how the art team represents urban geographies. More specifically, I want to consider how the artists visualize the U.S. cities attacked by the Ocean. To make an obvious but important point about U.S. cities, one that Aldama underscores, "Latinos have become the largest minority group in the United States, increasingly outnumbering the Anglo majority in more and more regions."[119] As

13. The Ocean attacks the surface world. "Throne of Atlantis, Chapter 1," Geoff Johns (writer), Ivan Reis (penciller), Joe Prado (inker), and Rod Reis (colorist), *Justice League* 2, no. 15, The New 52 (New York: DC Comics, December 2012 / February 2013).

Aldama repeats throughout his study, to represent a major U.S. city in the twenty-first century and fail to represent a vibrant Latinx community indicates "the creator's will to exclude and erase."[120] So how do Reis, Prado, and Reis represent U.S. urban geographies? When Orm leads the Ocean's attack on U.S. cities, he strikes Boston, Metropolis, and Gotham. Even though the latter two are fictional geographies, these are all large urban centers that, following U.S. demographic trends, should all be minority-majority geographies.

In representing these cities and their victims, Reis, Prado, and Reis do something perhaps unexpected. When the tidal waves devastate cities throughout the East Coast, the violence is presented as an abstract spectacle. When Metropolis is suddenly struck, Ivan Reis creates a two-page spread that shows the terrifying scale of the attack. The tremendous height of the waves swallow skyscrapers, and the waves' force throws massive military and industrial fishing ships from the Ocean into the heart of the city. What is remarkable about this two-page spread, though, is the absence of people (fig. 13).[121] We don't see the victims. In fact, throughout *Justice League* 15 (December 2012 / February 2013)—the first issue that visualizes the Ocean's attack on Humanity—the victims remain largely invisible. Instead, the visualization mostly emphasizes the awesome scope and scale of the attack. This aesthetic choice has tremendous allegorical import.

Reis, Prado, and Reis visualize the series' central allegory—the threat of ecological violence is imminent and threatens all biological humans. Rather than an example of slow violence, ecological devastation is visualized as an apocalypse that threatens to drown all lives, as signified by this two-page spread. American literature and ecological scholar Lawrence Buell writes, "Apocalypse is the single most powerful master metaphor that the contemporary environmental imagination has at its disposal."[122] This image of the tsunami—and there are many like it in the issues showing the attack—can be read as an allegory for the extreme weather threatening coastal cities throughout the Anthropocene. But this contemporary anxiety about extreme weather and the Anthropocene more generally is a privileged narrative.

In *A Billion Black Anthropocenes or None* Kathryn Yusoff powerfully argues, "If the Anthropocene proclaims a sudden concern with the exposures of environmental harm to white liberal communities, it does so in the wake of histories in which these harms have been knowingly exported to black and brown communities under the rubric of civilization, progress, modernization, and capitalism. The Anthropocene might seem to offer a dystopic future that laments the end of the world, but imperialism and ongoing (settler) colonialisms have been ending worlds for as long as they have been in existence."[123] Although "the Anthropocene proclaims the language of species life—*anthropos*—through a universalist geologic commons, it neatly erases histories of racism."[124] The Anthropocene, in its dominant form, is a project of whiteness that erases histories, epistemologies, and narratives from communities of color. Yusoff calls the dominant Anthropocene "White Geology," a project and structure built on and perpetuated by extracting "properties and personhood."[125] More specifically, white geology turns matter into property and Black and brown bodies into commodities.

In visualizing the cities of Gotham, Boston, and Metropolis, Reis, Prado, and Reis had the opportunity to critique the dominant Anthropocene. The Latinx artists had the opportunity to visualize that the communities at the frontlines of climate change are predominately Black and brown. Instead, the artists represent the cities as largely abstract and generalizable. For the most part, they refuse to visualize specific, material people victimized by this ecological apocalypse. It seems that the Ocean's attack is an empty spectacle rather than an aesthetic intervention; it seems that The New 52 *Aquaman* participates in Aldama's critique of mainstream comics' "willful erasure" of Latinx communities. But I want to suggest a different way—an allegorical way—to read these scenes.

The Ocean's attack on the U.S. East Coast was "the first major crisis" of the "modern era" demarcated by The New 52 publishing initiative.[126] As stated above, the "Throne of Atlantis" story line, which features the Ocean's attack on U.S. cities, is the first crossover event of The New 52. This Aquaman-centered narrative unfolded in *Aquaman* and in *Justice League* comics simultaneously. *Aquaman* 15 and *Justice League* 15 were both published in December 2012 / February 2013, establishing a publishing pattern that would last for three months. Prior to this crossover event, the first fifteen issues of The New 52 *Aquaman* were all created by Johns, Reis, Prado, and Reis. However, for the "Throne of Atlantis" narrative arc, Ivan Reis and Joe Prado were assigned to *Justice League* issues 15–17, and new artists were contracted to visualize *Aquaman* issues 15–17, with Paul Pelletier as penciller and Sean Parsons, Art Thibert, and Karl Kesel as inkers.[127] Only Rod Reis, the colorist, worked between *Justice League* and *Aquaman*. While Pelletier, Parsons, Thibert, and Kesel are all white, it should be stressed that economic exploitation and working-class precarity cut across all races and ethnicities. While The New 52 *Aquaman* was in production, *HuffPost* wrote an article on the comic artist Kesel, the inker for *Aquaman* during the "Throne of Atlantis" crossover event. The article focuses on Kesel, "the well-known DC and Marvel Comics writer/inker," because at the time, he was forced into "selling everything . . . in order to pay for the fees and medical bills that came along with the adoption of a 15-week-old baby who was born addicted to heroin."[128] Although Kesel is a "well-known" artist for both DC and Marvel, the structure of these corporations fail to provide the safety net for the preponderance of their workers.

Throughout the "Throne of Atlantis" story line, the millions of people drowned by the Ocean remain largely invisible. For example, in *Aquaman* 15, with artwork by Pelletier, Thibert, Kesel, and Reis, Mera attempts to save the untold number of victims drowning in the streets of Gotham, yet she ultimately capitulates and stares in horror: "Bodies. There are so many bodies down there."[129] Mera stares into the rushing and rising waters that conceal the hundreds of thousands—perhaps millions—of lives violently drowned, beyond visibility.

When the victims are shown in select panels, Pelletier, Thibert, Kesel, and Reis render them as obscure, anonymous, and faceless. On the opening pages of *Aquaman* 15, we see several bodies

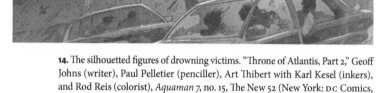

14. The silhouetted figures of drowning victims. "Throne of Atlantis, Part 2," Geoff Johns (writer), Paul Pelletier (penciller), Art Thibert with Karl Kesel (inkers), and Rod Reis (colorist), *Aquaman 7*, no. 15, The New 52 (New York: DC Comics, December 2012 / February 2013).

drowning in Gotham. Members of the Justice League do their best to rescue the victims, but the numbers are overwhelming. A horrified Commissioner Gordon, rescued from the Ocean by Aquaman, learns from Batman what has happened. When Gordon asks in horror "how many" people the Justice League were able to rescue, Batman despondently responds, "As many as we could."[130] When Batman states this, he looks into the tumultuous waters as if trying to imagine the countless victims drowning silently, invisibly, and inaudibly.

When the artists do show the drowning victims, they are mostly visualized in silhouette, which obscures their faces and any other defining features (fig. 14). These are abstract, nondifferentiated, interchangeable victims. This aesthetic strategy—this refusal to specify and concretize the victims in terms of race or ethnicity—is persistent throughout. While there is a generalizable horror at this unprecedented ecological violence, the victims remain largely anonymous and invisible.

I want to suggest that we can read these scenes allegorically. This apocalyptic event that killed millions discloses the social fault lines in the United States. U.S. cities are fast becoming—and in many cases, have already become—minority-majority geographies, yet in the dominant national culture, Black and brown communities remain largely unseen. In the dominant national narrative, such racialized communities are largely excluded and erased. In representing the victims of U.S. cities, Reis, Prado, and Reis set the template in the opening issues of the "Throne of Atlantis" story line by showing the scale of the Ocean's attack and by refusing to represent the victims in any specificity. This choice not to fully visualize the victims of this apocalyptic attack that devastates multiple U.S. cities encapsulates how the dominant U.S. culture sees communities of color—as invisible, as interchangeable, as disposable.

This visual allegory exemplifies and critiques how, in the dominant white capitalist culture, Black and brown lives don't matter. This spectacle of violence allegorizes the myriad ways in which white culture erases Black and brown communities from the national symbolic—an erasure that is the condition of possibility for multiple violences from the everyday to the structural. This white erasure is redoubled for brown and Black immigrant communities. In the *Journal of Immigrant and Migrant Health*, Francesca Gany, Patricia Novo, Rebecca Dobslaw, and Jennifer Leng write, "Mexican and Latino/Latina immigrants represent a rapidly growing population within the United States. The majority settle in urban areas. As a group . . . these immigrants often find work in hazardous jobs, with high injury and fatality rates. They often have inadequate or no safety training, no personal protective equipment, limited understanding of workers' rights, job insecurity, fear of report of undocumented

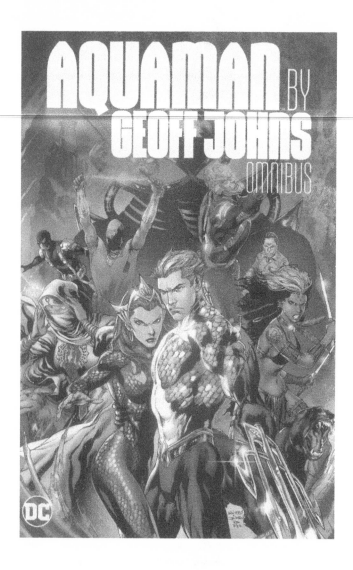

15. *Aquaman by Geoff Johns Omnibus* cover, which only recognizes the writer, not any of the artists. Geoff Johns (writer), Ivan Reis and Paul Pelletier (pencillers), Joe Prado and Sean Parsons (inkers), and Rod Reis (colorist), *Aquaman by Geoff Johns Omnibus* (Burbank CA: DC Comics, 2017).

status and lack health care benefits."[131] In a sense, Reis, Prado, and Reis can be understood as immigrant workers within DC Comics' international assembly line of production. All three artists live and work in Brazil, and all their labor enriches a U.S. corporation. Like immigrant workers throughout U.S. cities, Reis, Prado, and Reis work in relative invisibility, obscured by the hypervisibility of Geoff Johns (fig. 15).

New perspectives open by recognizing The New 52 *Aquaman* as a Latinx text and by recognizing Latinx labor, but in many ways, Humanity—both in the Anthropocene and in this comic series—remains a white imaginary. For the remainder of this book, I want to bring communities of color into clearer view and foreground how the franchise is explicitly becoming Black, brown, and Indigenous.

4
Allegories of White Supremacy

Black Manta and the Black Atlantic

The concluding narrative arc of Johns's multiyear run culminates in a surprising intersectional allegory of nationalism, white supremacy, and fascism. In the concluding arc, Arthur fulfills his birthright and assumes the throne of Atlantis. This assumption of power, though, comes at a cost. In becoming the ruler of Atlantis, Arthur learns that this position of power is organized by a politics of xenophobia and racism. Put differently, as Arthur discovers, Atlantis is a nation-state animated by the myths and practices of racial purity.

There are hints of Atlantis's racialized national identity strewn throughout the previous narrative arcs. During "Throne of Atlantis," for example, Arthur explains to Batman that when he first journeyed to Atlantis to assume the throne, which was legally his by "birthright" due to his mother's royal blood, he was initially embraced with open arms.[1] "But," as Aquaman shares, "within weeks, there was dissension. Some called me the impure king. A half-human surface dweller. There was a movement to change the laws and reinstate my younger brother [Orm] . . . A full Atlantean."[2] Atlantis's obsession with "pure" blood as the necessary condition for national belonging reads as an explicit allegory of many nation-states, but in this context, it registers as an allegory for U.S. nationalism. Both nation-states

16. Aquaman addresses a wide range of marine life, with the promise to serve as their protector. "Throne of Atlantis, Epilogue," Geoff Johns (writer), Paul Pelletier (penciller), Sean Parsons (inker), and Rod Reis (colorist), *Aquaman 7*, no. 17, The New 52 (New York: DC Comics, February/April 2013).

are racial formations predicated on a myth of purity, a fiction that must be continually policed, maintained, and preserved through multiple interlocking racialized institutions. In this racist logic, the dominant race—whiteness in the United States and Atlantean in Atlantis—is a state of purity that becomes defiled by a single drop of "impure" blood. National subjects must avoid intimate contact with racialized others, because such contact ideologically becomes a mark of permanent contamination. In their dominant formations, the United States and Atlantis are racist states, and Aquaman's mixed heritage—his mother is Atlantean and his father is Human—marks him as outside Atlantis's national project.

Despite being initially rejected by Atlantis because of his mixed heritage, Arthur returns to Atlantis at the end of Johns's multiyear run, because he recognizes that despite the racist politics of the underwater kingdom, the Ocean needs a protector against Humanity's increasingly aggressive, centuries-long war against all marine life. At the end of *Aquaman* 17 (February/April 2013), the epilogue to the "Throne of Atlantis" arc, Arthur makes explicit that the reason why he chooses to become King of Atlantis is to be the protector of the Ocean. Arthur is less concerned with the myopic politics of Atlantis and more concerned with the globe-spanning Ocean and its maritime multitudes. In a beautiful, two-page spread, with artwork by Paul Pelletier (penciller), Sean Parsons (inker), and Rod Reis (colorist), Arthur is surrounded by marine life of all shapes and sizes, representing the Ocean's incredible diversity. Arthur promises to all marine life, "I won't fail you again" (fig. 16).[3] This is to say, Arthur promises never to abandon the political project of defending the Ocean against Humanity's historical path of destruction that threatens all ecosystems and all life. Another name for this historical path is the Anthropocene.

Arthur's motivation for becoming king is to help maintain a diverse, capacious world where all life is respected and matters—not just Human life. As Arthur explains to Mera, he wants to be King of Atlantis because he wants to help construct a bridge of understanding between the Ocean and the surface world. Arthur elaborates, "I've been pushing these two worlds apart my entire life, but I need to bring them together somehow."[4] Arthur wants to become a new type of leader, one that builds new connections, new relationships, and new politics.

In working toward a new, post-Anthropocenic future, Arthur learns about his inherited past. Working toward this knowledge means learning to see beyond nationally sanctioned myths and official archives. Arthur must learn to see beyond what Vulko, an advisor to the throne, calls the "great lie" that organizes contemporary Atlantis.[5] In *Aquaman* issue 0 (September/November 2012), Vulko tries to persuade Arthur to leave his life on the surface world and become king. In words that eerily echo the language of future U.S. president Donald Trump, Vulko says, "Our people can be great again with a great leader."[6] These lines are repeated several months later in February/April 2013. Once again, Vulko tells Arthur, "Atlantis can be a great nation again but it needs your leadership. You need to embrace your birthright."[7] The politics of this racially charged language become explicit in Johns's final narrative arc of The New 52 *Aquaman*.

In the series' final narrative arc (March/May 2013–November 2013 / January 2014), Vulko tells Arthur that Arthur must speak to the "Dead King." The Dead King is kept in the underwater penal colony Xebel, located beyond the political and epistemic borders of Atlantis. When Arthur addresses the Dead King, the latter is exasperated by this moniker: "The Dead King? So they have erased my name from the Atlantean tomes as well? What were you told about me, Arthur?"[8] Arthur learns that the Dead King's actual name is Atlan, the founder and first ruler of

Atlantis. Listening to Atlan, Arthur learns to see beyond what Vulko calls "the great lie," a lie that, from the perspective of Atlantis's ruling class, functions as a noble lie. In *The Republic*, Plato introduces the concept of the "noble lie" to signify a myth that helps bind a political community together.[9] The noble lie is a false narrative that works to encourage citizens to love their political community. Atlantis's noble lie rewrites the history and founding of the underwater nation.

In *Aquaman* issue 0, Arthur learns about the founder and first King of Atlantis, Atlan, and a year later, in *Aquaman* 22 (July/September 2013), Arthur learns that the national narratives about Atlan are all fabricated myths. The modern-day nation of Atlantis is established and maintained by imprisoning and erasing its past and creating and perpetuating the great lie. The great lie is the fiction that Atlan's nationalistic vision was for an isolated, walled-in Atlantis rooted in nativism and obsessed with racial purity. Moreover, the great lie conceals the fact that Atlan was overthrown because of his politics of hospitality, diversity, and open borders.

In *Aquaman* 24 (October/December 2013), the penultimate issue of Johns's narrative run, the truth about Atlantis's history is disclosed. In the issue, Vulko takes Arthur to the "ancient tomes of Atlantis, deep within the trench," a space where secrets are "buried."[10] This disavowed history is buried at the bottom of the Ocean, saturated in darkness. Arthur learns how and why Atlantis transitioned from an island kingdom to an underwater kingdom. At the center of this buried archive is an ice-covered throne, which Vulko instructs Arthur to sit on. This is not an act of assuming the throne but, rather, capitulating to the agency of the throne—or, rather, of the ice. Vulko guides Arthur, "Let the ice take you," and he warns Arthur that this process "will be painful."[11] The notion that history is a painful process coheres with Jameson's famous maxim articulated in

The Political Unconscious: "History is what hurts."[12] This entire section is a rich allegory. The ice transports Arthur to the past, to see the ostensibly *real* Atlantis. In this figuration, the ice becomes agential. But the ice does not provide a simple window to the past. Rather, as the ice narrates history, it becomes clear that the ice is part of the propaganda machine that supports and maintains the great lie. The ice is the seemingly solidified narrative of history. But the brilliance of this allegory is that ice is malleable. The ice's seemingly fixed narrative can be melted away.

As Arthur learns from the ice, Atlantis was once one of the greatest surface nations on Earth. Initially, this story hews closely to Plato's allegory. Atlan, the "architect, the builder and the king of the nation of Atlantis," was a liberal ruler who respected, welcomed, and practiced a politics of diversity.[13] Atlan constructed Atlantis on the principle of radical hospitality. However, in the interpretive narrative offered by the ice, Atlan's actions were misguided and destructive to the health and well-being of Atlantis. Stories are not neutral. Rather, they emanate from particular actors and agents who project their own meanings, values, and ideas into narratives. The linking of stories to storytellers is brilliantly visualized by Pelletier, Parsons, and Reis. The artists consistently visualize the ice's narration within a speech bubble of various shades of blue that signifies the ice. Put differently, the blue speech bubble repeatedly reminds readers that the narrative is from the ice's perspective, not a neutral narrative (as if such a narrative could exist). The ice perpetuates a political narrative that is invested in maintaining the great lie.

In the ice's telling, Atlan's practice of political hospitality resulted in the nation's downfall. Atlan's vision was to "unite this world," to be a beacon where all peoples, practices, and communities would be embraced.[14] Atlan believed in democracy, in a government ruled by the people. In contrast to narrow forms of nationalism that posit a singular, homogenous demos, Atlan believed in a diverse, heterogenous, ever-expanding demos. The ice narrates, "The years passed and Atlantis grew. As did Atlan's tolerance for outsiders, inviting all people to join the great nation."[15] At every turn, the ice's diction conveys xenophobic and racist values. The ice refers to citizens who are not native to Atlantis as "outsiders," attempting to mark immigrants as permanently outside the nation's affective community. Moreover, the ice describes Atlan's embrace of difference and celebration of diversity as the ruler's "tolerance," a noun that implicitly posits an unbridgeable gap between insiders and those deemed outsiders. The thinly veiled hatred animating this narrative is juxtaposed by the visuals. When the ice bemoans that Atlantis continually grows with the arrival of outsiders, the panel shows a spacious Atlantis with no one in sight except the silhouetted figures of King Atlan and Queen Sala. The ice's racism becomes even more explicit in the next panel as it tells Arthur that King Atlan was "leading us towards a world of mongrels. He turned no one away from the city of Atlantis."[16] "Mongrel" is a keyword of white supremacy, and the use of this word underwrites how Atlantis becomes a conspicuous allegory of the United States. In her article "Mongrel Monstrosities," Abby L. Ferber writes that in the United States, "White supremacist publications are filled with images of 'mongrels'—feared and despised because they straddle and destabilize those racial boundaries essential to securing White identity and power."[17] "Mongrel" is an index of white supremacy, articulating the fantasy and fear of interracial intimacies. In this racial allegory, the ice's narrated history of Atlantis is analogous to U.S. history being narrated from the perspective of a white supremacist.

The ice's narration continues, "He had to be stopped."[18] The person who eventually "stopped" Atlan, the person who led the coup, was Atlan's brother, Orin. Orin declared to Atlan, "I will stop the madness of fusing races together. I will not stand by and watch as you lead us down a path of self-destruction!" "And," Orin continued, "neither will my people!" (fig. 17).[19] Orin ordered the murder of Atlan's wife and children, and Orin took it upon himself to fatally spear his own brother, justifying his actions because "we must preserve the races of the world!"[20] Orin led a coup of fascism. As he promised, Orin established a nation-state defined by strict borders and committed to purity. The ice narrates, "King Orin saved us from Atlan's misguided and dangerous dream."[21] The ice does not counter Orin's explicit racism; rather, the ice supports it. In this fascist logic, a commitment to diversity, to plurality, to open borders, is a "dangerous dream" that threatened to drown Atlantis's greatness. To justify the coup, the Atlantean elite forged the great lie that buried and silenced Atlan's progressive politics.

The New 52 *Aquaman*'s figuring of Atlantis as an allegory of fascism has a pronounced precedent. In the 1930s Hitler and other leading Nazis became obsessed with Atlantis and believed that the lost island was the origin of the Aryan race. In fact, Hitler financed a program for Nazis to find the historical Atlantis and hence "prove" that Aryans descended from a mighty and pure race.[22]

At the end of Johns's lengthy run, The New 52 *Aquaman* proves to be more than an ecological allegory; it is also an interlocking allegory of race, racism, nationalism, and fascism. At the conclusion, readers learn that it is not Arthur's birthright to become King of Atlantis. Arthur is not the descendent of Atlan; rather, he is the descendent of Orin. Put differently, Arthur is a descendent of a fascist who believed and institutionalized that Atlantis should be reserved for pure-blooded Atlanteans. At the end, the visuals of Reis, Pelletier, Prado, Parsons, and Reis call into question Arthur's canonical look.

17. Orin tells Atlan that he will lead a political coup. "Death of a King, Chapter 6: Secret of the Seven Seas," Geoff Johns (writer), Paul Pelletier (penciller), Sean Parsons (inker), and Rod Reis (colorist), *Aquaman 7*, no. 24, The New 52 (New York: DC Comics, October/December 2013).

When Orin—the ruler of Atlantis's state of fascism—is visualized, he looks nearly identical to Arthur (see fig. 17). Arthur's blond hair, blue eyes, and other Anglo features are no longer just traditional representations, but rather, they become markers of a fascist aesthetics. Although Arthur has a father from the surface world and, hence, in the racist logic of Atlantis, he is marked as a "half-breed," he still looks Aryan.

This twist changes how we read Arthur's ruling name—King Arthur conspicuously echoes the British king. Since the nineteenth century, narratives of King Arthur have been used and circulated to create a myth about England's origins.[23] As Jonathan Jones writes, "In many ways, the myth of Arthur created medieval civilization. It also helped create Britain as we know it. The British may have invented Arthur, but Arthur in turn legitimated the idea of Britain as a great nation."[24] England's King Arthur myth is analogous to Atlantis perpetuating what Vulko calls "the great lie."

The great lie attempts to bury history and replace it with a political myth that naturalizes fascist politics. The final narrative arc highlights how the dead refuse to stay dead, how the past haunts the present. Atlan was "buried deep within the trench," beyond the visibility and audibility of modern Atlantis.[25] This containment of the past, however, proves futile. In the final narrative arc, Atlan rises from the dead as the Dead King. This narrates, in the parlance of popular culture, Freud's thesis of the return of the repressed. The political repressed, the horrors and violences of history, refuse to stay buried.

Although Orin tried to kill his brother, Atlan survived the attack and went into hiding. Later, Atlan returned to Atlantis and murdered Orin and Orin's wife, plunging Atlantis into a civil war between citizens loyal to Atlan's politics of hospitality and Orin's politics of fascism.[26] In his final act, Atlan used all his strength and "arcane knowledge" to sink the kingdom he built to the Ocean's bottom.[27] The ice narrates, "Ninety percent of the population of Atlantis died as their lungs filled with water. . . . But there were those that survived."[28] Those that survived evolved and adapted to living underwater. Those who are "evolved," the ostensibly fittest to survive, adapted Orin's fascist politics and established the discourse of purity and isolationism as Atlantis's founding myth. As The New 52 *Aquaman* allegorizes, racism and fascism survive and continue to structure the modern world in all geographies, even at the bottom of the Ocean.

Intellectually, Johns's narrative displays an awareness of structural racism. But this interlocking allegory of race, racism, nationalism, and fascism becomes troubled by the figure of Black Manta, one of Aquaman's archnemeses and one of the few African American supervillains in Marvel and DC Comics.[29]

The Marcus Garvey of the Sea?

If The New 52 *Aquaman* is aware of myriad, interlocking forms of racism, then how does it represent Black Manta? If the series is creating a critical allegory of white supremacy and fascism, then how does it imagine and visualize Black life?

Created by (white) writer Bob Haney and (white) artist Nick Cardy, Black Manta debuted in *Aquaman* 35 (September/October 1967) as a ruthless underwater mercenary who is obsessed with killing Aquaman. For a decade, Black Manta was a cipher. He was not given an origin story or represented with any interiority or depth. In fact, for ten years, readers never even glimpsed his face. Black Manta was always visualized in full-body armor and with an oversized helmet that made him appear as an alien, beyond Human-organizing structures such as race, ethnicity, gender, and sexuality. Black Manta escaped all codes and conventions of Human classification and existed as the embodiment of evil. His sole desire was to kill Aquaman.

However, in *Adventure Comics* 452 (July/August 1977), a decade after his debut, Black Manta removed his helmet for the first time and revealed his face. In a shocking twist, Black Manta disclosed that he is Black. In revealing his face, Black Manta reveals that his chosen name is a racial signifier. In the issue in which he reveals his face, Black Manta articulates that his real objective is not simply to harm Aquaman but, rather, to transform an underwater city into a home for his "people," which would then serve as a "base for a new empire" (fig. 18).[30]

When Black Manta reveals these political plans, he remains fully armored, and hence, his racialized face and body are shrouded. Aquaman initially construes Black Manta's design as the latter's insatiable hunger for personal power. This narcissistic desire for power contrasts with superheroes, who use their power as a means toward achieving a greater, social good. In the next panel, Black Manta continues, "I've recruited enough of my own people to serve the purpose quite adequately" (fig. 18). At this juncture, Aquaman believes "my people" is a phrase synonymous with henchmen, similar to any other supervillain's disposable lackeys. Black Manta then removes his helmet and shows his face. In a panel located at the literal margins—at the bottom of the page and to the far right—readers see, for the first time, that Black Manta is Black. Black Manta's naked face disrupts DC's Oceanic world. Despite representing maritime multitudes, DC's Ocean, up to this point, had been represented as a white geography.

This one panel mandates that readers hear Black Manta's voice not as a generic supervillain but as an embodied Black man. While his face is visible for the first time, Black Manta states, "I mean exactly what I said: 'my people.' Or have you never wondered why I'm called—Black Manta—?" (fig. 18). On the next page, Black Manta elaborates: "Since Blacks have been suppressed for so long on the surface, they fight well for a chance to be 'masters' below!"[31] At this moment, Black Manta becomes legible as a political actor working toward Black nationalism. In the panel in which he discloses his drive for Black liberation, Black Manta's henchmen also remove their helmets for the first time. They are also African American. This issue posits that readers understand Black Manta as a radical figure of revolution. When Black Manta declares that an underwater city "shall be the base for a new empire," he means creating an autonomous Black nation. Black Manta becomes the Marcus Garvey of the sea.[32]

18. Black Manta reveals his face and his politics of Black nationalism. "Dark Destiny, Deadly Dreams," David Michelinie (writer), Jim Aparo (artist), Jerry Serpe (colorist), *Adventure Comics* 1, no. 452 (New York: DC Comics, July/August 1977).

Black Manta allegorizes Black nationalism and, in some ways, anticipates the influential theory of the Black Atlantic, famously developed by Paul Gilroy. Gilroy conceptually moves away from the dominant nation form and centers instead on the Atlantic Ocean, which Gilroy analyzes as a Black geography from which a new political imaginary can be developed, one defined by relationality, circulation, and fluidity. In Gilroy's theory, the Atlantic Ocean is recognized as a geography that connects Black subjects throughout the diaspora. The Atlantic Ocean is recognized as the foundation of the modern world—a world made by Black slavery—and it is a geography in which Black agency and collectivism can be reimagined and from which a new world order, one that centers on Blackness, can be born.[33]

In *Adventure Comics* 452 Black Manta becomes a powerful critique of Humanity, a category that structurally excludes

African Americans. As Black Manta articulates, the only place where Black lives can flourish is away from the surface world, away from a colonial-capitalist modernity founded on and perpetuating violence against Black communities. Only the Ocean, a space largely imagined as outside the project of Humanity, affords an opportunity for a Black nation to develop.[34] In this issue, Black Manta becomes a pop-culture icon of Black power.[35]

Black Manta is posited, or so it seems, as a Black revolutionary who is part of a robust genealogy that understands the Ocean as a source of Black politics, Black history, Black theory, Black possibilities, and Black imaginaries.[36] But this radical gesture is undercut from the outset. In the same issue that Black Manta reveals his racialized identity and his politics of Black power, he also commits one of the most shocking and barbaric crimes in DC Comics—he kills a baby. In the very same issue that Black Manta reveals his face and in which the dynamics of anti-Black racism are foregrounded for the first time in *Aquaman* comics, the comic creators narrate Black Manta as one of the most horrific supervillains in superhero comics. Rather than seriously engage with Black Manta's radical politics, the comic instead represents Black power as a fundamental threat to civilization and Humanity. Black Manta, in brief, is figured as a monster.

In the same issue in which Black Manta reveals that he is a Black subject committed to Black nationalism, we learn that Black Manta has kidnapped Aquaman and Mera's baby, Arthur Jr., whose nickname is "Aquababy." The narrative of a supervillain kidnapping a baby is shocking on its own. This shock of horror is enhanced when Aquaman discovers that Black Manta has entrapped Aquababy in a globe that can suffocate the infant. Black Manta explains his plans to Aquaman as follows: "The globe in which your whimpering offspring is encased is slowly filling with air. And given his size, I should think five minutes sufficient time for him to . . . suffocate!"[37]

(Aquababy is an aquatic being who gets his oxygen through water.) When explaining his plans of torture and death, Black Manta's erect arm points backward, an iconic gesture that looks like a reversed Nazi salute. Black Manta points at Aquababy in the globe with the water level dropping to the baby's knees. We both read and see this scene of suffocation.

The issue ends with Aquaman holding his dead son in his arms.

Even in superhero comics, where supervillains are common-place and evil plans are hatched regularly, Black Manta's act of infanticide exceeds all superhero comic norms. The article "10 Most Devastating Comic Book Endings" articulates the shock and horror of Black Manta's act: "Death is no stranger to super-hero comics. Half of all superheroes are born in response to a traumatic death, most superheroes have died themselves at one point or another, and their primary motivation almost always boils down to wanting to keep people from dying. So death in comic books, by murder, natural causes, or freak accidents, are not uncommon. However, there has only been one notable incident of direct infanticide."[38] It is important to emphasize (which the article does not) that this act of infanticide occurs in the same issue in which Black Manta reveals he is Black and committed to radical Black politics. The comic's cultural logic, therefore, reinforces the racist stereotype that Blackness is synonymous with barbarity and inhumanity.

This infanticide becomes the structuring event of subsequent *Aquaman* narratives and reboots. It is a trauma that extends over multiple issues of *Aquaman* comics and over multiple years. In *Justice League of America Annual* 2 (October 1984), which was published seven years after Black Manta killed Aquababy, this act of infanticide remains the defining event in Aquaman's and Mera's lives. The Aquaman-centric issue of *Justice League* delves into the ongoing pain and suffering of both Aquaman and Mera. After two decades of marital bliss—Aquaman and Mera were married in *Aquaman* 18 (November/December 1964)—Mera tells Aquaman in a recorded message, "We shared so much once—our thoughts as well as our love—but all that seemed to end when our son died. It's just taken me so long to accept it."[39] In this annual, double-sized issue featuring a major Justice League story—the dissolving of the Justice League of America—DC Comics highlights the lingering trauma of what can be argued as the greatest singular act of evil in DC history up to this point.

To make perhaps an obvious point, DC Comics' representation of Black Manta practiced and perpetuated anti-Black racism. In the same issue that visualizes Black Manta as African American, he becomes posited as evil incarnate. What could have been an opportunity to recognize structural racism and radical Black politics instead reinforces the racist ideology that equates Black men with incorrigible criminality.[40] *Adventure Comics* 452, the issue in which Black Manta reveals his race, positions African Americans as antithetical to civilization even before he kills Aquababy in the issue's last pages. The underwater city that Black Manta seeks to use as his base to build a Black empire is a city of "idylists," a community separate and distinct from Atlantis and one that practices a "religion" of pacifism and nonviolence.[41] In this racist allegory, Black Manta is posited as the opposite of the idylists, overtaking their city and literally turning their geography of nonviolence into one of violence. When Aquaman sees his son encased in the globe with diminishing water, Black Manta holds a button and says that he would "be happy to press the button to replenish the water" on the condition that Aquaman fights Aqualad, Aquaman's surrogate son. Black Manta uses his power to create the conditions in which white subjects are forced into nonchoices. Either Aquaman watches his baby suffocate to death, or Aquaman fights his surrogate son to death in order to save his biological infant. Aquaman apologizes to Aqualad for what he is about to do, but as he explains, he has no choice. He must do everything to save his baby. Tellingly, the arena in which this father and surrogate son combat is described as "an arena that once served as a discussion forum for the passive idylists."[42] Black Manta—and, by allegorical extension, Black power and Black nationalism—is narratively posited as antithetical to civilization and Humanity. A comic issue that had the potential to be a forum for radical Black politics instead becomes yet another example of anti-Blackness that is central to the modern world.[43]

Black Manta indexes the problematic history of Black representation in mainstream superhero comics. Modern Black superheroes only began to appear in DC and Marvel comics in the late 1960s and 1970s, a period marked by conspicuous racial strife, violence, and Black uprising.[44] During this period, multiple manifestations of Black power circulated in mass-market American culture, including in superhero comics, as evidenced by Black Panther (1966), the Falcon (1969), John Stewart as the Green Lantern (1971), Luke Cage (1972), Black Goliath (1975), Storm (1975), and Black Lightning (1977).[45] As the above list indicates, the racial identity of Black superheroes and supervillains frequently becomes signaled by their name, a pattern that extends to Black Manta. This linguistic marking of race is part of the complex, contradictory history of Blackness in mass-market superhero comics. Although Black Manta was revealed to be Black in 1977, his relation to Blackness since then has been virtually nonexistent, beyond the racist ideology that equates Blackness with criminality. While Black superheroes and supervillains exist in mass-market comics, they are frequently deracinated from Black community, Black culture, and Black epistemology. As Kenneth Ghee writes in his contribution to

Black Comics: Politics of Race and Representation, superhero comics are replete with Black superheroes who have "little or no reference to a sustaining Black family, a viable Black community, continuity with Black history or Black culture." Blackness becomes reduced to "color only."[46] Black Manta exemplifies this racist representation.

It wasn't until 1992, two decades after revealing his face, that Black Manta was even given a backstory.[47] *Aquaman* 6 (March/May 1992) shows Black Manta as a young boy who grew up in Baltimore and who loved the Ocean. One day, he was kidnapped by white sailors who made him into a slave on the high seas. As Black Manta narrates, he was forced to labor and constantly deprived of food and water. This narrative powerfully and explicitly evokes the Atlantic slave trade. Black Manta becoming a slave in the twentieth century gives popular form to the political philosophy of Afropessimism. This theory, developed within critical Black studies, analyzes how Black bodies are marked as Slaves throughout modernity.[48] As Christina Sharpe writes, modernity is defined by "the reappearances of the slave ship in everyday life in the form of the prison, the camp, and the school."[49] Racialized slavery does not exist exclusively in the past; rather, the present remains in slavery's "wake."[50] Black Manta's origin story could have been a powerful, popular representation of Afropessimism. However, this origin story, one that links Black Manta to this history of anti-Blackness and slavery, is a one-off. Rather than sustained attention to Black Manta's history as a victim of structural anti-Blackness and modern-day Black slavery, the comic series, once again, leaves Blackness behind. In fact, ten years later, Black Manta is given a new origin story. In *Aquaman* 8 (July/September 2003), Black Manta becomes narrated as an orphan on the autistic spectrum during a time when there "was little sympathy" for nonnormative children.[51] Black Manta's evil, it is suggested, is rooted in mental illness.

Although the new origin story tries to critique mental health discourses and apparatuses, it still pathologizes the Black body.

Black Manta's history has been defined by multiple, intersecting racist discourses. In fact, it wasn't until 2010, four decades after his debut, that Black Manta was given a name: David.[52] The author who named Black Manta, who began to recognize his Humanity, is Geoff Johns. In the issue in which Black Manta is given a name, he learns he has a son, Jackson, establishing the foundation for even further Humanization.[53] (The institution of the family, of course, is central to the ideological construct of the Human.) Black Manta learning he is a father and wrestling with his developing affection for his son goes a long way toward the Humanization of this supervillain, a theme I explore more fully when I turn to the animated television show *Young Justice* in my afterword.

Despite all the sea changes in Black Manta's history, his murder of Aquababy continues to reverberate throughout the decades. Through every reboot and reimagining, there is a fear that history will repeat itself. But Johns seemed intent on breaking this cycle. In the *Brightest Day* story line (2010–11), authored by Johns, Aquababy is not broached. Moreover, by giving Black Manta a name and giving him a son, Johns seemed to be on a narrative course to exploring Black Manta's complex interiority. The New 52 *Aquaman* was a chance to wipe the slate clean and move into the future as an antiracist corrective to the comic's past.

As argued in the previous section, Johns's allegory of Atlantis serves as evidence that he understands structural racism. Johns is a prolific writer for DC, so he knows Black Manta's history and moreover, we can assume, his responsibility for reimagining Black Manta. In The New 52 *Aquaman*, Black Manta is introduced in the second narrative arc, titled "The Others" (March/May 2012–October/December 2012). In this narrative arc, Johns gives Arthur a new history and creates a new superhero group whose name suggests that Johns is aware of the dynamics of race and racism. In this new iteration, before joining the Justice League, Arthur was part of a different superhero collective: the Others. The allegorical significance of this collective is made explicit in its naming, which links the group to critical race theory, a theory in which the concept of other is central for critiquing the interlinked processes of racialization and colonialism. Tellingly, the Others is composed primarily of Black and brown members. It is a racialized superhero group that has been othered by the dominant genre of the Human.[54]

However, this narrative, seemingly informed by critical race theory, reinforces the stereotype that Black Manta is evil incarnate. The arc begins with Kahina the Seer, an Iranian superhero and member of the Others, running through the jungles of Brazil. She is being hunted by Black Manta. Kahina is visualized as Muslim, wearing a niqab (a veil), leaving only her eyes uncovered. To reinforce her Muslim identity, Kahina's first words are "Salaam alaikum," which are spoken to a rampaging Black Manta.[55] Black Manta is posited, once again, as a figure of radical evil.

All members of the Others, including Kahina, are being systemically hunted down and ruthlessly murdered by Black Manta, because they are Aquaman's chosen family. Even in 2012, when "The Others" narrative arc was published, Black Manta remains defined by his maliciousness and his singular drive to hurt Aquaman in the most sadistic ways possible. In the opening pages of *Aquaman* 7 (March/May 2012), Black Manta corners Kahina and beats her into submission. While Kahina lies in defeat, Black Manta does everything in his power to humiliate and enhance Kahina's pain—physically, psychically, and spiritually. First, he pulls down her niqab, an act that is a conspicuous hate crime, targeting Kahina's religion and intentionally violating the sanctity that the niqab signifies. After this horrific act, Black Manta removes his helmet, an act that either informs or reminds readers that he is African American. Black Manta menacingly moves mere inches from Kahina's face and describes his premeditated plan: "After I kill you, I will go to Tehran and I will kill your family." Kahina stutters in disbelief, and tears stream down her face. Black Manta continues, making sure she knows that her family will be slowly and painfully tortured, "Your husband. Your children. I will clean them like a fish."[56] In this new, diverse reboot, The New 52 *Aquaman* still presents Black Manta without any interiority, without any complexity, without any layers. Whereas Johns represents Orm—Arthur's other archnemesis—with complex interiority (see chapter 3), Johns presents Black Manta as evil embodied, whose only drive and desire is to make Aquaman suffer in the most extreme ways imaginable, including torturing and killing Aquaman's loved ones and their extended families.

In The New 52 *Aquaman*, Black Manta is represented as a "Black Avenger," without any of the political dimensions associated with this term.[57] The so-called reason why Black Manta attempts to torture and kill all of Aquaman's family and friends is because, it is revealed late in Johns's narrative run, Aquaman accidentally killed Black Manta's father. Johns attempts to render the murderous feud between Black Manta and Arthur Curry in the mode of tragedy. In yet another new origin story, Johns presents Black Manta and his father as treasure hunters who journey the world's Oceans in search of valuables. One day, Black Manta was hired by a scientist to acquire a sample of Arthur's blood for the scientist to analyze Arthur's genetic makeup. When Black Manta snuck aboard Arthur's ship to gather a blood sample, he encounters Thomas Curry, Arthur's father. The two fight, and in the ensuing struggle, Thomas has a heart attack and dies three days later in a hospital.[58] Arthur blames Black Manta for this death, and after his father's funeral, Arthur becomes obsessed with vengeance.[59] When Arthur locates Black Manta's vessel, "he thought Manta was alone," but the caption box informs, "He wasn't."[60] At the time, Black Manta was out scavenging, and Black Manta's father—tellingly unnamed—was on board. In the darkness, Arthur chokes the life out of Black Manta's father, mistaking father for son. The most condemning reading of this murder is that Arthur treats all Black people as fungible, unable or unwilling to differentiate between father and son. But a more generous reading is that it was night, and the darkness led to this fatal mistake. The important point to emphasize, though, is that Johns makes the antagonism between Arthur Curry and Black Manta a form of tragedy, with vengeance becoming a trans-generational drive. As with all tragedies, this cycle of violence is senseless, and if it is not stopped, bloodshed will continue to pour across geographies and throughout generations.

What is telling is that Arthur is able, eventually, to move on from this tragedy. Arthur renounces his desire to seek revenge and, instead, dedicates his life to greater political and ecological causes, such as protecting the Oceans. In contrast, Black Manta remains mired in an ever-evolving revenge fantasy. In The New 52 *Aquaman*, Black Manta's entire reason for living is not only to exact revenge on Arthur but to ensure that everyone within Arthur's world suffers violently. Black Manta's vengeance, his hatred, exceeds the boundaries of normative genres such as tragedy.

Eventually, Black Manta is captured and incarcerated at Belle Reve supermax penitentiary. While there, Amanda Waller offers Black Manta a chance to join the Suicide Squad. Before making the offer, Waller attempts to probe Black Manta's interiority. *Aquaman* 23.1 (September/November 2013) begins with Waller addressing Black Manta: "Now, you try hard to come off as psycho, but you're way too focused, too controlled." Waller then identifies Black Manta as a "killing machine": "What you really are is the most highly disciplined killing machine who's ever occupied one of my cells."[61] At a prison designed for the most dangerous criminals in the DC universe, Black Manta is deemed one of the most, if not the most, vicious and violent. Several issues earlier, a character describes Belle Reve as a prison designed for "people more than human."[62] To be institutionalized at Belle Reve, in other words, is to be positioned and categorized outside the Human. The preponderance of criminals incarcerated in Belle Reve are superhumans (such as Orm). Black Manta, however, has no superpowers. Black Manta is just a Black man. However, as Waller's language makes clear, Black Manta is outside the regime of the Human. Waller calls him a "killing machine" programmed for one purpose. The categorization of Black Manta as evil beyond the genre of the Human reinforces the racist ideology that equates Blackness with inhuman criminality. This ideological equation has been used since the collapse of the Reconstruction era to justify the incarceration of African Americans at an increasingly disproportionate rate.[63] It is not surprising to see Black Manta in such a setting. The icon of a Black man incarcerated in a supermax prison has become a defining attribute of the American landscape.

Waller, though, offers Black Manta a way out of his imprisonment and, moreover, into the ideological category of the Human. Waller explains that the Suicide Squad will give Black Manta an opportunity to "be more than" a killing machine. As Waller elaborates, using the sanctioned discourse of psychology, the "only thing driving" Black Manta is his desire to kill Aquaman. But she asks, "Where do you direct all of this hate" when Aquaman is dead?[64] Rather than seeing Black Manta as having a rich interior life capable of experiencing a wide range of complex, diverse emotions, Waller reads Black Manta's life as defined and organized by "hate." Even with the offer to join the

Suicide Squad, Waller can't imagine any other driving emotion. Waller attempts to coax Black Manta as follows: "You work with me and we can redirect that hate."[65] In this psychology, Black Manta is exclusively defined by his hate. He becomes posited as hate embodied. A DC supervillain with no depth, complexity, and interiority may not seem like a big deal. However, Black Manta is one of the few African Americans in the DC universe. The burden of representation, therefore, is heightened. In his article "The Absence of Black Supervillains in Mainstream Comics," Phillip Lamarr Cunningham writes, "Both the DC and Marvel universes feature a litany of supervillains who wield great power and great intellect and who pose a true threat to the superheroes in these respective universes. However, relatively few of these supervillains are black."[66] Cunningham continues, "The scarcity of black supervillains is inextricably linked to the equal scarcity of black superheroes in mainstream comics, particularly those who have had an ongoing series. As one might imagine, black villains were created primarily as antagonists to those few black superheroes who have had their own ongoing series. . . . For example, most of Marvel's black villains originate from either the *Black Panther* series or the *Luke Cage* series, both of which feature black protagonists."[67] What differentiates Black Manta from so many mainstream Black supervillains in Marvel and DC is that his archnemesis is a white superhero. Black Manta and Aquaman are structurally opposed not just in their respective identities as supervillain and superhero but in their racial composition as well. Aquaman's blond hair, blue eyes, and Aryan features are set in contrast to Black Manta's physiognomy.

At the conclusion of Johns's run as sole writer of The New 52 *Aquaman*, Black Manta transforms from one costumed supervillain into a different costumed supervillain. At the end of the run, Black Manta is a felon. In fact, in the issue in which Waller attempts to recruit Black Manta to the Suicide Squad,

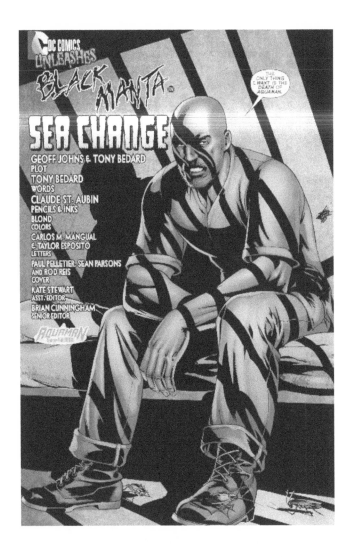

19. Black Manta incarcerated in a supermax prison. "Sea Change," Geoff Johns and Tony Bedard (plot), Tony Bedard (words), Claude St. Aubin (penciller and inker), Blond (colors), *Aquaman 7*, no. 23.1, The New 52 (New York: DC Comics, September/November 2013).

the splash page features a hypermasculine, muscular Black Manta in an orange jumpsuit. Black Manta is imprisoned, and the shadows of the prison bars bisect his body and face (fig. 19).

On this splash page, Black Manta is figured as a larger-than-life felon who embodies and perpetuates the racist trope of the Black man as a superpredator. The trope of Black criminality and the Black threat to (white) civil society is reinforced by representing white institutions (here prisons) as inadequate to contain and control the Black body. On this splash page, Black Manta's larger-than-life body threatens to break through the prison cell and the comic's cell. This image visualizes white anxiety about Black bodies and further fuels white investment in the prison industrial complex, a complex that normalizes and naturalizes Black surveillance, Black criminality, Black containment, and the destruction of Black communities everywhere.[68] In the dominant U.S. imaginary, Blackness—especially Black masculinity—has become synonymous with criminality, and The New 52 Black Manta perpetuates this anti-Black stereotype. In this sense, The New 52 is not a break from DC's racist past but a continuation of this troubling tradition.

However, Black Manta is not fixed. Characters are reimagined and reinvented all the time. So what happens when Black Manta becomes represented by James Wan, a Chinese Malaysian Australian filmmaker?

Confronting Anti-Black Racism

As already noted, The New 52 Aquaman became a primary source for the big-budget, 2018 DC movie Aquaman, for which Johns receives story credit and for which he was a cowriter. But Johns's voice is not the only one participating in the creative process of bringing Aquaman to the big screen. James Wan is also given story credit, and moreover, he is the movie's director. Many of the characters, visuals, and story lines introduced in The New 52 iteration are used in the movie, including the trench. But Wan's version is not a faithful translation. Rather, Wan reimagines Aquaman as a narrative about people of color and visualizes the Ocean as a space for Black and Indigenous liberation.

In this final section, I want to briefly consider how Wan represents Black Manta and, in just one scene, gives more depth, compassion, and history to the character than in any previous comic iteration. In just one scene, Wan did more for the character of Black Manta than decades of comic book representations up to that point.

In the 2018 movie, just as in The New 52 version, Black Manta's hatred for Aquaman is because the latter killed his father. But in Wan's version, Black Manta, from the outset, is treated with compassion. Wan wants viewers to understand, empathize with, and, even more, root for this ostensible supervillain. Brandon Zachary, an associate writer for Comic Book Resources, argues that the movie *Aquaman* succeeds by making Black Manta "the hero of his own story." Zachary continues, "One of the most compelling elements of director James Wan's *Aquaman* isn't the titular hero or the undersea kingdom of Atlantis. It's Black Manta."[69] In many ways, Zachary observes, Black Manta is analogous to Marvel's Erik Killmonger in *Black Panther*. Both characters are driven by a sense of justice.

Wan's *Aquaman* troubles the waters of whiteness. With Wan at the movie's helm, no character of color becomes a caricature. In Wan's adaptation, Black Manta is created with complexity, interiority, and a history, all of which are inextricable from his Blackness. This symbolic victory is achieved in one scene.

Similar to Johns's origin story in The New 52, Black Manta and his father are pirates. But Wan does something from the outset that Johns fails to do—he gives both Black Manta and his father full names, David and Jesse Kane, respectively. Early in the movie, Jesse Kane (played by Michael Beach) and his son David Kane (Yahya Abdul-Mateen II) overtake a submarine. This scene of Black criminality, though, is undercut when Wan allows the action to stop for Jesse to address his son. This address, while brief, intimates at how these characters have struggled to survive in a world defined by anti-Blackness. Jesse gifts David a knife and explains, "This was your grandfather's. He was one of the navy's first frogmen during World War II. He was so stealthy in the war, his unit nicknamed him Manta. But after the war, his country forgot about him, so he went back to the sea, scavenging and surviving with his wit and this knife. He gave it to me when I was your age, and now it's yours, son." This monologue roots Jesse and David's shared history in institutional racism. The moniker adopted by David, "Black Manta," is an homage to his grandfather and an acknowledgment of the state-sponsored, structural racism his grandfather experienced in the military. In *Torchbearers of Democracy* Chad L. Williams analyzes the complex and contradictory role of African American soldiers during World War I: "African American servicemen embodied the inherent tensions of fighting for a country that denied democracy to its own citizens and the dilemma of remaining loyal to both nation and race."[70] During World War II, African Americans were still treated like second-class citizens. Although more than 1.2 million African Americans fought for the United States, they were segregated from their white counterparts. Even when fighting totalitarianism, Jim Crow culture ruled the day.[71] As the scene in *Aquaman* intimates, structural racism is intergenerational and, moreover, it is suggested, the reason why Jesse and David are pirates in the first place. The reason why father and son turned to the informal economy is because the formal economy remains a white structure in which the opportunities for African Americans are limited at best.

This small scene opens and deepens Black Manta in ways that years of comic books failed to do. Representation matters in popular culture, but who is creating the popular culture—who is behind the camera, who is writing the screenplay, who is creating comic book art—often matters more. In the afterword, I briefly sketch how The New 52 *Aquaman* led to a range of diverse *Aquaman* cultural producers, including Wan, committed to making the Oceans visible as a Black, brown, Indigenous, and queer geography.

20. Jackson Hyde, the new Aquaman, swims through the Ocean. "The Confluence, Part 1," Brandon Thomas (writer), Daniel Sampere (artist), Adriano Lucas (colorist), *Aquaman*, no. 1, Future State (Burbank CA: DC Comics, January/March 2021).

Afterword

The Ocean's Black, Queer, Brown, and Indigenous Futures

A decade after the launch of The New 52, DC Comics introduced a new initiative, Future State, which narrates various superheroes in the near and distant future. In the twenty-four titles that compose this initiative, the future appears radically open. In Future State *Aquaman* 1 (January/March 2021), Aquaman is no longer figured as a traditional, white-appearing superhero. Rather, in the future, Aquaman is now Jackson Hyde, an African American who proudly claims his Black heritage. The opening splash page, with artwork by Daniel Sampere, features Jackson forcefully swimming through the water, stretching toward the top corner of the page as his long dreadlocks flow behind him. Sampere draws Jackson in loving, attentive detail (fig. 20).

Sampere's splash page exemplifies what Frederick Luis Aldama theorizes as the "will to style." The phrase "will to style," as Aldama writes, "is shorthand for identifying the responsibility of the creator (or creators) in understanding well the building blocks of reality that they are reconstructing."[1] The artist's social responsibility becomes pronounced when they visualize characters of color. A comic's racial politics, in other words, does not work exclusively at the level of narrative but also at the level of artwork. Artists must recognize this responsibility and commit to appropriately, respectfully, and humbly visualizing characters of color. This aesthetic commitment is the artist's "will to style." Aldama theorizes, "The more present the will to style, the more likely [... the comic will] *make new* our perception, thought, and feeling about the world we live in."[2] About Latinx superheroes specifically, Aldama writes, "The choice of shape, line, perspective (and ink and color) plays a significant role in determining whether readers experience any given Latinx superhero as complex."[3] This theory is exemplified by Sampere's opening splash page. The page features Jackson forcefully swimming away from five massive sharks, each commanded by a militaristic figure. Despite the hectic, multidirectional action, the page's focal point is Jackson's dreadlocks. Sampere draws the reader's eyes away from the action and toward the richness and beauty of Black culture. Each dreadlock is individualized and stylized with tremendous detail, care, and love. Sampere respects dreadlocks as a salient icon of Black identity and signification.[4]

Future State *Aquaman*, featuring an African American as the titular character, is written by Brandon Thomas, the first African American to author the aquatic superhero. Thomas gives Jackson depth and nuance, and moreover, he creates a narrative that is radically ecological. In Future State *Aquaman*, Thomas introduces the concept of "the Confluence," a progressive conception of space-time that exceeds Human categories. In the series, the Ocean is not only a living, interconnected geography on Earth but, moreover, a geography that extends across and connects all galaxies. The Confluence is the watery means through which this new Aquaman and Andy Curry—daughter of The New 52 iteration of Aquaman and Mera—journey across space and time. This new imaginary is animated by the ecological philosophy of the interconnectivity of all things—even beyond Earth's borders. The connectivity of all Oceans throughout the galaxy foregrounds the ontological limits of Earthbound creatures.

Traveling across intergalactic space and time through connected Oceanways, Jackson and Andy implicitly learn that knowledge is not a domain to be mastered. Instead, knowledge becomes figured as contingent, provisional, and conditional. Humanism and all Human systems are washed away in the Confluence.

In the future, not only is Aquaman African American, but moreover, the next individual to assume the Aquaman mantle defies the masculine normativity inscribed into the name. In Future State *Justice League* 1 (January/March 2021), set thirty years in the future, the new members of the Justice League queer and refigure canonical iterations of this supergroup. In the future, Green Lantern is a Black woman; the Flash is Black and nonbinary; and one canonical character gets a new name. The new iteration of the Justice League features not a new man occupying the role of Aquaman but, rather, Andy Curry, whose superhero moniker is Aquawoman.

The "future state" of Aquaman suggests an Oceanic future defined by radical diversity, which manifests itself in myriad ways, including, most conspicuously, through race and gender. But how diverse is Aquaman, really? Comic superheroes have become "multi-million-dollar corporate properties."[5] Given the financial value of superheroes, Douglas Wolk, author of *Reading Comics*, writes that "significant lasting change is almost impossible to get past the marketing department."[6] While this cynical take is warranted, superheroes are not reified. Artistic energies can override corporate containment.

Since The New 52, Aquaman has become defined by progressive tides in nearly all media, from comics and graphic novels to television and blockbuster movies. On December 19, 2018, mere days before the release of the blockbuster *Aquaman* movie and four years removed from Geoff Johns's extended run, Kelly Sue DeConnick became the first woman to become the chief writer for an extended *Aquaman* narrative run. DeConnick is a self-proclaimed feminist who has vociferously critiqued the patriarchy rampant at all levels of mass-market comics. DeConnick, for example, established and popularized the Sexy Lamp test. As DeConnick explains, "If you can take out your female character and replace her with a sexy lamp and your plot still functions, you're doing it wrong."[7] The reason why DeConnick had to establish this aesthetic test is because of the pervasive sexism in superhero comics. Her test has become an important method for feminists everywhere to call out writers, editors, story lines, and publishers. But DeConnick has also recognized that mass-market comics are not categorically patriarchal. Rather, DeConnick also invests energy and time in making visible the central role of women to the production of comics. In March 2016, for example, DeConnick started the #VisibleWomen movement on Twitter, "to disabuse hiring professionals of the notion that women comic artists are rare and to raise awareness of said women with readers."[8]

DeConnick's feminism makes clear that while representation matters, what matters even more is who is doing the representing. DeConnick began her *Aquaman* run with Rebirth issue 43 (December 2018 / February 2019) and concluded two years later with issue 65 (November 2020 / January 2021). In DeConnick's narrative run, a significant portion is devoted to Mera working to abolish the Atlantean monarchy and establishing a democratic political order. Near the end of DeConnick's politically charged run, Mera delivers a speech to an enormous assembly of the Ocean's inhabitants, who gathered for what they believed to be a royal wedding to secure and protect the monarchy. Mera proclaims to the shocked audience, "No more kings! No more queens! We must give our power to our people!"[9] DeConnick makes Mera into a revolutionary figure.

These progressive tides animate not only DC comic books but nearly all media featuring Aquaman. Whereas, prior to The

New 52 iteration, Aquaman was posited as a joke by multiple media texts, since The New 52, Aquaman has become, for the most part, a figure of respect and importance. On November 26, 2010, the serialized cartoon *Young Justice* premiered on Cartoon Network, focusing on teenage superheroes in training who are members of a covert collective that work in concert with, yet independent from, the Justice League. The members of Young Justice continually expand and evolve, but the founding members are Kid Flash, Speedy, Robin, and the group's chosen leader, Aqualad. Aqualad has been a staple in Aquaman comics since *Adventure Comics* 269 (December 1959 / February 1960). The first Aqualad, Garth, is Aquaman's white protégé, created by writer Robert Bernstein and artist Ramona Fradon. In 2010 Brandon Vietti, Greg Weisman, and Phil Bourassa introduced a new Aqualad, whose name is Kaldur'ahm and whose nickname is Kaldur. In contrast to Garth, the new Aqualad is Black, and in episode 4 of *Young Justice*, "Drop-Zone" (January 28, 2011), Kaldur is unanimously chosen by his peers to be the team leader. The show was canceled after two seasons (2010–13), but due to fan activism, it was renewed. The show's third season (2019) opens with Kaldur having become the new Aquaman and the cochair of the Justice League. The world of superheroes, previously saturated in whiteness, became, in the television show, led by an African American.

While Kaldur was created for television, a slightly modified version of Kaldur appeared several months prior in Geoff Johns and Ivan Reis's *Brightest Day* 4 (June/August 2010). When Johns saw the design of Kaldur for the cartoon, he adapted the character for his crossover series *Brightest Day* (2010–11) with a new name, Jackson Hyde. Despite the name differences, both Kaldur and Jackson are similar in myriad ways: both are Black; both are Aqualad; both can control water; both have complex tattoos covering their arms; both have similar costumes; and both learn that Black Manta is their father. However, the cartoon traveled where the comics refused to go.

The preponderance of *Young Justice* season 2 (2012–13) is devoted to exploring the complex relationship between Kaldur and his biological father. In the second season, Kaldur goes undercover and pretends to ally with Black Manta and his secret, malicious organization, the Light. This mission becomes complicated, however, as Black Manta develops affection and even love for his estranged son, and similarly, Kaldur develops fondness for his estranged father. Not only did such a complex relationship not make its way into Johns's script, but moreover, Johns excluded Jackson as a character all together in The New 52 *Aquaman*. Whereas Kaldur remained a central part of *Young Justice*, Johns's version of Aqualad disappeared almost immediately after his introduction. In fact, Jackson Hyde would not be part of The New 52 universe, even with an unprecedented fifty-two different comic lines running simultaneously. It would not be until the DC 2016 reboot, Rebirth, that Jackson reappeared.

In the comic series *Teen Titans*, part of DC's Rebirth, Jackson is reintroduced and made more intersectional. Jackson is now a Black, gay superhero. However, such a complex identity is largely marginalized in the comic series. There are no story lines exploring Jackson's sexual identity nor any story lines even suggesting that Jackson could be in an intimate relationship. This marginalization is corrected, however, in the graphic novel *You Brought Me the Ocean* (2020), part of the DC imprint DC Ink, which produces young adult graphic novels. *You Brought Me the Ocean* is a collaboration between Lambda Award–winning writer Alex Sanchez and artist Jul Maroh. Sanchez is perhaps best known for the young-adult novel *So Hard to Say*, while Maroh is perhaps best known for being both the writer and artist of the award-winning 2010 graphic novel *Blue Is the*

Warmest Color (*Le bleu est une couleur chaude*). Both creators are openly queer, and both have won multiple awards recognizing their creative commitment to queer representation. In their collaborative origin story for Jackson Hyde, nicknamed Jake, Sanchez and Maroh make central an aspect of Jackson's identity that had only been marginal in the comics: Jackson's queerness.

It is a long-practiced superhero trope that a teenager learning to harness and control their emerging superpowers is a metaphor for a teenager learning the complexities and contradictions of their identity within the dominant social order. In this sense, superpowers have been read as a metaphor for sexuality, gender, and race. In *You Brought Me the Ocean*, Jake Hyde explicitly struggles to embrace his powers to control water, and he explicitly struggles to embrace his sexuality. In other words, Sanchez and Maroh make the superhero and queer narratives mirror and reinforce each other. For Jake, the narrative of his emerging superpowers is parallel to and inextricable from his emerging queerness. In a world that polices and insists on Humanism, Jake Hyde is a metahuman; in a world of whiteness, Jake Hyde is Black; and in a world of heteronormativity, Jake Hyde is gay. The story, set in New Mexico, posits queerness as a trope for superpowers, and it posits superpowers as a trope for queerness. Just as queerness seems invisible in the heteronormative small town in rural New Mexico that Jake calls home, so too does water, in this setting, seem invisible. But such are false ways of seeing. Queerness, like water, is everywhere. You just need to learn how to see it. Moreover, water, like identity, is fluid and dynamic. Jake Hyde—Black, queer, small-town kid, future Aquaman—defies all identity categories.

Two years prior to *You Brought Me the Ocean*, perhaps the most impactful reimagining of Aquaman occurred with the release of James Wan's 2018 movie *Aquaman*. The most revolutionary aspect of James Wan's *Aquaman, perhaps,* is the casting of Joseph Jason Namakaeha Momoa, better known as Jason Momoa, in the titular role. Momoa is openly "proud of his Hawaiian and Polynesian" heritage, a heritage that becomes explicit in the movie.[10] In this 2018 iteration, Aquaman becomes an explicit mixed-race superhero.[11]

Whereas in previous iterations, including The New 52, Aquaman was metaphorically a mixed-race superhero, Wan's *Aquaman* literalizes this identity. As Wan explains, "What I love about Jason's background of being biracial is that he's the perfect guy for this character who . . . is biracial, except for Aquaman his biracial-ness stems from being half-Atlantean and half-surface dweller. And I think that is something that Jason can relate to, and it's something that I think is very important."[12] Momoa's Aquaman is "the first mixed-race superhero in the DC Extended Universe, and possibly in the whole of the superhero film franchises."[13]

More specifically, Aquaman becomes a Hapa superhero. *Hapa* is the Hawaiian word used to describe someone of mixed heritage. Hapa was originally a derogatory term used to describe "mixed-race children of plantation guest workers from the Philippines, Korea, China and Japan, and the women they married in Hawai'i in the early part of the 20th century."[14] Today, though, Hapa has become a term proudly embraced as an identity by mixed-race Hawaiians.[15] In *Hapa Mag*, Melissa Slaughter celebrates that *Aquaman* is "Hapa AF."[16] Slaughter writes, "Momoa's background influenced the look and costume design for Arthur; he threw Hawaiian phrases into Arthur's dialogue; he did a haka [a ceremonial dance in Māori culture] at the L.A. premiere."[17] Moreover, Momoa's casting became generative in creating a nonwhite movie. Because of Momoa's casting, three other nonwhite actors were cast in the movie: Temuera Morrison (Māori), who plays Arthur's father, Thomas

Curry, and newcomers Kaan Guldur and Otis Dhanji, who play Arthur at ages nine and thirteen respectively.[18] The presence of these actors all actively shape the story world.

In the movie, Momoa and Morrison make Arthur and Thomas Curry explicitly Māori. Momoa intentionally adopted a Māori identity to play Arthur in order to honor Morrison. As a young boy in Iowa (after his parents divorced, Momoa and his mother left Hawai'i), Momoa saw the 1994 film *Once Were Warriors*, which centers on a Māori family and stars Morrison. Morrison explains, "Jason [Momoa] saw *Once Were Warriors* when he was growing up in Iowa and because his father's Hawaiian, it really impinged on his cultural consciousness and identity. It was a powerful film for him and inspired him to get into the business."[19] In fact, it was Momoa who wanted Morrison to be cast as Thomas Curry.[20] Momoa shares, "I love Temuera Morrison, he was one of my idols."[21]

While filming *Aquaman* in the Gold Coast, Momoa's embrace of Māori culture deepened. Morrison recalls, "There were a number of times when we went out for a fancy dinner and I'd end up giving him taiaha [spear] lessons on the street while everyone else was eating. . . . I feel quite proud Jason has adopted it as his culture too."[22] Evidence of Aquaman's Māori identity is prevalent throughout the movie: Momoa is marked with tāmoko, Māori "tattoos"; he wears a pounamu around his neck, a greenstone that is sacred in Māori culture; and he greets his dad with a hongi, a traditional Māori greeting in which people press their noses together. Morrison credits Momoa with "embracing the Māori culture he encountered during filming on the Gold Coast."[23] This embrace included incorporating the Māori language into the movie. During a fight scene early in the movie, when Aquaman saves Russian sailors, he cries out, "Ona Takai," which is a Māori phrase.[24] Momoa explains his decision to use the Māori language as an homage to Morrison: "He was my father in the movie. I wanted him to play my dad, so I thought it would be good to just use Māori for it instead of Hawaiian. There's no such thing as Hawaiian, it's 'Nā Kānaka Maoli' with an L. That's what Hawaiian means. That's where the Māoris came from. So, I thought it was all right to go 'Ono Takai,' which means '*You deserve this,*' and I think it's kind of neat to add a little more flavor in there, you know what I mean."[25]

Momoa's decision to make Arthur Curry Māori brings to the surface a salient aspect of Aquaman's politics: the sacredness of water. For Māori peoples, water (*wai*) is the essence of life, and all water has *mauri* ("life essence").[26] As Indigenous activist and writer Tina Ngata (Ngāti Porou) shares, "When I speak to wai I speak to myself—and that is not only to acknowledge the inherent understanding that many Māori carry, which is 'Ko wai mātou—we are water'—but also that my knowing of wai has been developed through my own distinct exposure to elders, experts and experience. This linguistic relationship can also help us to understand our traditional perspectives, and the central role that water has played in our sense of identity and well-being. 'Ko wai mātou' also means 'Who are we.'"[27] As Māori and Indigenous people everywhere recognize, water is sacred and water is life, including human life.

While Momoa and Morrison embrace the Indigenous worldview that water is sacred and a symbol of the interconnection of all things, Wan stages the Ocean as an ideological battlefield. In contrast to Aquaman's Indigenous perspective, his half-brother Orm is obsessed with racial purity. As Slaughter writes, "Like an underwater Nazi," Orm "rules the sea with bleach-blonde hair and blue eyes."[28] One of the movie's central conflicts is the battle between Orm's vision of a pure Atlantean society and Arthur's status as mixed-race. In an early sequence, this ideological conflict is literalized as Orm demands a battle to take place in the heart of Atlantis. This battle is staged as a spectacle similar to a U.S. sports event. The field of combat is surrounded by thousands of emotionally charged Atlanteans, and a giant screen—similar to screens at NFL games—contextualizes the battle. On the screen, posited as a neutral source of information, Arthur is identified as a "half-breed." Adjacent to Arthur's image on the screen is a list of his pros and cons. According to this public medium of information, Arthur has no pros, and two of his three "cons" refer to his mixed-race status: "surface dweller," "half breed," and "drunk." Like the history of racism everywhere, racial hierarchies are ideologically justified by texts (here a screen) positing people deemed racially inferior as being morally inferior. Arthur's racial status, in other words, is inextricable from what is perceived as a moral flaw, which in this case is his ostensible inebriation.

Throughout the movie, Arthur is called variations of "half-breed." When Arthur, for example, encounters the monster Karathen, the monster insults him as follows: "You dare come here with your tainted mongrel blood to claim Atlantis's greatest treasure?" (Ironically, Karathen is voiced by Julie Andrews, famous for her iconic role in *The Sound of Music*, a movie about the rise of Nazism.) Such racist insults are strewn throughout the movie. Arthur is called a "half-breed abomination," "mongrel," "tainted," and "unworthy." The movie charts Arthur's journey to become King of Atlantis and, moreover, to embrace his mixed-race status as a source of strength and world-making power. Mera (played by Amber Heard) tells Arthur, "You think you're unworthy to lead because you're of two different worlds, but that's exactly why you are worthy. You are the bridge between land and sea." Arthur is a bridge to a new world order, a new ecological world order that delinks from whiteness, from colonialism, from the excesses of global capitalism. In the movie's final scene, Arthur embraces his mixed-race identity with pride, an embrace that is simultaneous with and inextricable from his embracing his role as the Ocean's protector. In the movie's final moment, Arthur declares, "I am Aquaman."

Momoa not only represents a new iteration of Aquaman; he is the first Indigenous mainstream superhero. In an interview for *Hapa Mag*, Slaughter asked Momoa about being a "Hapa man with a Hapa family" and playing the first Hapa superhero. Momoa replied, "Honestly, to be the first mixed-race superhero in 2018 is like, 'Really?' Is there not one? And that's a huge honor."[29] Slaughter concludes her essay by turning to the personal, which, of course, is inextricable from the political: "To be completely honest, I cried throughout the film. *Hapa Mag* editor Lauren Hardie sat beside me, tears in her eyes, and we had a Hapa moment. Every 'half-breed' and 'unworthy' moment we felt in our souls. And in the end, when Arthur stood up to defeat the Big Bad and take his rightful place as the King of the Atlantis, we cheered for Aquaman, our new Hapa hero."[30]

This new Aquaman is a symbol that recognizes Indigenous strength and power and, equally important, Indigenous science and epistemology. Indigenous philosopher and environmental justice scholar Kyle Powys Whyte (Citizen Potawatomi Nation) writes that Indigeneity "modifies knowledge." Whyte asserts, "Indigenous knowledges often refer to observations of species and the environment over a long time scale in a particular place," which "Indigenous peoples use . . . to support their sustenance and self-determination."[31] Indigenous knowledges are inextricable from Indigenous stewardship. Such knowledges center "on protecting intergenerational systems of place-based relationships from being obstructed by globalization and other political, social, and economic forces."[32] Knowing, being, and becoming are interwoven. As an example of such Indigenous knowledge, Whyte turns to Māori epistemology: "Māori organizing, including the Waitangi Tribunal, has helped establish the legal personhood of the Whanganui River in the New Zealand settler nation-state, thus establishing respect for the rivers' rights and interests as a living system."[33] Water scientist, legal scholar, and policy expert Kelsey Leonard (Shinnecock Indian Nation) insists, "Water is a living relation" that must be granted "legal personhood."[34]

Momoa becoming Aquaman gives popular form to Indigenous knowledge. Like the character he plays, Momoa, in real life, is a self-identified water activist. In 2019 Momoa addressed the United Nations on the existential and interlinked crises of Ocean pollution, climate change, and environmental inequities that disproportionally affect people of color. Momoa offered, as a path forward, Indigenous ways of knowing and being: "We are the living consequence of forgotten traditions. We suffer a collective amnesia of a truth that was once understood. The truth that to cause irreversible damage to the earth, is to bring the same unto ourselves. We the island nations—and all coastal communities—are the front lines in this environmental crisis. The Oceans are in a state of emergency. Entire marine ecosystems are vanishing with the warming of the seas. And as the waste of the world empties into our waters, we face the devastating crisis of plastic pollution."[35]

The same year that Momoa addressed the United Nations, he launched a more sustainable water company, Mananalu, which is committed to eliminating single-use plastic bottles. Instead of plastic bottles, Mananalu uses aluminum, which Momoa describes as "infinitely recyclable."[36] Momoa explains his company name as follows: "*Mana* is a very sacred word in Hawaiian. It means 'spirit of life'—it's a whole energy force. *Nalu* means wave. Mananalu represents an unstoppable wave of change. I want to create a wave of change."[37] In 2020 Momoa "donated drinking water to the Navajo Nation, an Indigenous community of some 200,000 people in the Southwest that was not only ravaged by COVID-19, but also has struggled histori-cally to gain reliable access to clean water."[38] Momoa posted on Instagram, "My water company is still small but I'm doing what I can to help those that need it the most."[39]

Momoa's commitment to water activism and this understand-ing of the interconnections of water and human flourishing is rooted in his Indigeneity. Momoa was born in Honolulu, and on the islands, he stresses, "water is life. Every aspect of life is tied to the water."[40] In an interview, Momoa explains,

> I was born in Hawaii. I'm basically from Waianae, Nanakuli, the west side, Makaha. . . . My dad grew up in a Quonset hut on Hakimo Road. . . . I would spend my summers there and it was very, very different growing up in Nanakuli, which is beautiful, with the most loving family, with all my cousins there, because there's not too many white people down there. But my mom made it over there in the '70s and met an amaz-ing Hawaiian family and had me. That marriage never made it but she came home to a very, very white family in a place called Iowa, where it is awesome. I love the Midwest, and it's the same people (as in Hawaii)—people who don't want to leave their land, who are very content where they're at. They take great pride in being farmers. It's the same thing; it's people who love being where they're from, but there's just not a lot of diversity.[41]

In college, Momoa studied marine biology and wildlife biology.[42] Journalist Maggie Fazeli Fard writes of Momoa, "Amid all his success, he never lost sight of his heritage or his connection to his family, to his island, and to the water. His most prominent tattoo, a sleeve on his left arm, is a pattern of repeating rows of shark teeth. He explains that it's a tribute to the shark, which is his family's *aumakua*, a guardian spirit and the Momoa family crest."[43]

Indigenous politics and Ocean scholar Karin Amimoto Ingersoll describes the "seascape epistemology" of the Kānaka Maoli (Indigenous Hawaiians) as "revealing hidden linkages between water and land that speak to Indigenous ways of knowing and being, to historical means of political, social, and cultural survival."[44] Addressing the United Nations, Momoa emphasized that "the Oceans are in a state of emergency." The reason for this state of emergency, Momoa makes clear, is Humans. "We are a disease that is infecting our planet."[45]

Human society must change, and that change, Momoa insists, "cannot come in 2050, or 2030, or even 2025." Rather, "the change must come today."[46] Essential to such large-scale change is storytelling. In *Braiding Sweetgrass* Robin Wall Kimmerer (Citizen Potawatomi Nation) emphasizes the importance of stories to creating and maintaining healthy, flourishing ecosystems. Kimmerer writes that we need "healing stories that allow us to imagine a different relationship, in which people and land are good medicine for each other."[47] Such stories are a form of activism. The future of Aquaman, in all media, will hopefully offer more explicit and engaged "healing stories" for the Oceans and for the planet as a whole.

NOTES

INTRODUCTION

1. Bradley, "A Brief History of Pop Culture Dumping on Aquaman."
2. *Aquaman: A Celebration*, 66.
3. "The Trench, Part 1," 15.
4. "The Trench, Part 1," 15.
5. "The Trench, Part 1," 15.
6. There is an important, growing body of scholarship that examines comics in an ecological context, including King and Page, *Posthumanism and the Graphic Novel in Latin America*; Menga and Davies, "Apocalypse Yesterday"; Perry, "Anthroposcenes"; and J. Scott, *The Posthuman Body in Superhero Comics*.
7. Mladenov, *Marine Biology*, 1.
8. Roorda, *The Ocean Reader*, 3–4.
9. P. Steinberg, *The Social Construction of the Ocean*.
10. See P. Steinberg, "Of Other Seas."
11. Rozwadowski, *Vast Expanses*, 7.
12. Mentz, *At the Bottom of Shakespeare's Ocean*, ix.
13. Roorda, *The Ocean Reader*, 1.
14. Zalasiewicz, Williams, and Waters, "Anthropocene," 14.
15. Zalasiewicz, Williams, and Waters, "Anthropocene," 14.
16. Zalasiewicz, Williams, and Waters, "Anthropocene," 14.
17. For more on utopian narratives and their world-making capability, see Wegner, *Imaginary Communities*. Also see Jameson, *The Political Unconscious*, especially 291–92. Jameson recognizes utopian texts as working at an allegorical level. Jameson, *The Political Unconscious*, 291.
18. "Death of a King, Chapter 7," 20.
19. Gillis, "The Blue Humanities." For an important critique of Gillis and the blue humanities more generally, see Bakker, "Offshore."
20. Kolbert, *The Sixth Extinction*, 107.
21. Forsythe, "Meet the Aquaman Comics Artist."
22. Forsythe, "Meet the Aquaman Comics Artist."

23. For more on mixed-race superheroes, see Dagbovie-Mullins and Berlatsky, *Mixed-Race Superheroes*.

24. Momoa debuted as Aquaman in Zack Snyder's *Batman v Superman: Dawn of Justice* (2016).

25. Slaughter, "The 'Aquaman' Movie Is Hapa A F."

26. Laughlin, "'Half Asian'? 'Half White'? No—'Hapa.'"

27. Laughlin, "'Half Asian'? 'Half White'? No—'Hapa.'"

28. Wynter, "Unsettling the Coloniality." As Braidotti writes in her posthumanist critique, the Human "is a normative convention" that functions as "a systematized standard of recognizability—of Sameness—by which all others can be assessed, regulated, and allotted to a designated social location." Braidotti, *The Posthuman*, 26 (capitalization in original).

29. Berlatsky and Dagbovie-Mullins, "The Whiteness of the Whale," 46.

30. "Single Wet Female."

31. Robinson, "All Hail the Harpoon-Handed Aquaman."

32. "The Trench, Part 1," 6, 9.

33. "The Trench, Part 1," 3.

34. "The Trench, Part 1," 5.

35. "The Trench, Part 1," 9.

36. Hood, "Aquaman Now Highest-Grossing DC Film Ever."

37. Mladenov capitalizes "Global Ocean" throughout *Marine Biology*.

38. Some comics scholars critique allegorical readings of superheroes for how such readings flatten and reduce the structures and lived experiences of race and racism. See Lund, "The Mutant Problem"; Shyminsky, "Mutant Readers, Reading Mutants."

39. DeLoughrey, *Allegories of the Anthropocene*, 10.

40. Roorda, *The Ocean Reader*, 1.

41. Rediker, *The Slave Ship*, 10.

42. Sekula and Burch, *The Forgotten Space*.

43. P. Steinberg, *The Social Construction of the Ocean*, 14.

44. Sekula and Burch, *The Forgotten Space*.

45. DeLoughrey, "Submarine Futures," 34.

46. DeLoughrey, "Submarine Futures," 34.

47. Gange, "Seeing from the Sea."

48. Gange, "Seeing from the Sea."

49. Oreskes, "The Scientific Consensus on Climate Change," 138.

50. Chakrabarty, "The Climate of History," 207.

51. For an accessible account of this new form of genocide, see Kolbert, *The Sixth Extinction*.

52. Doyle, "UN Urges World to Slow Extinctions." Also see Dobson, "Biodiversity."

53. "How Many Species Are We Losing?"

54. Doyle, "UN Urges World to Slow Extinctions."

55. Doyle, "UN Urges World to Slow Extinctions."

56. May, "Why Worry about How Many Species and Their Loss?"

57. May, "Why Worry about How Many Species and Their Loss?"

58. May, "Why Worry about How Many Species and Their Loss?"

59. National Oceanic and Atmospheric Administration, "What Is the Census of Marine Life?"

60. Mora et al., "How Many Species Are There on Earth and in the Ocean?"

61. Gillis, "The Blue Humanities."

62. Young, "Making Aquaman Cool Again" (capitalization in original).

63. Mladenov, *Marine Biology*, 1. This fact launches Dan Abnett's run of Rebirth *Aquaman*. See "Prologue: After the Deluge."

64. Mladenov, *Marine Biology*, 1.

65. National Oceanic and Atmospheric Administration, "How Much Oxygen Comes from the Ocean?"

66. Crutzen and Stoermer, "The Anthropocene," 17.

67. Jackson, *Becoming Human*, 25.

68. See Jackson, *Becoming Human*, 23.

69. Adamson, "We Have Never Been Anthropos"; Whyte, "Indigenous Science (Fiction) for the Anthropocene"; Wynter and McKittrick, "Unparalleled Catastrophe."

70. Boatner, "Sub-Mariner," 360.

71. Boatner, "Sub-Mariner," 360.

72. Boatner, "Sub-Mariner," 360.

73. Daniels, *Marvel*, 10.

74. Daniels, *Marvel*, 27.

75. Maslon and Kantor, *Superheroes!*, 136.

76. Boatner, "Sub-Mariner," 361.

77. Boatner, "Sub-Mariner," 360.

78. Fighting Nazis on the Ocean became a common trope at the time. For example, in *Superman* 12 (September–October 1941), Superman fights what are clearly supposed to be Nazis on the seas. See Lund, *Re-Constructing the Man of Steel*, 116.

79. See Lund, "Comics Activism," for more on this concept.

80. Spiegelman, "Golden Age Superheroes."

81. C. Scott, "Written in Red, White, and Blue," 328.

82. Fingeroth, *Disguised as Clark Kent*; Royal, "Jewish Comics," 6; Weinstein, *Up, Up, and Oy Vey!* For a critique of Superman's rootedness in Judaism, see Lund, *Re-Constructing the Man of Steel*.

83. For more on how comic books were forms of propaganda during World War II, see Goodnow and Kimble, *The 10 Cent War*.

84. "The Submarine Strikes."

85. "The Submarine Strikes."

86. "The Submarine Strikes."

87. Ogilvie and Miller, *Refuge Denied*.

88. I am indebted to Martin Lund for this important point.

89. Greenberg, *Four Fish*, 12.

90. See Mentz, *Ocean*, xv.

91. "Throne of Atlantis, Epilogue."

92. "Throne of Atlantis, Epilogue," 2.

93. Greenberg, *Four Fish*, 139–40.

94. Greenberg, *Four Fish*, 10.

95. "Throne of Atlantis, Epilogue," 9.

96. "The Facts."

97. Tsing, *The Mushroom at the End of the World*, 19.

98. "Throne of Atlantis, Epilogue," 2.

99. "Throne of Atlantis, Epilogue," 3.

100. "Throne of Atlantis, Epilogue," 4–5.

101. "Throne of Atlantis, Epilogue," 4–5.

102. "Throne of Atlantis, Epilogue," 7.

103. "Throne of Atlantis, Epilogue," 3.

104. "Throne of Atlantis, Epilogue," 7.

105. "Throne of Atlantis, Epilogue," 7.

106. Braverman and Johnson, *Blue Legalities*.

107. Cited in Edrén and Teilmann, "Humpback Whale," 899.

108. The above two paragraph are indebted to Rothenberg, "Nature's Greatest Hit."

109. Rothenberg, "Nature's Greatest Hit."

110. Rothenberg, "Nature's Greatest Hit."

111. "Throne of Atlantis, Epilogue," 8.

112. "Throne of Atlantis, Epilogue," 8.

113. "Death of a King, Chapter 7," 20.

114. Johns, "The New 52 Interviews."

115. Tambling, *Allegory*, 6.

116. Benjamin, *The Origin of Tragic German Drama*, 177.

117. DeLoughrey, *Allegories of the Anthropocene*, 10.

118. For more on the central role allegories play in narrating, interrogating, and imagining beyond the Anthropocene, see DeLoughrey, *Allegories of the Anthropocene.*

119. Jameson, *Allegory and Ideology*, 10.

120. For a critique of such perfect translatability, see Spivak, "Can the Subaltern Speak?"

121. See, for example, Jameson, *Allegory and Ideology*, 10–11.

122. Jameson, *Allegory and Ideology*, 10.

123. Jameson, *Allegory and Ideology*, 34.

124. See DeLoughrey, *Allegories of the Anthropocene*, 9.

125. See Jameson, *The Political Unconscious*, 10, 29.

126. Jameson, *Allegory and Ideology*, 52.

127. Jameson, *Allegory and Ideology*, 25.

128. Jameson, *The Political Unconscious*, 29.

1. DEEP IN THE TRENCHES

1. *National Ocean Conference.*

2. *National Ocean Conference.*

3. Earle, *Sea Change*, xii (emphasis in original).

4. Cited in Helmreich, *Alien Ocean*, 10.

5. For a study of Freud's complicated conception of "oceanic feeling," see Ackerman, "Exploring Freud's Resistance."

6. See Griswold, "How 'Silent Spring' Ignited the Environmental Movement."

7. See Helmreich, *Alien Ocean.*

8. "The Trench, Part 1," 1.

9. P. Steinberg, "Of Other Seas," 157.

10. P. Steinberg, "Of Other Seas," 157.

11. Helmreich, *Alien Ocean*, 34, see also 171–211.

12. Wilderson, *Red, White, and Black*, 38.

13. Glissant, *Poetics of Relation*, 6.

14. Glissant, *Poetics of Relation*, epigraph page (capitalization in original).

15. Glissant, *Poetics of Relation*, dedication page to Michael Smith.

16. Walcott, "The Sea Is History" (capitalization in original).

17. Glissant, *Poetics of Relation*, 49.

18. Glissant, *Poetics of Relation*, 49.

19. Baucom, *Specters of the Atlantic*, 24.

20. Baucom, *Specters of the Atlantic*, 321.

21. "The Trench, Part 1," 2.

22. See for example, "The Trench, Part 2."

23. In *On Monsters*, Stephen T. Asma writes, "We still employ the term and concept [monster] to apply to *inhuman* creatures of every stripe, even if they come from our own species." Asma, *On Monsters*, 7 (emphasis in original).

24. Foucault, *The Order of Things*, 387.

25. Adamson, "We Have Never Been Anthropos."

26. Braidotti, *The Posthuman*, 15.

27. Braidotti, *The Posthuman*, 15.

28. "The Trench, Part 2," 13.

29. "The Trench, Part 2," 10–11.

30. "The Trench, Part 2," 12.

31. "The Trench, Part 2," 13.

32. For more on this trope, see Dagbovie-Mullins and Berlatsky, *Mixed-Race Superheroes*.

33. "Lost," 13.

34. "Lost," 13.

35. See Wilderson, *Afropessimism*.

36. Mentz, *Ocean*, xv.

37. Mentz, *Ocean*, xv–xvi.

38. Braidotti, *The Posthuman*, 15.

39. "The Trench, Part 2," 13.

40. "The Trench, Part 2," 14.

41. "The Trench, Part 1," 20.

42. J. Jackson, "The Rise of Slime," 494.

43. Various authors, "The First Dead Zone," 485.

44. National Oceanic and Atmospheric Administration, "What Is a Dead Zone?"

45. Roorda, *The Ocean Reader*, 483.

46. Various authors, "The First Dead Zone," 484.

47. National Oceanic and Atmospheric Administration, "What Is a Dead Zone?"

48. "The Trench, Part 2," 19.

49. "The Trench, Part 3," 9.

50. See P. Steinberg, *The Social Construction of the Ocean*, 16–20.

51. Cited in P. Steinberg, *The Social Construction of the Ocean*, 17.

52. "The Trench, Part 3," 9.

53. Earle, *Sea Change*, xii.

54. "The Trench, Part 3," 8.

55. Kendi, *Stamped from the Beginning*, 49, 210.

56. "The Trench, Part 3," 13.

57. "Single Wet Female," 21.

58. For more on panel rhetoric, see Gavaler, *Superhero Comics*, 215–22.

59. "The Trench, Part 3," 13.

60. "The Trench, Part 3," 13.

61. "The Trench, Part 3," 13.

62. "Aquaman Goes to College!"

63. "The Trench, Part 3," 11.

64. "The Trench, Part 3," 17.

65. Petersen, "Exploring Deep-Ocean Trenches."

66. "Ocean Trenches."

67. Petersen, "Exploring Deep-Ocean Trenches."

68. "Ocean Trenches."

69. "The Submarine Strikes," 1.

70. "The Submarine Strikes," 4.

71. "The Submarine Strikes," 8.

72. "The Submarine Strikes," 1.

73. Coletta, "Aquaman," 15.

74. Gavaler, *Superhero Comics*, 206.

75. Gavaler, *Superhero Comics*, 210.

76. Mack, *The Sea*.

77. "The Trench, Part 3," 20.

78. "The Trench, Part 3," 20.

79. Alaimo, "Dispersing Disaster," 184.

80. "The Trench, Conclusion," 1.

81. C. Moore, "The First Trash Vortex," 488.

82. Qiu, "Man-Made Pollutants Found in Earth's Deepest Ocean Trenches."

83. C. Moore, "The First Trash Vortex," 490.

84. Mathuros, "More Plastic than Fish in the Ocean by 2050."

85. C. Moore, "The First Trash Vortex," 490.

86. C. Moore, "The First Trash Vortex," 491.

87. Roorda, *The Ocean Reader*, 116.

88. Roorda, *The Ocean Reader*, 116; Condliffe, "Descent to the Deepest Deep," 117.

89. Condliffe, "Descent to the Deepest Deep," 117.

90. "The Trench, Conclusion," 5.

91. "The Trench, Conclusion," 4.

92. J. Jackson, "The Rise of Slime," 496.

93. Earle, "Walking on the Seafloor," 115.

94. J. Jackson, "The Rise of Slime," 495.
95. "The Trench, Conclusion," 11.
96. Or so the reader and Arthur are led to believe. The trench return at the end of Johns's narrative run, as I will explore later.
97. "The Trench, Conclusion," 19.
98. "Lost," 5.
99. "The Trench, Conclusion," 9.
100. See Spivak, "Can the Subaltern Speak?"
101. Z. Jackson, *Becoming Human*, 25.
102. Davies, *Humanisms*, 141, cited in Braidotti, *The Posthuman*, 15.
103. Cary Wolfe, "Posthumanities," cited in Braidotti, *The Posthuman*, 1.

2. WAVES OF FEMINISM

1. "The Trench, Part 2," 12.
2. "Deserted!," 4.
3. Cocca, *Superwomen*, 12.
4. Phelan, *Unmarked*, 6.
5. Cocca, *Superwomen*, 11.
6. Cocca, *Superwomen*, 11.
7. Cocca, *Superwomen*, 12.
8. "The Trench, Part 1," 18.
9. "The Trench, Part 1," 19.
10. "The Trench, Part 1," 19.
11. "The Doom from Dimension Aqua," 6.
12. "The Doom from Dimension Aqua," 7.
13. "The Wife of Aquaman."
14. "The Trench, Part 1," 19.
15. "The Trench, Conclusion," 21.
16. "Lost," 22.
17. See Kern, *Feminist City*. Kern suggests that all capitalist urban spaces are defined and structured by patriarchy. Capitalism and patriarchy are inextricable structures.
18. "Deserted!," 3.
19. "Deserted!," 3.
20. "Deserted!," 3.
21. "Deserted!," 3.
22. "Deserted!," 3.
23. See Gay, *Not That Bad*.
24. "Deserted!," 4.
25. "Deserted!," 4.

26. "Deserted!," 5.
27. "Deserted!," 5.
28. "Deserted!," 5.
29. "Deserted!," 5.
30. "Deserted!," 5.
31. "Deserted!," 5.
32. "Deserted!," 6.
33. "Deserted!," 6.
34. "Deserted!," 6.
35. "Deserted!," 11.
36. "Deserted!," 11.
37. Rogers, "Requiem for The New 52."
38. Tucker, *Slugfest*, 248.
39. Tucker, *Slugfest*, 248.
40. Hyde, "Super Hero Fans Expected to Line-Up Early."
41. S. Steinberg, "DC Comics Offers Digital Comics Same Day as Print."
42. Truitt, "DC Comics Unleashes a New Universe of Superhero Titles."
43. Truitt, "DC Comics Unleashes a New Universe of Superhero Titles."
44. Melrose, "DC Announces Post-'Flashpoint' Details."
45. Peeples, "Up, Up and Out of the Closet."
46. Peeples, "Up, Up and Out of the Closet."
47. See Austin and Hamilton, *All New, All Different?*, 295–96.
48. Hudson, "Marvel Editors Discuss Women."
49. Brienza, "Men of Wonder."
50. Hudson, "The Big Sexy Problem" (emphasis in original).
51. Brienza, "Men of Wonder."
52. Brienza, "Men of Wonder."
53. Hudson, "The Big Sexy Problem."
54. ". . . And Most of the Costumes Stay On . . . ," 19.
55. ". . . And Most of the Costumes Stay On . . . ," 19.
56. ". . . And Most of the Costumes Stay On . . . ," 19.
57. Hudson, "The Big Sexy Problem."
58. Hudson, "The Big Sexy Problem."
59. Hudson, "The Big Sexy Problem."
60. Sneddon, "Women in Comics: Women in the New 52 Reviewed."
61. Sneddon, "Women in Comics: Women in the New 52 Reviewed."
62. MacDonald, "What Really Happened."
63. Hudson, "Answering Dan DiDio."
64. Hudson, "Answering Dan DiDio."
65. Hudson, "Answering Dan DiDio."

66. MacDonald, "What Really Happened."

67. E. Brown, "Hire More Women."

68. E. Brown, "Hire More Women."

69. Morrison, "Geoff Johns Steps Down."

70. Lee and DiDio, "We Hear You."

71. Lee and DiDio, "We Hear You."

72. Hudson, "'We Hear You.'"

73. Shendruk, "Analyzing the Gender Representation."

74. Shendruk, "Analyzing the Gender Representation."

75. Shendruk, "Analyzing the Gender Representation."

76. Shendruk, "Analyzing the Gender Representation."

77. Shendruk, "Analyzing the Gender Representation."

78. S. Scott, "Fangirls in Refrigerators," 22.

79. S. Scott, "Fangirls in Refrigerators," 3.

80. "The Trench, Part 1," 12.

81. "The Trench, Part 1," 12.

82. "Waiters and Waitresses."

83. Cooper, "One in Nine U.S. Workers"; Tepper, "Lowest Paying Jobs in America."

84. "Waiters and Waitresses."

85. "The Trench, Part 1," 12.

86. Kheel, "From Heroic to Holistic Ethics," 258–59.

87. Kheel, "From Heroic to Holistic Ethics," 258.

88. Gaard, "Ecofeminism," 68. The concept of "entangled empathy" comes from Lori Gruen's "Navigating Difference."

89. Gaard, "Ecofeminism," 69.

90. Garrard, *Ecocriticism*, 26–30.

91. Mies and Shiva, *Ecofeminism*, xvi.

92. Cocca, *Superwomen*, 7.

93. See, for example, S. Scott, "Fangirls in Refrigerators."

3. THE APOCALYPTIC OCEAN

1. "The Others," 13.

2. "The Others," 13.

3. Nixon, *Slow Violence*, 2.

4. Nixon, *Slow Violence*, 2.

5. See Woloch, *The One vs. the Many*.

6. "New Fish," 1.

7. "New Fish," 1.

8. "New Fish," 1–2.

9. "Deserted!," 4.
10. Roorda, *The Ocean Reader*, 486.
11. Abbing, *Plastic Soup*, 1.
12. Abbing, *Plastic Soup*, 6.
13. Abbing, *Plastic Soup*, 1.
14. Abbing, *Plastic Soup*, 1.
15. Abbing, *Plastic Soup*, 14.
16. Mathuros, "More Plastic than Fish in the Ocean by 2050."
17. C. Moore, "The First Trash Vortex," 490.
18. Abbing, *Plastic Soup*, 6, 10.
19. Hervey, "The Plastic in Our Bodies."
20. Neill, "Confluence."
21. Reid, "Solwara 1 and the Sessile Ones," 27.
22. Mossler, "The Footprint of Bottom-Trawl Fishing."
23. "Bottom Trawling."
24. "Bottom Trawling."
25. Clover, *The End of the Line*, 1–2.
26. Clover, *The End of the Line*, 2.
27. "Thorne of Atlantis, Chapter 3," 7. Also see "Throne of Atlantis, Chapter 5," 13.
28. "Throne of Atlantis, Chapter 3," 7.
29. Abbing, *Plastic Soup*, 1.
30. "New Fish," 15.
31. "Throne of Atlantis, Chapter 1."
32. Garrard, *Ecocriticism*, 23.
33. Cartwright, "Atlantis."
34. Plato, *Critias* 108e–109a, cited in Cartwright, "Atlantis."
35. Plato, *Critias* 121b, cited in Cartwright, "Atlantis."
36. Cartwright, "Atlantis."
37. This project to attain national recognition continues beyond The New 52. Dan Abnett's opening run for DC Universe Rebirth, the reboot following The New 52, begins with Arthur opening Spindrift Station, an embassy trying to foster peaceful relations and understanding between the surface and watery world. As Arthur explains, the embassy "is a link between . . . land and sea . . . like the shore." See "The Drowning, Part 1," 6.
38. See Arendt, *The Origins of Totalitarianism*.
39. "Throne of Atlantis, Part 2," 10.
40. "Throne of Atlantis, Part 2," 11.
41. "Throne of Atlantis, Part 2," 15.

42. "Throne of Atlantis, Part 2," 15.

43. "Throne of Atlantis, Epilogue," 13.

44. E. Johnson and Braverman, "Blue Legalities," 2.

45. E. Johnson and Braverman, "Blue Legalities," 2.

46. P. Steinberg, *The Social Construction of the Ocean*.

47. Cited in P. Steinberg, *The Social Construction of the Ocean*, 91.

48. E. Johnson and Braverman, "Blue Legalities," 12.

49. E. Johnson and Braverman, "Blue Legalities," 12.

50. E. Johnson and Braverman, "Blue Legalities," 12.

51. P. Steinberg, *The Social Construction of the Ocean*, 13.

52. Yusoff, *A Billion Black Anthropocenes*, 4,

53. DeLoughrey, "Submarine Futures," 32. See also DeLoughrey, *Routes and Roots*.

54. Hugh, "The Truman Proclamation."

55. DeLoughrey, "Submarine Futures," 32.

56. Margolies, "Jurisdiction in Offshore Submerged Lands," 447.

57. "Geological Survey—Supplemental Estimate," cited in Margolies, "Jurisdiction in Offshore," 447.

58. United Nations Convention on the Law of the Sea, Article 77, para. 1, 54, cited in Hugh, "The Truman Proclamation."

59. "The Deep Green Sea," 4, cited in P. Steinberg, *The Social Construction of the Ocean*, 173.

60. P. Steinberg, *The Social Construction of the Ocean*, 90.

61. P. Steinberg, *The Social Construction of the Ocean*, 96.

62. P. Steinberg, *The Social Construction of the Ocean*, 139.

63. "Throne of Atlantis, Chapter 1."

64. "Throne of Atlantis, Part 2," 20.

65. "Throne of Atlantis, Part 2," 20.

66. Proctor and Schiebinger, *Agnotology*, cited in E. Johnson and Braverman, "Blue Legalities," 6.

67. Boonshoft, "From Boston's Resistance" (emphasis in original).

68. "Throne of Atlantis, Part 2," 20.

69. Schmitt, *The Nomos of the Earth*, 43, cited in Braverman and Johnson, "Blue Legalities," 1.

70. Braverman and Johnson, "Blue Legalities," 1.

71. "Death of a King, Chapter 2," 5.

72. Anderson, *Imagined Communities*.

73. DeLoughrey, "Submarine Futures," 32.

74. Schrader, "Marine Microbiopolitics," 258.

75. Schrader, "Marine Microbiopolitics," 258.

76. Schrader, "Marine Microbiopolitics," 258.

77. Earle, "'Mission Blue' Warning," cited in Braverman and Johnson, "Blue Legalities," 9.

78. Schmitt, *The Nomos of the Earth*, 43.

79. Schmitt, *Land and Sea*, 11.

80. "Thorne of Atlantis, Chapter 3."

81. Schmitt, *The Concept of the Political*, 26.

82. See "Throne of Atlantis, Chapter 5"; "Death of a King, Chapter 7."

83. "New Fish," 15.

84. See Mbembe, *Necropolitics*.

85. Butler, *Precarious Life*, 20 (emphasis in original).

86. Weheliye, *Habeas Viscus*, 135.

87. J. Moore, "The Rise of Cheap Nature," 87 (emphasis in original).

88. J. Moore, "The Rise of Cheap Nature," 87 (capitalization in original). Also see Adamson, "We Have Never Been Anthropos"; Davis and Todd, "On the Importance of a Date"; Wynter and McKittrick, "Unparalleled Catastrophe."

89. "New Fish," 17.

90. "New Fish," 18 (capitalization in original).

91. "Death of a King, Chapter 7."

92. As Laura Gómez argues, "Latino" is a U.S.-produced category that seeks to homogenize and unify a diverse community that, until coming to the United States, never self-identified as Latino/a/x. I follow Gómez's essential argument that "Latino" has become a racialized identity. Gómez's book *Inventing Latinos* "explains how and why Latino became cognizable as a racial group . . . that is other and inferior to Whites." As Gómez elaborates, "Latino" is a category that is both "fabricated and flexible." Gómez, *Inventing Latinos*, 4, 5.

93. "Ivan Reis."

94. Lamar, "Ivan Reis."

95. Andrade, "Brazilian Artists Bring Super Heroes to Life."

96. Andrade, "Brazilian Artists Bring Super Heroes to Life."

97. Andrade, "Brazilian Artists Bring Super Heroes to Life."

98. Forsythe, "Meet the Aquaman Comics Artist."

99. Mello, "Contractor or Employee in Brazil."

100. Global Post Guest, "The Brazilian Economy—What Went Wrong?"

101. Harper, "Comics and the Diminishing Role of Artists" (capitalization in original).

102. Harper, "Comics and the Diminishing Role of Artists."

103. MacDonald, "Does Anyone Care about the Artists."

104. MacDonald, "Does Anyone Care about the Artists."

105. De Blieck, "Seriously, Don't Be a Comic Book Artist."

106. De Blieck, "Seriously Don't Be a Comic Book Artist."

107. De Blieck, "Seriously Don't Be a Comic Book Artist."

108. Hanley, "Gendercrunching June 2014."

109. Morrison, "Goeff Johns Steps Down."

110. Polo, "After Justice League and Aquaman, Geoff Johns Returns."

111. See "*Aquaman* (2018): Full Cast and Crew."

112. Forsythe, "Meet the Aquaman Comics Artist."

113. Aldama, *Latinx Superheroes*, 3.

114. La Jeunesse, "Latinx People."

115. La Jeunesse, "Latinx People."

116. Aldama, *Latinx Superheroes*, 4.

117. Aldama, *Latinx Superheroes*, 4.

118. La Jeunesse, "Latinx People."

119. See Aldama, *Latinx Superheroes*, 8, 6, 27, 162–64.

120. Aldama, *Latinx Superheroes*, 163.

121. See "Throne of Atlantis, Chapter 1."

122. Buell, *The Environmental Imagination*, 285.

123. Yusoff, *A Billion Black Anthropocenes*, xiii.

124. Yusoff, *A Billion Black Anthropocenes*, 2.

125. Yusoff, *A Billion Black Anthropocenes*, xii (capitalization in original).

126. Jaffe, "Aquaman Comes Through."

127. Pelletier and Parsons continued through to the end of Johns's tenure, except for issues 20, 23.1, and 23.2, for a total of ten issues.

128. "Karl Kesel, Marvel Comics Writer, Sells Comic Book Collection."

129. "Throne of Atlantis, Part 2," 6.

130. "Throne of Atlantis, Part 2," 3–4.

131. Gany et al., "Urban Occupational Health," 846.

4. ALLEGORIES OF WHITE SUPREMACY

1. "Throne of Atlantis, Chapter 5," 24.

2. "Throne of Atlantis, Part 2," 11.

3. "Throne of Atlantis, Epilogue," 18–19.

4. "Throne of Atlantis, Chapter 5," 28.

5. "Death of a King, Chapter 3."

6. "Underwater," 18.

7. "Throne of Atlantis, Chapter 5," 24.

8. "Death of a King, Chapter 4," 3.

9. Plato, *The Republic*, 414b–415d.

10. "Death of a King, Chapter 6," 2.
11. "Death of a King, Chapter 6," 9.
12. Jameson, *The Political Unconscious*, 102.
13. "Death of a King, Chapter 6," 10.
14. "Death of a King, Chapter 6," 11.
15. "Death of a King, Chapter 6," 11.
16. "Death of a King, Chapter 6," 11.
17. Ferber, "Mongrel Monstrosities," 57.
18. "Death of a King, Chapter 6," 12.
19. "Death of a King, Chapter 6," 12.
20. "Death of a King, Chapter 6," 13.
21. "Death of a King, Chapter 6," 13.
22. Kurlander, *Hitler's Monsters*; Ratner, "Why the Nazis Were Obsessed."
23. See Barczewski, *Myth and National Identity*; Manheim, "The Dark Link"; McLeod, "Ideology and Racial Myth."
24. Jones, "King Arthur Forged Our Britain."
25. "Death of a King, Chapter 6," 2.
26. "Death of a King, Chapter 6."
27. "Death of a King, Chapter 6," 15.
28. "Death of a King, Chapter 6," 18.
29. See Cunningham, "The Absence of Black Supervillains."
30. "Dark Destiny, Deadly Dreams," 9.
31. "Dark Destiny, Deadly Dreams," 10.
32. J. Johnson, "*Aquaman* Wants to Be Obama."
33. While the dominant U.S. culture projects the Ocean as a white space and Oceanic occupations as largely white, scholars such as W. Jeffrey Bolster reveal how in antebellum America, Blacks were at the center of the "Age of Sail." Bolster, *Black Jacks*, 2.
34. For more on how Blacks are positioned as outside the project of Humanity, see Wilderson, *Afropessimism*.
35. For a terrific overview of the Black power movement and its wide-ranging impact on all aspects of social, cultural, and political life, see Joseph, *The Black Power Movement*.
36. In this sense, Black Manta can be placed in conversation with Gilroy, *The Black Atlantic*; Glissant, *Poetics of Relation*; and Sharpe, *In the Wake*.
37. "Dark Destiny, Deadly Dreams," 13.
38. Segall, "10 Most Devastating Comic Book Endings."
39. "The End of the Justice League!," 6.
40. Muhammad, *The Condemnation of Blackness*.

41. "Dark Destiny, Deadly Dreams."
42. "Dark Destiny, Deadly Dreams," 13.
43. See Wilderson, *Afropessimism*.
44. See Nama, *Super Black*.
45. For a history of early mainstream U.S. Black superheroes, see J. Brown, *Black Superheroes*, 15–26; Nama, *Super Black*.
46. Ghee, "Will the Real Black Superheroes," 232.
47. "The End of a Road."
48. See Wilderson, *Afropessimism*; Wilderson, *Red, White, and Black*. Wilderson capitalized "Slave" and "Slavery" throughout his writings.
49. Sharpe, *In the Wake*, 21.
50. Sharpe, *In the Wake*, 2.
51. "Paint It Black!," 1.
52. "Lost and Found."
53. Jackson was first introduced, albeit briefly, in *Brightest Day* 4 (July/August 2010). "Thresholds."
54. See Wynter, "Unsettling the Coloniality."
55. "The Others," 5.
56. "The Others," 8.
57. For more on the politics of this trope, see Pierrot, *The Black Avenger in Atlantic Culture*.
58. "The Others, Chapter 3."
59. "The Others, Chapter 4."
60. "The Others, Chapter 4," 16.
61. "Sea Change," 1.
62. "Death of a King, Chapter 3," 14.
63. See Alexander, *The New Jim Crow*.
64. "Sea Change," 3.
65. "Sea Change," 3.
66. Cunningham, "The Absence of Black Supervillains," 51.
67. Cunninghmam, "The Absence of Black Supervillains," 54.
68. See Alexander, *The New Jim Crow*.
69. Zachary, "Aquaman Villain Black Manta Is the Hero of His Own Story."
70. Williams, *Torchbearers of Democracy*, 6.
71. Guglielmo, *Divisions*, 6.

AFTERWORD

1. Aldama, *Latinx Superheroes*, 4.
2. Aldama, *Latinx Superheroes*, 4, 96 (emphasis in original).
3. Aldama, *Latinx Superheroes*, 97.

4. Kuumba and Ajanaku, "Dreadlocks."

5. Oyola, "Marked for Failure," 22.

6. Wolk, *Reading Comics*, 102, cited in Oyola, "Marked for Failure," 22.

7. Dockterman, "Meet Captain Marvel," cited in Cocca, *Superwomen*, 220.

8. McKenney, "#VisibleWomen."

9. "Echoes of a Life Lived Well, Part 4," 18.

10. Jean-Philippe, "How Jason Momoa's Hawaiian and Polynesian Roots."

11. For more on this trope, see Dagbovie-Mullins and Berlatsky, *Mixed-Race Superheroes*.

12. Wan, "How 'Furious 7' Helped James Wan."

13. Slaughter, "The 'Aquaman' Movie Is Hapa AF."

14. Laughlin, "'Half Asian'? 'Half White'? No—'Hapa.'"

15. Laughlin, "'Half Asian'? 'Half White'? No—'Hapa.'"

16. Slaughter, "The 'Aquaman' Movie Is Hapa AF."

17. Slaughter, "The 'Aquaman' Movie Is Hapa AF."

18. Slaughter, "The 'Aquaman' Movie Is Hapa AF."

19. Van der Zwan, "Why Jason Momoa Fought for Temuera Morrison."

20. Van der Zwan, "Why Jason Momoa Fought for Temuera Morrison."

21. Barrow, "How Jason Momoa and James Wan Incorporated Polynesia Culture."

22. Van der Zwan, "Why Jason Momoa Fought for Temuera Morrison."

23. Van der Zwan, "Why Jason Momoa Fought for Temuera Morrison."

24. Barrow, "How Jason Momoa and James Wan Incorporated Polynesia Culture."

25. Barrow, "How Jason Momoa and James Wan Incorporated Polynesia Culture."

26. Ngata, "Wai Māori."

27. Ngata, "Wai Māori."

28. Slaughter, "The 'Aquaman' Movie Is Hapa AF."

29. Slaughter, "The 'Aquaman' Movie' Is Hapa AF."

30. Slaughter, "The 'Aquaman' Movie' Is Hapa AF."

31. Whyte, "Indigeneity," 145.

32. Whyte, "Indigeneity," 145.

33. Whyte, "Indigeneity," 145.

34. Leonard, "Why Lakes and Rivers Should Have the Same Rights as Humans."

35. Weekes, "Jason Momoa Continues Being the Living Embodiment of Aquaman."

36. Fard, "Water Warrior."

37. Fard, "Water Warrior."

38. Fard, "Water Warrior."

39. Stoney and Hofmann, "These Celebrities Are Helping Navajo Nation Efforts."

40. Fard, "Water Warrior."

41. Wilson, "Hawaii-Born Actor Jason Momoa's 'Aquaman' Role."

42. Hacker, "The 1 Thing about Jason Momoa That You Might Not Know."

43. Fard, "Water Warrior."

44. Ingersoll, *Waves of Knowing*, 20.

45. Fard, "Water Warrior."

46. Fard, "Water Warrior."

47. Kimmerer, *Braiding Sweetgrass*, x.

BIBLIOGRAPHY

Abbing, Michiel Roscam. *Plastic Soup: An Atlas of Ocean Pollution*. Washington DC: Island Press, 2019. Originally published in Dutch, in 2018, by Uitgeverij Lias.

Ackerman, Sarah. "Exploring Freud's Resistance to the Oceanic Feeling." *Journal of the American Psychoanalytic Association* 65, no. 1 (February 2017): 9–31.

Adamson, Joni. "We Have Never Been Anthropos: From Environmental Justice to Cosmopolitics." In *Environmental Humanities: Voices from the Anthropocene*, edited by Serpil Oppermann and Serenella Iovino, 155–73. New York: Roman and Littlefield, 2016.

Alaimo, Stacy. "Dispersing Disaster: The Deepwater Horizon, Ocean Conservation, and the Immateriality of Aliens." In *American Environments: Climate-Cultures-Catastrophe*, edited by Christof Mauch and Sylvia Mayer, 177–93. Heidelberg, Germany: Universitätsverlag Winter, 2012.

Aldama, Frederick Luis. *Latinx Superheroes in Mainstream Comics*. Tucson: University of Arizona Press, 2017.

Alexander, Michelle. *The New Jim Crow: Mass Incarceration in the Age of Colorblindness*. New York: The New Press, 2010.

Anderson, Benedict. *Imagined Communities: Reflections on the Origin and Spread of Nationalism*. London: Verso, 1983.

". . . And Most of the Costumes Stay On . . ." Judd Winick (writer) and Guillem March (artist). *Catwoman* 4, no. 1. The New 52. New York: DC Comics, September/November 2011.

Andrade, Renato. "Brazilian Artists Bring Super Heroes to Life." Reuters, January 31, 2007. https://www.reuters.com/article/us-brazil-cartoons /brazilian-artists-bring-super-heroes-to-life-idUSN1842303220070131.

"Aquaman (2018): Full Cast and Crew." IMDb, accessed November 29, 2020. https://www.imdb.com/title/tt1477834/fullcredits?ref_=tt_cl_sm#cast.

Aquaman: A Celebration of 75 Years. Burbank CA: DC Comics, 2016.

"Aquaman Goes to College!" Joe Samachson (writer) and Louis Cazeneuve (artist). *Adventure Comics* 1, no. 120. New York: DC Comics, September 1947.

Arendt, Hannah. *The Origins of Totalitarianism*. New York: Schocken Books, 1951. Reprinted in 2004, with a new introduction by Samantha Power. Citations are to the 2004 edition.

Asma, Stephen T. *On Monsters: An Unnatural History of Our Worst Fears*. Oxford: Oxford University Press, 2011.

Associated Press. "Warner's DC Comic-Book Unit Leaving Gotham." *San Diego Union-Tribune*, October 29, 2013. https://www.sandiegouniontribune.com/sdut-warners-dc-comic-book-unit-leaving-gotham-2013oct29-story.html.

Austin, Allan W., and Patrick L. Hamilton. *All New, All Different? A History of Race and the American Superhero*. Austin: University of Texas Press, 2019.

Bakker, Justine M. "Offshore: Descending into the Blue Humanities." *Counterpoint: Navigating Knowledge*, November 6, 2019. https://www.counterpointknowledge.org/offshore-descending-into-the-blue-humanities/.

Barczewski, Stephanie L. *Myth and National Identity in Nineteenth-Century Britain: The Legends of King Arthur and Robin Hood*. Oxford: Oxford University Press, 2000.

Barrow, Jerry L. "How Jason Momoa and James Wan Incorporated Polynesian Culture into 'Aquaman.'" *BET*, December 20, 2018. www.bet.com/celebrities/exclusives/aquaman-jason-momoa-entourage.html.

Baucom, Ian. *Specters of the Atlantic: Finance Capital, Slavery, and the Philosophy of History*. Durham NC: Duke University Press, 2005.

Benjamin, Walter. *The Origin of Tragic German Drama*. Translated by John Osborne. New York: Verso, 1998.

Berlatsky, Eric, and Sika Dagbovie-Mullins. "The Whiteness of the Whale and the Darkness of the Dinosaur: The Africanist Presence in the Superhero Comics from *Black Lightening* to *Moon Girl*." In *Unstable Masks: Whiteness and American Superhero Comics*, edited by Sean Guynes and Martin Lund, 38–56. Columbus: The Ohio State University Press, 2020.

Boatner, Charlie. "Sub-Mariner." In *Comics through Time: A History of Icons, Idols, and Ideas*, vol. 1, *1800–1960*, edited by M. Keith Booker, 360–62. Santa Barbara CA: Greenwood, 2014.

Bolster, W. Jeffrey. *Black Jacks: African American Seamen in the Age of Sail*. Cambridge MA: Harvard University Press, 1997.

Boonshoft, Mark. "From Boston's Resistance to an American Revolution." *New York Public Library* (blog), February 28, 2017. https://www.nypl.org/blog/2017/02/28/boston-resistance-american-revolution.

"Bottom Trawling." Oceana, accessed May 2, 2020. https://usa.oceana.org /bottom-trawling.

Bradley, Laura. "A Brief History of Pop Culture Dumping on Aquaman." *Vanity Fair*, December 12, 2018. https://www.vanityfair.com/hollywood /2018/12/aquaman-jokes-family-guy-big-bang-theory-south-park.

Braidotti, Rosi. *The Posthuman*. Cambridge, UK: Polity Press, 2013.

Braverman, Irus, and Elizabeth R. Johnson, eds. *Blue Legalities: The Life and Laws of the Sea*. Durham NC: Duke University Press, 2020.

Brienza, Casey. "Men of Wonder: Gender and American Superhero Comics." University of Cambridge, November 1, 2011. https://www.cam .ac.uk/research/discussion/men-of-wonder-gender-and-american -superhero-comics.

Brown, Elliott. "Hire More Women—Here's a Few To Get You Started." Change.org, 2011. https://www.change.org/p/co-publisher-dc-comics -hire-more-women-heres-a-few-to-get-you-started.

Brown, Jeffrey A. *Black Superheroes, Milestone Comics, and Their Fans*. Jackson: University of Mississippi Press, 2001.

Buell, Lawrence. *The Environmental Imagination: Thoreau, Nature Writing, and the Formation of American Culture*. Cambridge MA: Harvard University Press, 1995.

Butler, Judith. *Precarious Life: The Powers of Mourning and Violence*. London: Verso, 2004.

Carson, Rachel. *The Edge of the Sea*. Boston MA: Houghton Mifflin, 1955.

——. *The Sea around Us*. Oxford: Oxford University Press, 1951.

——. *Under the Sea-Wind: A Naturalist's Picture of Ocean Life*. New York: Simon and Schuster, 1941.

Cartwright, Mark. "Atlantis." *World History Encyclopedia*, April 8, 2016. https://www.ancient.eu/atlantis/.

Chakrabarty, Dipesh. "The Climate of History: Four Theses." *Critical Inquiry* 35, no. 2 (Winter 2009): 197–222.

Clover, Charles. *The End of the Line: How Overfishing Is Changing the World and What We Eat*. New York: The New Press, 2006.

Cocca, Carolyn. *Superwomen: Gender, Power, and Representation*. New York: Bloomsbury, 2016.

Coletta, Charles. "Aquaman." In *Comics through Time: A History of Icons, Idols, and Ideas*, vol. 1, *1800–1960*, edited by M. Keith Booker, 14–16. Santa Barbara CA: Greenwood, 2014.

Condliffe, Jamie. "Descent to the Deepest Deep." In *The Ocean Reader: History, Culture, Politics*, edited by Eric Paul Roorda, 116–17. Durham NC: Duke University Press, 2020.

"The Confluence, Part 1." Brandon Thomas (writer), Daniel Sampere (artist), and Adriano Lucas (colorist). *Aquaman*, no. 1. Future State. Burbank CA: DC Comics, January/March 2021.

Cooper, David. "One in Nine U.S. Workers Are Paid Wages That Can Leave Them in Poverty, Even When Working Full Time." Economic Policy Institute, June 15, 2018. https://www.epi.org/publication /one-in-nine-u-s-workers-are-paid-wages-that-can-leave-them-in -poverty-even-when-working-full-time/.

Crutzen, Paul J., and Eugene F. Stoermer. "The Anthropocene." *IGBP Newsletter* 41 (2000): 17–18.

Cunningham, Phillip Lamarr. "The Absence of Black Supervillains in Mainstream Comics." *Journal of Graphic Novels and Comics* 1, no. 1 (2010): 51–62.

Dagbovie-Mullins, Sika A., and Eric L. Berlatsky, eds. *Mixed-Race Super-heroes*. New Brunswick NJ: Rutgers University Press, 2021.

Daniels, Les. *Marvel: Five Fabulous Decades of the World's Greatest Comics*. New York: Harry N. Abrams, 1991.

"Dark Destiny, Deadly Dreams." David Michelinie (writer), Jim Aparo (artist), and Jerry Serpe (colorist). *Adventure Comics* 1, no. 452. New York: DC Comics, July/August 1977.

Davies, Tony. *Humanisms*. London: Routledge, 1997.

Davis, Heather, and Zoe Todd. "On the Importance of a Date, or, Decolonizing the Anthropocene." *ACME* 16, no. 4 (2017): 761–80.

"Death of a King, Chapter 1." Geoff Johns (writer), Paul Pelletier (penciller), Sean Parsons (inker), and Rod Reis (colorist). *Aquaman* 7, no. 18. The New 52. New York: DC Comics, March/May 2013.

"Death of a King, Chapter 2." Geoff Johns (writer), Paul Pelletier (penciller), Sean Parsons (inker), and Rod Reis (colorist). *Aquaman* 7, no. 19. The New 52. New York: DC Comics, May/June 2013.

"Death of a King, Interlude: The Return of The Others." John Ostrander (writer), Manuel Garcia (penciller), Wayne Faucher, Sandra Hope, Ray McCarthy, and Rob Hunter (inkers), and Pete Pantazis (colorist). *Aquaman* 7, no. 20. The New 52. New York: DC Comics, May/July 2013.

"Death of a King, Chapter 3: Confrontation." Geoff Johns (writer), Paul Pelletier (penciller), Sean Parsons (inker), and Rod Reis (colorist). *Aquaman* 7, no. 21. The New 52. New York: DC Comics, June/August 2013.

"Death of a King, Chapter 4." Geoff Johns (writer), Paul Pelletier (penciller), Sean Parsons (inker), and Rod Reis (colorist). *Aquaman* 7, no. 22. The New 52. New York: DC Comics, July/September 2013.

"Death of a King, Chapter 5: Dead End." Geoff Johns (writer), Paul Pelletier (penciller), Sean Parsons (inker), and Rod Reis (colorist). *Aquaman 7*, no. 23. The New 52. New York: DC Comics, August/October 2013.

"Death of a King, Chapter 6: Secret of the Seven Seas." Geoff Johns (writer), Paul Pelletier (penciller), Sean Parsons (inker), and Rod Reis (colorist). *Aquaman 7*, no. 24. The New 52. New York: DC Comics, October/December 2013.

"Death of a King, Chapter 7: Baptism of Fire." Geoff Johns (writer), Paul Pelletier (penciller), Sean Parsons (inker), and Rod Reis (colorist). *Aquaman 7*, no. 25. The New 52. New York: DC Comics, November 2013 / January 2014.

De Blieck, Augie, Jr. "Seriously, Don't Be a Comic Book Artist. Just Don't." *Pipeline Comics*, October 18, 2018. https://www.pipelinecomics.com /seriously-dont-be-a-comic-book-artist-just-dont/.

"The Deep Green Sea." *Economist*, May 23, 1998.

DeLoughrey, Elizabeth M. *Allegories of the Anthropocene*. Durham NC: Duke University Press, 2019.

———. *Routes and Roots: Navigating Caribbean and Pacific Island Literature*. Honolulu: University of Hawai'i Press, 2007.

———. "Submarine Futures of the Anthropocene." *Comparative Literature* 69, no. 1 (2017): 32–44.

"Deserted!" Geoff Johns (writer), Ivan Reis (breakdowns), Joe Prado (artist), and Rod Reis (colorist). *Aquaman 7*, no. 6. The New 52. New York: DC Comics, February/April 2012.

Dobson, Andy. "Biodiversity." In *Keywords for Environmental Studies*, edited by Joni Adamson, William A. Gleason, and David N. Pellow, 17–19. New York: New York University Press, 2016.

Dockterman, Eliana. "Meet Captain Marvel: Fighter Pilot, Feminist and Marvel's Biggest Gamble." *Time*, November 4, 2014. https://time.com /3554606/captain-marvel-movie-kelly-sue-deconnick/.

"The Doom from Dimension Aqua." Jack Miller (writer) and Nick Cardy (artist). *Aquaman 1*, no. 11. New York: DC Comics, September/October 1963.

Doyle, Alister. "U.N. Urges World to Slow Extinctions: 3 Each Hour." Reuters, May 22, 2007. https://www.reuters.com/article/us-climate -extinctions/u-n-urges-world-to-slow-extinctions-3-each-hour -idUSL2253331920070522.

"The Drowning, Part 1: The End of Fear." Dan Abnett (writer), Brad Walker (penciller), Andrew Hennessy (inker), and Gabe Eltaeb (colorist). *Aquaman 8*, no. 1. Rebirth. Burbank CA: DC Comics, June/August 2016.

Earle, Sylvia A. "'Mission Blue' Warning: The Ocean Is Not Too Big to Fail." *Daily Beast*, August 15, 2014. https://www.thedailybeast.com /mission-blue-warning-the-ocean-is-not-too-big-to-fail.

———. *Sea Change: A Message of the Oceans*. New York: Ballantine Books, 1996.

———. "Walking on the Seafloor." In *The Ocean Reader: History, Culture, Politics*, edited by Eric Paul Roorda, 111–15. Durham NC: Duke University Press, 2020.

"Echoes of a Life Lived Well, Part 4." Kelly Sue DeConnick (writer), Miguel Mendonça (artist), and Romula Fajardo Jr. (colorist). *Aquaman* 8, no. 61. Rebirth. Burbank CA: DC Comics, July/September 2020.

"Eco-Wars, Part 1." Shaun McLaughlin (writer), Vince Giarrano (penciller and inker), and Tom McCraw (colorist). *Aquaman* 4, no. 9. New York: DC Comics, June/August 1992.

Edrén, Susi M. C., and Jonas Teilmann. "Humpback Whale." In *Encyclopedia of the Arctic*, edited by Mark Nuttall, 898–99. New York: Routledge, 2004.

"The End of a Road." Shaun McLaughlin (writer), Ken Hooper (penciller), Bob Dvorak (inker), and Tom McCraw (colorist). *Aquaman* 4, no. 6. New York: DC Comics, March/May 1992.

"The End of the Justice League!" Gerry Conway (writer), Chuck Patton (penciller), David Hunt (inker), and Carl Gafford (colorist). *Justice League of America Annual* 1, no. 2. New York: DC Comics, October 1984.

"The Facts." Plastic Oceans International, accessed June 30, 2022. https:// plasticoceans.org/the-facts/.

Fard, Maggie Fazeli. "Water Warrior: Jason Momoa." *Experience Life*, August 20, 2020. https://experiencelife.lifetime.life/article/water -warrior-jason-momoa/.

Ferber, Abby L. "Mongrel Monstrosities." In *Multiculturalism in the United States: Current Issues, Contemporary Voices*, edited by Peter Kivisto and Georganne Rundblad, 57–70. Thousand Oaks CA: Pine Forge Press, 2000.

Fingeroth, Danny. *Disguised as Clark Kent: Jews, Comics, and the Creation of the Superhero*. New York: Continuum, 2007.

Forsythe, Dana. "Meet the Aquaman Comics Artist Who Inspired the New Movie." *SyFy Wire*, December 18, 2018. https://www.syfy.com /syfywire/meet-the-aquaman-comics-artist-who-inspired-the-new -movie (accessed November 26, 2010, site discontinued).

Foucault, Michel. *The Order of Things: An Archeology of the Human Sciences*. Translated by Alan Sheridan. New York: Vintage, 1994. Originally published in French, in 1966, as *Les Mots et les choses*, by Éditions Gallimard.

Gaard, Greta. "Ecofeminism." In *Keywords for Environmental Studies*, edited by Joni Adamson, William A. Gleason, and David N. Pellow, 68–70. New: New York University Press, 2016.

Gange, David. "Seeing from the Sea." *Critical Fish*, July 30, 2020. https://thecriticalfish.co.uk/seeing-from-the-sea/.

Gany, Francesca, Patricia Novo, Rebecca Dobslaw, and Jennifer Leng. "Urban Occupational Health in the Mexican and Latino/Latina Immigrant Population: A Literature Review." *Journal of Immigrant and Minority Health* 16, no. 5 (2014): 846–55.

Garrard, Greg. *Ecocriticism*. London: Routledge, 2012.

Gavaler, Chris. *Superhero Comics*. London: Bloomsbury Academic, 2018.

Gay, Roxane, ed. *Not That Bad: Dispatches from Rape Culture*. New York: Harper Perennial, 2018.

"Geological Survey—Supplemental Estimate for 'Geological Surveys, 1948'—$2,750,000 / Geological Survey of the Continental Shelf." Continental Shelf Record Group 57: Records of the Geologic Survey, Geologic Division, Fuels Branch, General Administrative Files, 1943–53.

Ghee, Kenneth. "Will the Real Black Superheroes Please Stand Up?! A Critical Analysis of the Mythological and Cultural Significance of Black Superheroes." In *Black Comics: Politics of Race and Representation*, edited by Sheena C. Howard and Ronald L. Jackson II, 223–37. London: Bloomsbury, 2013.

Gillis, John R. "The Blue Humanities." *Humanities* 34, no. 3 (May/June 2013). https://www.neh.gov/humanities/2013/mayjune/feature/the -blue-humanities.

Gilroy, Paul. *The Black Atlantic: Modernity and Double Consciousness*. Cambridge MA: Harvard University Press, 1993.

Glissant, Édouard. *Poetics of Relation*. Translated by Betsy Wing. Ann Arbor: University of Michigan Press, 1997.

Global Post Guest. "The Brazilian Economy—What Went Wrong?" *World*, March 17, 2012. https://theworld.org/stories/2012-03-17/brazilian -economy-what-went-wrong.

Gómez, Laura E. *Inventing Latinos: A New Story of American Racism*. New York: The New Press, 2020.

Goodnow, Trischa, and James J. Kimble, eds. *The 10 Cent War: Comic Books, Propaganda, and World War II*. Jackson: University Press of Mississippi, 2016.

Greenberg, Paul. *Four Fish: The Future of the Last Wild Food*. New York: Penguin Press, 2010.

Griswold, Eliza. "How 'Silent Spring' Ignited the Environmental Movement." *New York Times*, September 21, 2012. https://www.nytimes.com/2012/09/23/magazine/how-silent-spring-ignited-the-environmental-movement.html.

Gruen, Lori. "Navigating Difference (Again): Animal Ethics and Entangled Empathy." In *Strangers to Nature: Animal Lives and Human Ethics*, edited by Gregory R. Smulewciz-Zucker, 213–33. Lanham MD: Lexington Books, 2012.

Guglielmo, Thomas A. *Divisions: A New History of Racism and Resistance in American's World War II Military*. New York: Oxford University Press, 2021.

Guynes, Sean, and Martin Lund, eds. *Unstable Masks: Whiteness and American Superhero Comics*. Columbus: The Ohio State University Press, 2020.

Hacker, Caitlin. "The 1 Thing about Jason Momoa That You Might Not Know." *Yahoo Life*, April 1, 2017. https://www.yahoo.com/lifestyle/1-thing-jason-momoa-might-173800153.html.

Hanley, Tim. "Gendercrunching June 2014—Including Nationality and Ethnicity at the Big Two." *Bleeding Cool*, August 29, 2014. https://bleedingcool.com/comics/recent-updates/gendercrunching-june-2014-including-nationality-and-ethnicity-at-the-big-two/.

Harper, David. "Comics and the Diminishing Role of Artists in a Visual Medium." *Multiversity Comics*, February 11, 2014. http://www.multiversitycomics.com/longform/diminishing-role-of-artists/.

Helmreich, Stefan. *Alien Ocean: Anthropological Voyages in Microbial Seas*. Berkeley: University of California Press, 2009.

Hervey, Ginger. "The Plastic in Our Bodies." *Politico*, May 5, 2019. https://www.politico.eu/article/the-plastic-in-our-bodies-health/.

Hood, Cooper. "Aquaman Now Highest-Grossing DC Film Ever, Passing Dark Knight Rises." *Screen Rant*, January 27, 2019. https://screenrant.com/aquaman-highest-grossing-dc-film-ever/.

"How Many Species Are We Losing?" World Wildlife Fund, accessed April 8, 2020. https://wwf.panda.org/discover/our_focus/biodiversity/biodiversity/#:~:text=These%20experts%20calculate%20that%20between,2%2C000%20extinctions%20occur%20every%20year.

Hudson, Laura. "Answering Dan DiDio: The Problem with Having Only 1% Female Creators at DC Comics." *Comics Alliance*, July 28, 2011. https://comicsalliance.com/dc-dan-didio-female-creators/.

———. "The Big Sexy Problem with Superheroines and Their 'Liberated Sexuality.'" *Comics Alliance*, September 22, 2011. https://comicsalliance.com/starfire-catwoman-sex-superheroine/.

———. "Marvel Editors Discuss Women in Comics and the Lack of Female-Led Titles." *Comics Alliance*, December 8, 2011. https://comicsalliance.com/marvel-women-comics-editors/.

———. "'We Hear You': DC Comics Responds to Concerns about Few Female Creators." *Comics Alliance*, July 30, 2011. https://comicsalliance.com/dc-comics-we-hear-you-female-creators/#ixzz1TmCmPXrF.

Hugh, Laura. "The Truman Proclamation and the Rule of Law." Rule of Law Education Centre, September 28, 2016. https://www.ruleoflaw.org.au/truman-proclamation-rule-law/.

Hyde, David. "Super Hero Fans Expected to Line-Up Early as DC Entertainment Launches New Era of Comic Books." DC Comics, August 17, 2011. https://www.dccomics.com/blog/2011/08/17/super-hero-fans-expected-to-line-up-early-as-dc-entertainment-launches-new-era-of-comic-books.

Ingersoll, Karin Amimoto. *Waves of Knowing: A Seascape Epistemology*. Durham NC: Duke University Press, 2016.

"Ivan Reis." Comic Vine, accessed August 14, 2020. https://comicvine.gamespot.com/ivan-reis/4040-40487/.

Jackson, Jeremy. "The Rise of Slime." In *The Ocean Reader: History, Culture, Politics*, edited by Eric Paul Roorda, 494–96. Durham NC: Duke University Press, 2020.

Jackson, Zakiyyah Iman. *Becoming Human: Matter and Meaning in an Antiblack World*. New York: New York University Press, 2020.

Jaffe, Alex. "Curry Comes Through: Five Times Aquaman Saved the Justice League." DC Universe, September 1, 2021. https://www.dccomics.com/blog/2021/09/01/curry-comes-through-five-times-aquaman-saved-the-justice-league.

Jameson, Fredric. *Allegory and Ideology*. London: Verso, 2019.

———. *The Political Unconscious: Narrative as a Socially Symbolic Act*. Ithaca NY: Cornell University Press, 1981.

Jean-Philippe, McKenzie. "How Jason Momoa's Hawaiian and Polynesian Roots Have Impacted His Career." *Oprah Magazine*, August 19, 2019. https://www.oprahmag.com/life/a28747843/jason-momoa-ethnicity/.

Johns, Geoff. "The New 52 Interviews: Aquaman." Interview by Joey Esposito. *IGN*, September 27, 2011. Last updated January 18, 2012. https://www.ign.com/articles/2011/09/27/the-new-52-interviews-aquaman.

Johns, Geoff (writer), Ivan Reis and Paul Pelletier (pencillers), Joe Prado and Sean Parsons (inkers), and Rod Reis (colorist). *Aquaman by Geoff Johns Omnibus*. Burbank CA: DC Comics, 2017.

Johnson, Elizabeth R., and Irus Braverman. "Blue Legalities: Governing More-Than-Human Oceans." In *Blue Legalities: The Life and Laws of the Sea*, edited by Irus Braverman and Elizabeth R. Johnson, 1–24. Durham NC: Duke University Press, 2020.

Johnson, Jason. "*Aquaman* Wants to Be Obama for the Seven Seas but the People Wanted Trump." *Root*, December 21, 2018. https://www.theroot.com/aquaman-wants-to-be-obama-for-the-seven-seas-but-the-pe-1831250320.

Jones, Jonathan. "King Arthur Forged Our Britain—English Heritage Is Right to Celebrate Him." *Guardian*, March 23, 2016. https://www.theguardian.com/artanddesign/jonathanjonesblog/2016/mar/23/king-arthur-tintagel-english-heritage.

Joseph, Peniel E., ed. *The Black Power Movement: Rethinking the Civil Rights–Black Power Era*. New York: Routledge, 2006.

Jue, Melody. *Wild Blue Media: Thinking through Seawater*. Durham NC: Duke University Press, 2020.

"Karl Kesel, Marvel Comics Writer, Sells Comic Book Collection for Adoption of Baby with Heroin Exposure (VIDEO)." *HuffPost*, August 26, 2012. https://www.huffpost.com/entry/karl-kesel-marvel-comics-writer-sells-comic-collection-adopt-baby_n_1830335.

Kendi, Ibram X. *Stamped from the Beginning: The Definitive History of Racist Ideas in America*. New York: Nation Books, 2016.

Kern, Leslie. *Feminist City: Claiming Space in a Man-Made World*. London: Verso, 2020.

Kheel, Marti. "From Heroic to Holistic Ethics: The Ecofeminist Challenge." In *Ecofeminism: Women, Animals, Nature*, edited by Greta Gaard, 243–71. Philadelphia: Temple University Press, 1993.

Kimmerer, Robin Wall. *Braiding Sweetgrass: Indigenous Wisdom, Scientific Knowledge, and the Teaching of Plants*. Minneapolis MN: Milkweed Editions, 2013.

King, Edward, and Joanna Page. *Posthumanism and the Graphic Novel in Latin America*. London: UCL Press, 2017.

Kolbert, Elizabeth. *The Sixth Extinction: An Unnatural History*. New York: Picador, 2014.

Kurlander, Eric. *Hitler's Monsters: A Supernatural History of the Third Reich*. New Haven CT: Yale University Press, 2017.

Kuumba, M., and Femi Ajanaku. "Dreadlocks: The Hair Aesthetics of Cultural Resistance and Collective Identity Formation." *Mobilization* 3, no. 2 (1998): 227–43.

La Jeunesse, Marilyn. "Latinx People Helped Build the World of Comic Books—While Often Being Left Out of the Pages." *Teen Vogue*, October 10, 2019. https://www.teenvogue.com/story/latinx-representation -comic-books.

Lamar, Andre. "Ivan Reis: Making a Splash with Aquaman." *Comics Bulletin*, September 28, 2011. http://comicsbulletin.com/ivan-reis-making -splash-aquaman/ (accessed November 28, 2010, site discontinued).

Laughlin, Alex. "'Half Asian'? 'Half White'? No—'Hapa.'" *Code Switch*, December 15, 2014. https://www.npr.org/sections/codeswitch/2014/12 /15/370416571/half-asian-half-white-no-hapa.

Lee, Jim, and Dan DiDio. "We Hear You." *DC* (blog), July 29, 2011. https:// www.dccomics.com/blog/2011/07/29/we-hear-you.

Leonard, Kelsey. "Why Lakes and Rivers Should Have the Same Rights as Humans." Filmed December 2019. TED video, 13:12. https://www.ted .com/talks/kelsey_leonard_why_lakes_and_rivers_should_have_the _same_rights_as_humans?language=en#t-142015.

"Lost." Geoff Johns (writer), Ivan Reis (penciller), Joe Prado and Eber Ferreira (inkers), and Rod Reis (colorist). *Aquaman 7*, no. 5. The New 52. New York: DC Comics, January/March 2012.

"Lost and Found." Geoff Johns and Peter J. Tomasi (writers), Ivan Reis, Patrick Gleason, and Joe Prado (pencillers), Rebecca Buchman, Keith Champagne, Tom Nguyen, and Ivan Reis (inkers), and Aspen MLT's Peter Steigerwald (colorist). *Brightest Day*, no. 9. New York: DC Comics, September/November 2010.

Lund, Martin. "Comics Activism, a (Partial) Introduction." *Scandinavian Journal of Comic Art* 3, no. 2 (Spring 2018): 39–54. https://mau.diva -portal.org/smash/get/diva2:1399831/FULLTEXT01.pdf.

———. "The Mutant Problem: X-Men, Confirmation Bias, and the Methodology of Comics and Identity." *European Journal of Comics Art* 10, no. 2 (2015). https://doi.org/10.4000/ejas.10890.

———. *Re-Constructing the Man of Steel: Superman 1938–1941, Jewish American History, and the Invention of the Jewish-Comics Connection*. New York: Palgrave Macmillan, 2016.

MacDonald, Heidi. "Does Anyone Care about the Artists on Comics Any More?" *The Beat* (blog), July 22, 2015. https://www.comicsbeat.com /does-anyone-care-about-the-artists-on-comics-any-more/.

———. "What Really Happened at the Infamous Dan DiDio / Hire More Women Incident." *The Beat* (blog), July 29, 2011. https://www .comicsbeat.com/scoop-what-really-happened-at-the-infamous-dan -didiohire-more-women-incident/.

Mack, John. *The Sea: A Cultural History*. London: Reaktion Books, 2011.

Manheim, Noa. "The Dark Link between the Nazis and the Legend of Atlantis." *Haaretz*, January 24, 2019. https://www.haaretz.com/jewish /holocaust-remembrance-day/.premium-the-dark-link-between -nazis-and-atlantis-1.6870036.

Margolies, Daniel. "Jurisdiction in Offshore Submerged Lands and the Significance of the Truman Proclamation in Postwar U.S. Foreign Policy." *Diplomatic History* 44, no. 3 (June 2020): 447–65.

Maslon, Laurence, and Michael Kantor. *Superheroes! Capes, Cowls, and the Creation of Comic Book Culture*. New York: Crown Archetype, 2013.

Mathuros, Fon. "More Plastic than Fish in the Ocean by 2050: Report Offers Blueprint for Change." World Economic Forum, January 19, 2016. https://www.weforum.org/press/2016/01/more-plastic-than -fish-in-the-ocean-by-2050-report-offers-blueprint-for-change/.

May, Robert M. "Why Worry about How Many Species and Their Loss?" *PLOS Biology* 9, no. 8 (2011). https://www.ncbi.nlm.nih.gov/pmc /articles/PMC3160330/.

Mbembe, Achille. *Necropolitics*. Translated by Steven Corcoran. Durham NC: Duke University Press, 2019.

McKenney, Kyle. "#VisibleWomen Twitter Trend Dispels Myth That There Aren't Many Women Working in Comics." *Paste*, August 5, 2016. https://www.pastemagazine.com/comics/kelly-sue-deconnick /visiblewomen-trending-on-twitter-highlights-women/.

McLeod, Ken. "Ideology and Racial Myth in Purcell's 'King Arthur' and Arne's 'Alfred.'" *Restoration* 34, no. 1 (2010): 83–102.

Mello, Juliana. "Contractor or Employee in Brazil." *Brazil Business*, January 28, 2014. https://thebrazilbusiness.com/article/contractor-or -employee-in-brazil.

Melrose, Kevin. "DC Announces Post-'Flashpoint' Details, Relaunches All Titles." *Comic Book Resources*, May 31, 2011. https://www.cbr.com/dc -announces-post-flashpoint-details-relaunches-all-titles/.

Menga, Filippo, and Dominic Davies. "Apocalypse Yesterday: Posthumanism and Comics in the Anthropocene." *Environment and Planning E: Nature and Space* 3, no. 3 (2020): 663–87.

Mentz, Steve. *At the Bottom of Shakespeare's Ocean*. New York: Continuum, 2009.

———. *Ocean*. New York: Bloomsbury Academic, 2020.

Mies, Maria, and Vandana Shiva. *Ecofeminism*. London: Zed Books, 1993. Reprinted in 2014, with a foreword by Ariel Salleh. Citations are to the 2014 edition.

Mladenov, Philip V. *Marine Biology: A Very Short Introduction*. Oxford: Oxford University Press, 2013.

Moore, Charles. "The First Trash Vortex." In *The Ocean Reader: History, Culture, Politics*, edited by Eric Paul Roorda, 486–93. Durham NC: Duke University Press, 2020.

Moore, Jason W. "The Rise of Cheap Nature." In *Anthropocene or Capitalocene? Nature, History, and the Crisis of Capitalism*, edited by Jason W. Moore, 78–115. Oakland CA: PM Press, 2016.

Mora, Camilo, Derek P. Tittensor, Sina Adl, Alastair G. B. Simpson, and Boris Worm. "How Many Species Are There on Earth and in the Ocean?" *PLOS Biology* 9, no. 8 (2011). https://journals.plos.org/plosbiology/article/file?type=printable&id=10.1371/journal.pbio.1001127.

Morrison, Matt. "Geoff Johns Steps Down as DC's Chief Creative Officer." *Screen Rant*, June 11, 2018. https://screenrant.com/geoff-johns-dc-entertainment-comics-role/.

Mossler, Max. "The Footprint of Bottom-Trawl Fishing." Sustainable Fisheries, October 8, 2018. https://sustainablefisheries-uw.org/the-footprint-of-bottom-trawl-fishing/.

Muhammad, Khalil Gibran. *The Condemnation of Blackness: Race, Crime, and the Making of Modern Urban America*. Cambridge MA: Harvard University Press, 2019.

Nama, Adilifu. *Super Black: American Pop Culture and Black Superheroes*. Austin: University of Texas Press, 2011.

National Ocean Conference: Oceans of Commerce, Oceans of Life. Washington DC: U.S. Department of Commerce; Monterey CA: U.S. Department of the Navy, 1998. Published in conjunction with the National Ocean Conference, July 11–12, 1998, Monterey, California.

National Oceanic and Atmospheric Administration. "How Much Oxygen Comes from the Ocean?" National Ocean Service, last updated February 26, 2021. https://oceanservice.noaa.gov/facts/ocean-oxygen.html.

———. "What Is a Dead Zone?" National Ocean Service, last updated February 26, 2021. https://oceanservice.noaa.gov/facts/deadzone.html.

———. "What Is the Census of Marine Life?" National Ocean Service, last updated August 8, 2021. https://oceanservice.noaa.gov/facts/marine-census.html.

Neill, Peter. "Confluence." *Medium*, June 23, 2020. https://medium.com/@TheW2O/confluence-436d605babac.

"New Fish." Geoff Johns and Tony Bedard (plot), Tony Bedard (words), Geraldo Borges (penciller), Ruy José (inker), and Rod Reis (colorist). *Aquaman* 7, no. 23.2. The New 52. New York: DC Comics, September/November 2013.

Ngata, Tina. "Wai Māori: A Māori Perspective on the Freshwater Debate." *Spinoff*, November 6, 2018. https://thespinoff.co.nz/atea/06-11-2018/wai-maori-a-maori-perspective-on-the-freshwater-debate/.

Nixon, Rob. *Slow Violence and the Environmentalism of the Poor*. Cambridge MA: Harvard University Press, 2011.

"Ocean Trenches." Woods Hole Oceanographic Institution, accessed May 18, 2020. https://www.whoi.edu/know-your-ocean/ocean-topics/seafloor-below/ocean-trenches/.

Ogilvie, Sarah A., and Scott Miller. *Refuge Denied: The St. Louis Passengers and the Holocaust*. Madison: University of Wisconsin Press, 2010.

Oppermann, Serpil. "Storied Seas and Living Metaphors in the Blue Humanities." *Configurations* 27, no. 4 (Fall 2019): 443–61.

Oreskes, Naomi. "The Scientific Consensus on Climate Change: How Do We Know We're Not Wrong?" In *Climate Change: What It Means for Us, Our Children, and Our Grandchildren*, edited by Joseph F. C. DiMento and Pamela Doughman, 105–48. Cambridge MA: MIT Press, 2014.

"The Others." Geoff Johns (writer), Ivan Reis (penciller), Joe Prado (inker), and Rod Reis (colorist). *Aquaman* 7, no. 7. The New 52. New York: DC Comics, March/May 2012.

"The Others, Chapter 2." Geoff Johns (writer), Ivan Reis (penciller), Joe Prado and Ivan Reis (inkers), and Rod Reis (colorist). *Aquaman* 7, no. 8. The New 52. New York: DC Comics, April/June 2012.

"The Others, Chapter 3." Geoff Johns (writer), Ivan Reis (penciller), Joe Prado, Oclair Albert, and Andy Lanning (inkers), and Rod Reis (colorist). *Aquaman* 7, no. 9. The New 52. New York: DC Comics, May/July 2012.

"The Others, Chapter 4." Geoff Johns (writer), Ivan Reis (penciller), Joe Prado and Andy Lanning (inkers), and Rod Reis (colorist). *Aquaman* 7, no. 10. The New 52. New York: DC Comics, June/August 2012.

"The Others, Chapter 5." Geoff Johns (writer), Ivan Reis (penciller), Joe Prado, Jonathan Glapion, and Andy Lanning (inkers), and Rod Reis (colorist). *Aquaman* 7, no. 11. The New 52. New York: DC Comics, July/September 2012.

"The Others, Chapter 6." Geoff Johns (writer), Ivan Reis (penciller), Joe Prado, Oclair Albert, and Andy Lanning (inkers), and Rod Reis (colorist). *Aquaman 7*, no. 12. The New 52. New York: DC Comics, August/October 2012.

"The Others: Conclusion." Geoff Johns (writer), Ivan Reis (penciller), Joe Prado and Julio Ferreira (inkers), and Rod Reis (colorist). *Aquaman 7*, no. 13. The New 52. New York: DC Comics, October/December 2012.

Oyola, Osvaldo. "Marked for Failure: Whiteness, Innocence, and Power in Defining Captain America." In *Unstable Masks: Whiteness and American Superhero Comics*, edited by Sean Guynes and Martin Lund, 10–37. Columbus: The Ohio State University Press, 2020.

"Paint It Black!" Rick Veitch (writer), Yvel Guichet (penciller), and Mark Propst (inker). *Aquaman 6*, no. 8. New York: DC Comics, July/September 2003.

Peeples, Jase. "Up, Up and Out of the Closet." *Advocate*, July 18, 2011. https://www.advocate.com/arts-entertainment/features/2011/07/18/and-out-closet.

Perry, Laura. "Anthroposcenes: Towards an Environmental Graphic Novel." *C21 Literature* 6, no. 1 (2018). https://c21.openlibhums.org/article/id/517/.

Petersen, Carolyn Collins. "Exploring Deep-Ocean Trenches." ThoughtCo., December 5, 2018. thoughtco.com/ocean-trench-definition-4153016.

Phelan, Peggy. *Unmarked: The Politics of Performance*. New York: Routledge, 1993.

Pierrot, Grégory. *The Black Avenger in Atlantic Culture*. Athens: University of Georgia Press, 2019.

Plato. *The Republic*. Translated by Paul Shorey. In *The Collected Dialogues of Plato, Including the Letters*, edited by Edith Hamilton and Huntington Cairns, 575–844. Princeton NJ: Princeton University Press, 1989.

Polo, Susana. "After Justice League and Aquaman, Geoff Johns Returns with His Most Personal Project." *Polygon*, May 7, 2020. https://www.polygon.com/tv/2020/5/7/21248635/geoff-johns-dc-comics-luke-wilson-joker-aquaman-justice-league-society-stargirl.

Proctor, Robert N., and Londa Schiebinger. *Agnotology: The Making and Unmaking of Ignorance*. Stanford CA: Stanford University Press, 2008.

Qiu, Jane. "Man-Made Pollutants Found in Earth's Deepest Ocean Trenches." *Nature*, June 21, 2016. Reprinted in *Scientific American*, https://www.scientificamerican.com/article/man-made-pollutants-found-in-earth-s-deepest-ocean-trenches/.

Ratner, Paul. "Why the Nazis Were Obsessed with Finding the Lost City of Atlantis." *Big Think*, November 26, 2018. https://bigthink.com /culture-religion/why-the-nazis-were-obsessed-with-finding-the -lost-city-of-atlantis.

Rediker, Marcus. *The Slave Ship: A Human History*. New York: Viking Press, 2007.

Reid, Susan. "Solwara 1 and the Sessile Ones." In *Blue Legalities: The Life and Laws of the Sea*, edited by Irus Braverman and Elizabeth R. Johnson, 25–44. Durham NC: Duke University Press, 2020.

Robinson, Ashley V. "All Hail the Harpoon-Handed Aquaman." DC (blog), May 24, 2018. https://www.dccomics.com/blog/2018/05/24/all-hail -the-harpoon-handed-aquaman.

Rogers, Vaneta. "Requiem for The New 52: The Life and Times of DC's Controversial Reboot." *Newsarama*, March 1, 2016. https://www .newsarama.com/28202-dc-s-new-52-remembered.html (accessed November 21 2019, site discontinued).

Roorda, Eric Paul, ed. *The Ocean Reader: History, Culture, Politics*. Durham NC: Duke University Press, 2020.

Rothenberg, David. "Nature's Greatest Hit: The Old and New Songs of the Humpback Whale." *Wire*, September 2014. https://www.thewire.co .uk/in-writing/essays/nature_s-greatest-hit_the-old-and-new-songs -of-the-humpback-whale.

Royal, Derek Parker. "Jewish Comics; or, Visualizing Current Jewish Narrative." *Shofar* 29, no. 2 (Winter 2011): 1–12.

Rozwadowski, Helen M. *Vast Expanses: A History of the Oceans*. London: Reaktion Books, 2018.

Sanchez, Alex, and Jul [Julie] Maroh. *You Brought Me the Ocean*. Burbank CA: DC Comics, 2020.

Schmitt, Carl. *The Concept of the Political*. Translated by George Schwab. Expanded ed. Chicago: University of Chicago Press, 1996. Originally published in German, in 1932, as *Der Begriff des Politischen*, by Duncker and Humblot.

———. *The Land and the Sea: A World Historical-Meditation*. Translated by Samuel Garrett Zeitlin. Edited and with introductions by Russel A. Berman and Samuel Garrett Zeitlin. Candor: New York: Telos Press Publishing, 2015. Originally published in German, in 1942, as *Land und Meer: Eine weltgeschichtliche Betrachtung*, by Klett-Cotta.

———. *The Nomos of the Earth in the International Law of the Jus Publicum Europaeum*. Translated by G. L. Ulmen. New York: Telos, 2003.

Originally published in German, in 1950, as *Der Nomos der Erde im Völkerrecht des Jus Publicum Europaeum.*

Schrader, Astrid. "Marine Microbiopolitics: Haunted Microbes before the Law." In *Blue Legalities: The Life and Laws of the Sea*, edited by Irus Braverman and Elizabeth R. Johnson, 255–73. Durham NC: Duke University Press, 2020.

Scott, Cord. "Written in Red, White, and Blue: A Comparison of Comic Book Propaganda from World War II and September 11." *Journal of Popular Culture* 40, no. 2 (2007): 325–43.

Scott, Jeffery. *The Posthuman Body in Superhero Comics: Human, Superhuman, Transhuman, Post/Human.* New York: Palgrave Macmillan, 2016.

Scott, Suzanne. "Fangirls in Refrigerators: The Politics of (In)visibility in Comic Book Culture." *Transformative Works and Cultures* 13 (2013): 1–30.

"Sea Change." Geoff Johns and Tony Bedard (plot), Tony Bedard (words), Claude St. Aubin (penciller and inker), and Blond (colorist). *Aquaman* 7, no. 23.1. The New 52. New York: DC Comics, September/November 2013.

Segall, Mason. "10 Most Devastating Comic Book Endings." *What Culture*, March 31, 2020. https://whatculture.com/comics/10-most-devastating-comic-book-endings.

Sekula, Allan, and Noël Burch. *The Forgotten Space.* Amsterdam: Doc.Eye Film, 2010.

Sharpe, Christina. *In the Wake: On Blackness and Being.* Durham NC: Duke University Press, 2016.

Shendruk, Amanda. "Analyzing the Gender Representation of 34,476 Comic Book Characters." *Pudding*, July 2017. https://pudding.cool/2017/07/comics/.

Shyminsky, Neil. "Mutant Readers, Reading Mutants: Appropriation, Assimilation, and the X-Men." *International Journal of Comic Art* 8, no. 2 (Fall 2006): 387–405.

"Single Wet Female." Peter David (writer), Martin Egeland (penciller), Brad Vancata (inker), and Tom McCraw (colorist). *Aquaman* 5, no. 2. New York: DC Comics, August/September 1994.

Slaughter, Melissa. "The 'Aquaman' Movie Is Hapa AF." With Lauren Hardie. *Hapa Mag*, December 23, 2018. https://www.hapamag.com/issue-006/the-aquaman-movie-is-hapa-af.

Sneddon, Laura. "Women in Comics: The New 52 and the Batgirl of San Diego." *Comicbook Grrrl*, July 24, 2011. www.comicbookgrrrl.com

/2011/07/24/women-in-comics-the-new-52-and-the-batgirl-of-san
-diego/ (accessed February 19, 2021, site discontinued).

———. "Women in Comics: Women in the New 52 Reviewed." *Comicbook Grrrl*, October 9, 2011. http://www.comicbookgrrrl.com/2011/10/09 /women-in-comics-women-in-the-new-52-reviewed/ (accessed February 19, 2021, site discontinued).

Spiegelman, Art. "Golden Age Superheroes Were Shaped by the Rise of Fascism." *Guardian*, August 17, 2019. https://www.theguardian.com /books/2019/aug/17/art-spiegelman-golden-age-superheroes-were -shaped-by-the-rise-of-fascism.

Spivak, Gayatri Chakravorty. "Can the Subaltern Speak?" In *Marxism and the Interpretation of Culture*, edited by Cary Nelson and Lawrence Grossberg, 271–313. Urbana: University of Illinois Press, 1988.

Steinberg, Philip E. "Of Other Seas: Metaphors and Materialities in Maritime Regions." *Atlantic Studies* 10, no. 2 (2013): 156–69.

———. *The Social Construction of the Ocean*. Cambridge: Cambridge University Press, 2001.

Steinberg, Scott. "DC Comics Offers Digital Comics Same Day as Print." *Rolling Stone*, September 15, 2011. https://www.rollingstone.com /culture/culture-news/dc-comics-offers-digital-comics-same-day-as -print-67421.

Stoney, Alyssa, and Chelsea Hofmann. "These Celebrities Are Helping Navajo Nation Efforts to Fight Coronavirus." *Arizona Republic*, April 21, 2020. Last updated May 27, 2020. https://www.azcentral .com/story/news/local/arizona-health/2020/04/21/coronavirus -jason-momoa-mark-ruffalo-paul-rudd-navajo-nation-covid-19 /5169401002/.

"The Submarine Strikes." Mort Weisinger (writer) and Paul Norris (artist). *More Fun Comics* 1, no. 73. New York: DC Comics, September/ November 1941.

Tambling, Jeremy. *Allegory*. London: Routledge, 2010.

Tepper, Rachel. "Lowest Paying Jobs in America: 7 Out of 10 Are in the Food Industry." *HuffPost*, April 2, 2013. https://www.huffpost.com /entry/lowest-paying-jobs-food-industry_n_2999799.

"Thresholds." Geoff Johns and Peter J. Tomasi (writers), Ivan Reis, Ardian Syaf, Scott Clark, and Oclair Albert (pencillers), Vicente Cifuentes and David Beaty (inkers), and Aspen MLT's Peter Steigerwald and John Starr (colorists). *Brightest Day*, no. 4. New York: DC Comics, June/August 2010.

"Throne of Atlantis, Prologue." Geoff Johns (writer), Pete Woods and
    Pere Perez (pencillers), Marlo Alquiza, Ruy José, Sean Parsons, Pere
    Perez, and Cam Smith (inkers), and Tony Avina (colorist). *Aquaman*
    7, no. 14. The New 52. New York: DC Comics, November 2012 / Janu-
    ary 2013.
"Throne of Atlantis, Chapter 1." Geoff Johns (writer), Ivan Reis (penciller),
    Joe Prado (inker), and Rod Reis (colorist). *Justice League* 2, no. 15.
    The New 52. New York: DC Comics, December 2012 / February 2013.
"Throne of Atlantis, Part 2." Geoff Johns (writer), Paul Pelletier (penciller),
    Art Thibert and Karl Kesel (inkers), and Rod Reis (colorist). *Aqua-
    man* 7, no. 15. The New 52. New York: DC Comics, December 2012 /
    February 2013.
"Throne of Atlantis, Chapter 3: Friends and Enemies." Geoff Johns
    (writer), Ivan Reis (penciller), Joe Prado and Ivan Reis (inkers), and
    Rod Reis (colorist). *Justice League* 2, no. 16. The New 52. New York:
    DC Comics, January/March 2013.
"Throne of Atlantis, Chapter 4." Geoff Johns (writer), Paul Pelletier (pen-
    ciller), Sean Parsons (inker), and Rod Reis (colorist). *Aquaman* 7, no.
    16. The New 52. New York: DC Comics, January/March 2013.
"Throne of Atlantis, Chapter 5." Geoff Johns (writer), Ivan Reis and Paul
    Pelletier (pencillers), Joe Prado, Oclair Albert, and Sean Parsons
    (inkers), and Rod Reis and Nathan Eyring (colorists). *Justice League*
    2, no. 17. The New 52. New York: DC Comics, February/April 2013.
"Throne of Atlantis, Epilogue." Geoff Johns (writer), Paul Pelletier (pencil-
    ler), Sean Parsons (inker), and Rod Reis (colorist). *Aquaman* 7, no.
    17. The New 52. New York: DC Comics, February/April 2013.
"The Trench, Part 1." Geoff Johns (writer), Ivan Reis (penciller), Joe Prado
    (inker), and Rod Reis (colorist). *Aquaman* 7, no. 1. The New 52. New
    York: DC Comics, September/November 2011.
"The Trench, Part 2." Geoff Johns (writer), Ivan Reis (penciller), Joe Prado
    (inker), and Rod Reis (colorist). *Aquaman* 7, no. 2. The New 52. New
    York: DC Comics, October/December 2011.
"The Trench, Part 3." Geoff Johns (writer), Ivan Reis (penciller), Joe Prado
    (inker), and Rod Reis (colorist). *Aquaman* 7, no. 3. The New 52. New
    York: DC Comics, November 2011 / January 2012.
"The Trench, Conclusion." Geoff Johns (writer), Ivan Reis (penciller), Joe
    Prado and Eber Ferreira (inkers), and Rod Reis (colorist). *Aquaman*
    7, no. 4. The New 52. New York: DC Comics, December 2011 / Febru-
    ary 2012.

Truitt, Brian. "DC Comics Unleashes a New Universe of Superhero Titles." *USA Today*, May 31, 2011. https://usatoday30.usatoday.com/life /comics/2011-05-31-dc-comics-reinvents_n.html (accessed May 26, 2020, site discontinued).

Tsing, Anna Lowenhaupt. *The Mushroom at the End of the World: On the Possibility of Life in Capitalist Ruins*. Princeton NJ: Princeton University Press, 2017.

Tucker, Reed. *Slugfest: Inside the Epic Fifty-Year Battle between Marvel and DC*. New York: Da Capo Press, 2017.

"Underwater." Geoff Johns (writer), Ivan Reis and Joe Prado (artists), and Rod Reis (colorist). *Aquaman* 7, no. 0. The New 52. New York: DC Comics, September/November 2012.

United Nations Convention on the Law of the Sea. December 10, 1982, 1833 UNTS 397. https://www.un.org/depts/los/convention _agreements/texts/unclos/unclos_e.pdf.

van der Zwan, Sebastian. "Why Jason Momoa Fought for Temuera Morrison to Be Cast in Aquaman." *Now to Love*, December 29, 2018. https://www.nowtolove.co.nz/celebrity/movies/jason-momoa -temuera-morrison-aquaman-40125.

Various authors. "The First Dead Zone." In *The Ocean Reader: History, Culture, Politics*, edited by Eric Paul Roorda, 483–85. Durham NC: Duke University Press, 2020.

"Waiters and Waitresses." Data USA, accessed May 26, 2020. https:// datausa.io/profile/soc/waiters-waitresses.

Walcott, Dereck. "The Sea Is History." Poets.org, accessed May 8, 2020. https://poets.org/poem/sea-history. Originally published in *Selected Poems*, in 2007, by Farrar, Straus, Giroux.

Wan, James, dir. *Aquaman*. With Jason Momoa, Temuera Morrison, Nicole Kidman, and Yahya Abdul-Mateen II. Burbank CA: DC Films, 2018.

———. "How 'Furious 7' Helped James Wan Get His Feet Wet for 'Aquaman' and Why He'd Like to Make a Rom-Com [Interview]." By Hoai-Tran Bui. *SlashFilm* (blog), December 18, 2018. https://www .slashfilm.com/james-wan-interview-aquaman/.

Weekes, Princess. "Jason Momoa Continues Being the Living Embodiment of Aquaman with a UN Speech on Climate Change." *Mary Sue*, September 30, 2019. https://www.themarysue.com/jason-momoa-is -aquaman-talks-climate-change-with-un/.

Wegner, Philip. *Imaginary Communities: Utopia, the Nation, and the Spatial Histories of Modernity*. Berkeley: University of California Press, 2002.

Weheliye, Alexander G. *Habeas Viscus: Racializing Assemblage, Biopoli-tics, and Black Feminist Theories of the Human*. Durham NC: Duke University Press, 2014.

Weinstein, Simcha. *Up, Up, and Oy Vey! How Jewish History, Culture, and Values Shaped the Comic Book Superhero*. Baltimore MD: Leviathan Press, 2006.

Whyte, Kyle Powys. "Indigeneity." In *Keywords for Environmental Studies*, edited by Joni Adamson, William A. Gleason, and David N. Pellow, 143–46. New York: New York University Press, 2016.

———. "Indigenous Science (Fiction) for the Anthropocene: Ancestral Dystopias and Fantasies of Climate Change Crises." *Environment and Planning E: Nature and Space* 1, nos. 1–2 (March 2018): 224–42. https://journals.sagepub.com/doi/10.1177/2514848618777621.

"The Wife of Aquaman." Jack Miller (writer) and Nick Cardy (artist). *Aquaman* 1, no. 18. New York: DC Comics: November/December 1964.

Wilderson, Frank B., III. *Afropessimism*. New York: W. W. Norton and Company, 2020.

———. *Red, White, and Black: Cinema and the Structure of U.S. Antago-nisms*. Durham NC: Duke University Press, 2010.

Williams, Chad L. *Torchbearers of Democracy: African American Soldiers in the World War I Era*. Chapel Hill: University of North Carolina Press, 2010.

Wilson, Christie. "Hawaii-Born Actor Jason Momoa's 'Aquaman' Role Par-allels Own Upbringing." *Star Advertiser*, December 16, 2018. https://www.staradvertiser.com/2018/12/16/hawaii-news/hawaii-born-actor-jason-momoas-role-in-aquaman-parallels-his-own-upbringing/.

Wolfe, Cary. "Posthumanities." http://www.carywolfe.com/post_about.html (accessed January 2, 2012, site discontinued).

Wolk, Douglas. *Reading Comics: How Graphic Comics Work and What They Mean*. Cambridge MA: Da Capo Press, 2007.

Woloch, Alex. *The One vs. the Many: Minor Characters and the Space of the Protagonist in the Novel*. Princeton NJ: Princeton University Press, 2003.

Wynter, Sylvia. "Unsettling the Coloniality of Being/Power/Truth/Free-dom: Towards the Human, after Man, Its Overrepresentation—An Argument." *CR* 3, no. 3 (Fall 2003): 257–337.

Wynter, Sylvia, and Katherine McKittrick. "Unparalleled Catastrophe for Our Species? Or to Give a Humanness a Different Future: Conver-sations." In *Sylvia Wynter: On Being Human as Praxis*, edited by Katherine McKittrick, 9–89. Durham NC: Duke University Press, 2015.

Young, Bryan. "Making Aquaman Cool Again: An Interview with Geoff Johns." *HuffPost*, November 29, 2011. Last updated January 29, 2012. https://www.huffpost.com/entry/making-aquaman-cool-again_b _1108263.

Yusoff, Kathryn. *A Billion Black Anthropocenes or None*. Minneapolis: University of Minnesota Press, 2018.

Zachary, Brandon. "Aquaman Villain Black Manta Is the Hero of His Own Story." *Comic Book Resources*, December 28, 2018. https://www.cbr .com/aquaman-black-manta-hero/.

Zalasiewicz, Jan, Mark Williams, and Colin N. Waters. "Anthropocene." In *Keywords for Environmental Studies*, edited by Joni Adamson, William A. Gleason, and David N. Pellow, 14–16. New York: New York University Press, 2016.

INDEX

In the Encapsulations: Critical Comics Studies series

Aquaman and the War against Oceans: Comics Activism and Allegory in the Anthropocene
Ryan Poll

To order or obtain more information on these or other University of Nebraska Press titles, visit nebraskapress.unl.edu.